Shadé
So... you finally ca[...]
yourself a cookie a[...]
7 years later and we still talk, wow.
Time sure flies.
I appreciate your support and love as I do always and forever
stay cool and beautiful and don't be a stranger.
I know you'll enjoy the read.
7 years will turn into infinity ☺
Peace!!!

I HATE MY JOB

King Dhakir

FIRST EDITION - FIRST PRINTING
MARCH 20, 2009

PUBLISHING CONSULTANT
H. KHALIF KHALIFAH
khalifahpublishing@khabooks.com

ISBN # 1 - 56411-504-6 ybbg# 0000

Published by Creative Souls Multimedia®
P.O. Box 2038
Hempstead, NY 11551

Contact King Dhakir @ http://www.kingdhakir.com

Printed in Canada

I Hate My Job credits:

The Players:

Story/Written by: King Dhakir
Cover Concept by: King Dhakir
Cover Design by: Macario James
(http://www.macariojamesdesign.com)
Heart Drawn by: Alex (Uniondale, NY Tattoo artist)
Author Photo by: Sun Tzu Shan

TM

The **B**.est **U**.nder **R**.ated **N**.ow **U**.nified Movement
http://www.theburnumovement.com

TM
Creative Souls Multimedia

Dedicated to my moms, pops, sisters, and the rest of family and friends who stuck by me thru thick and thin. If we talk on the regular basis, then you know who you are.

:)

Also…this book is for those who feel like walking out their jobs in the middle of the work day…the treat's on me.

wink

In memory of:
Christine Holt (grandma)
Judy Holt (auntie)
Arthur Alford (granddad)

TABLE OF JEWELS

King Dhakir

I HATE MY JOB BOOK 1: (The Flame)

Prologue: Mama's Sun

Coldness inside the jail chilled my bones, and I wobbled my legs to keep warm. Wintry air swarmed near the holding cell and seeped through my long johns. I clenched my fists and winced angrily while digging my clipped nails into my palms. Harboring thoughts of running away, I sat calm with my patience riding on fumes. My mind drifted to ignore the cold, shielding myself from freezing.

Rats almost the size of cats played freeze tag inside an empty cell beside me. The game of hide-and-seek between cracks of the concrete amused me as they fought over crumbs. The stronger rat took home the prize while the weak starved after the squabble. My eyes smothered the fight, and the episode reminded me of how folks in my 'hood lived amongst each other.

The rats crawled back into the giant hole when a white police van zipped outside the precinct. The van stopped for a line of men dressed in street clothes to ship them off to Rikers Island, New York City's largest jail facility. Rusted chains locking their ankles to their wrists clanked on the concrete, and the prisoners strolled together, shivering from the cold.

I exchanged stares with a tall, lanky dark-skinned man with messy cornrows. He was in bad need of a shave, and his face looked like wavy clay with a crooked nose. I clenched my fists tighter as we grilled each other. Staring at the brother for a few seconds, he smiled and blew a kiss. I unclenched my fists and shot him the middle finger.

A short, stocky police officer witnessing the scene slapped the prisoner across the back of his head.

"Knock it off, wise guy." The officer scowled, and the prisoner disappeared inside the bus headed to Rikers. I wasn't locked up behind bars or anything like that, but sitting across from the holding cell in the police control room was chilling enough.

I turned to my side, and my eyes lit up with joy. The cocoa-skinned woman sporting a naturally wavy, brunette afro walked out the ladies' bathroom and beckoned me to follow her.

"Come here, my chocolate handsome prince." She smiled, but I sat annoyed.

"What took you so long?" I asked, visibly vexed.

"Mama had to take care of some business, baby."

"I'm cold, and you got me cooped up in this joint." I shuddered.

"Yeah, I know. I'm sorry. The meeting ran longer than I'd expected. Do you forgive me?"

I looked down, and raised my head to glance at her brown eyes. "Yeah, I forgive you."

She smiled and pinched my cheek. "Now let's go so I can show you around."

She grabbed her police jacket and gun, and we jetted out the precinct in her unmarked car. I hated police stations, and refused to step near a cell as a long as I breathed.

Mama sped through the Bronx and weaved between cars driving slowly on the Bruckner Expressway. I job shadowed her for the day while she patrolled the South Bronx. I always feared for her safety. Stick-up kids and murderous crews ran the area and banged on anyone who got in their way. Many apartment buildings rotted from fires of the '70s as pockets knotted when drug crews took over blocks. The flames charcoaled bricks that were once red, and wooden boards substituted for glass in windows, spanning from west to east. Some made it out those conditions while others didn't. The city was a funnel that swallowed its own as only a few escaped from the belly of the beast.

Anger streaked through my body because no one cared about the South Bronx, or any other 'hood in NYC. The 'hood was the bastard child of the American dream.

I'm sure you've heard the story a million times. I wanted to *change* the story. I just couldn't figure out *how*.

"Mama, do you love your job?" I asked out of the blue.

She thought before answering. Her eyes stayed on the road and she tapped on the steering wheel. "Yeah, I love my job. I always wanted to be a police officer."

"Why?"

"Well, Justice, I felt no one cared about serving my people. And if we're not going to care about ourselves, then who will?"

"Some people hate their job."

"Not all people hate their job."

"When I ride the bus, I always see people frowning with their heads slumped over, looking depressed," I countered.

"Well, you have people who love their job and others who hate them, but they don't know how to go about doing what they want to do."

My mind raced with other questions to ask Mama. I was interested in going to law school, but classes bored me. I couldn't relate to the teachers, lessons, and played-out slave stories. School felt as if I was learning a different language in every subject. Sitting in a classroom was no fun, especially when teachers only worked to collect a paycheck.

"So how did you become a cop?" I asked.

"I went to school."

"Did you like school?"

"It was cool. I did my *time* and now it's paying off."

"I don't like going to school."

"Yeah, I understand. But it's good to be educated. It's free, and your people fought for you to learn." Her eyes never left the road. "Find something you like to learn and stick with that. It's easier to trick a fool than someone with intelligence."

That made sense. But law school was a long way for someone in the middle of his high school years.

"So that's why you like your job, because you wanna make a difference?"

"Yeah, you can say that. I wouldn't trade my job for anything in the world."

I reclined in my seat, and closed my eyes. Daydreaming of winning court cases ran through my mind; shutting down lies from motor-mouthed prosecutors rallying against my clients. Defendants with short pockets caught the bad end of the game. Mad dudes from my 'hood got long jail sentences in the football numbers for petty crimes, or for crimes they didn't commit. I felt for some of them, and leveling the playing field in the court of law burned a passion in me to become an attorney.

I jumped when static from the police radio derailed my train of thought. My heart skipped a beat as Mama slowly cruised on the expressway.

"Officer King, we got a 10-30 at a clothing store on Southern Boulevard between East 163rd and Aldus streets." The dispatcher repeated the call, and Mama picked up speed on the Bruckner.

"I'm off-duty today!" Mama snapped.

"All of the Bronx police departments are short staffed, and we need emergency assistance for officers closer to that area."

Mama paused for a moment and huffed. She glanced at me while biting her lower lip, wishing the call was a bluff.

"Alright, I'm there," she muttered, and sped on the expressway.

True to her job, Mama always took on tough assignments. She'd won several medals of Honor and garnered a reputation throughout the police force citywide. I wasn't sure what was going on, but I excitedly looked on without knowing my life was possibly in danger.

"Strap on your seat belt, honey," Mama warned, and I braced myself for my first taste of action. "We're going in."

"Ayo, what's a 10-30?" I asked.

"It's a code for robbery in progress."

Mama cheated death on the Bruckner, swerving past cars and narrowly crashing into other bumpers. My legs numbed, and my toes twitched as she dodged other cars to switch lanes. Blood rushed through my veins when she lost control of the car. Sweat drenched my hands with needle-like pains flooding my feet. I sunk in my seat when Mama exited to the street from the e-way.

Death crashed before my eyes and fear forced me to close them. Pain drummed my head to the sum of sirens. I felt light as a feather. I later opened my eyes and saw nothing but strips of buildings passing us by. Beads of sweat slid down my nose while Mama surged through side streets. Hushing my mind from fright with stress rushing in the pit on my stomach, I couldn't wait for brake pads and tires to meet.

"Hold tight, baby." Mama screeched the car to a halt. "Whatever you do, stay in the car and wait for me. Don't move a muscle." She kissed my forehead and rushed out the gray compact car. She parked two blocks away from the scene to shelter me from possible danger.

I straightened my slouch for a clear view of the area. My throat dried, and I tried swallowing spit to moisten my cottoned mouth. My hands shuffled on the door opener and my heart flew south. I unbuckled the seat belt and readied to sprint out the car in case shots flared toward me.

Shoppers stormed frantically inside stores and hid beside cars as shots rang out.

CLACK!!! CLACK!!! CLACK!!!

A chorus of children's screams heightened my anxiety. I crouched under the dashboard when guns sung songs of violence. People aimlessly scattered around the block, and some dashed inside buses that crashed with other vehicles scrambling.

My lips quivered, and questions swirled around me.

Did Mama get shot? Did she shoot them? Is she dead or alive? Should I grab the gun in the glove compartment?

My hands fumbled with opening the glove compartment lock. I dropped the thought of grabbing the gun and peeked over the dashboard. My eyes widened. Mama was crouched on the side of a car trading shots with the goons.

Schpow!!! Schpow!!! Schpow!!!

Shots missed Mama and shattered store windows behind her. Nestled close to a war zone between my blood and unknown robbers was a nightmare in living color. Fear buttered my nerves when shots toasted the block. My stomach dropped as I sat straight with my eyes combing the area like a wide screen.

The robbers dashed from the scene. No other cop cars were seen, but I heard sirens echo from a distance. My eyes followed a man dressed in all black shadowing Mama from the side. Conscientiously, I grabbed the .45-millimeter handgun from the glove compartment and crept out the car door. Straddling a thin line by heading toward drama, Mama didn't have police back-up, and *that* sparked my anger. The fear of losing my old earth had pushed me to follow her and do the unthinkable, and I wasn't looking back.

Rain poured like a giant waterfall and clouds blackened. Thunder cracked the sky and rumbled like earthquakes. My head pounded like a drum kick, and I was in dire need of aspirins. There was no time for whining, so I jogged down Southern Boulevard and turned on East 163rd Street to catch up with Mama. I saw the man in black clutching his gun, and I stood ready to draw and take the law into my own hands.

The robber Mama was chasing darted across the courtyard of a dead end on Simpson Street. He tripped and fell on his face. Mama jumped on top of him and sprayed him with mace as he groaned in pain. He struggled to throw her off as she pinned him down. She flipped him around and stamped her knee on his back. I heard a loud crack when his arm twisted.

"Aaah, shit!" The robber yelled, and Mama slapped cuffs on his wrist.

My eyes lost his partner, the man in black, until I spotted him hiding behind a garbage dumpster. I hungered to burn him like the hottest summer, but my trigger finger frozen. The man paced closer behind Mama and lifted his arm. He aimed, knelt down, and leaned forward. The scene felt unreal, as if I was trapped in a whirlwind sandwiched between darkness.

The man cocked his gun, and my senses heightened. I could hear the clicks even when I stood far away from him. A hurricane of pain wrapped around my body when I collapsed on the pavement.

"Mama!" I screamed through tightened jaws, but the yell fell short. She never heard the shot. She shook and dropped on the concrete as the spark from the gun flashed in slow motion. The man clapped three shots into her back and stood over her. He pumped four more shots around her chest as distress inoculated my face.

"No," I cried, and tears drove down my cheeks. The last ounce of energy I had was the crutch for me to stand. My right hand gorilla gripped the .45-millimeter and aimed at the man. He spotted me aiming, and my hands shook as I closed my eyes.

click

Damn! The gun was on safety.

I fumbled to unlock the gun. My eyes caught the man reloading his piece. Numbness crammed inside my trigger hand and I aimed to shoot, hoping the gun wouldn't jam. Without looking, seven shots blazed when I squeezed the trigger from a visceral motion. My ears rang when the gun cried and let off tears of hate. The kick from the gun knocked me backward, and I clashed onto a gate. Struggling to hold my balance, my eyes opened and found him snaking on the floor. His gun slid away from him. I charged at him like a wild boar.

The .45 stared between his eyes, but I turned when coughs of Mama echoed near me. Blood oozed out her mouth after shots had pierced through her bulletproof vest. Worms of smoke seeped through the holes from her chest as shell casings littered the concrete. The shooter just missed hitting her head by an inch, and I saw the burn mark near her temple.

"Mama…Mama…" I panicked, and she shook violently. Tears soaked my cheeks and my head spun around, searching for anyone walking the streets.

"I need help!" I yelled, but no one answered. Simpson Street was deserted, and I doubted anyone living in surrounding buildings had heard the gun spray. Thunder had sweatered the shots as lightning masked the flashing of guns.

"J-J-Justice," she whispered, and her hand slid down the side of my face. Her eyelids kept opening and closing. I hugged her while battling the thought of losing my old earth.

"Don't say nothin', Mama." I sobbed, and gripped her jacket. My hands trembled with dread, and my mind was like a speeding car without brakes in rush hour.

Watching Mama's life slip away heated my skin. She shook less when I heard sirens screeching toward the courtyard.

Now those assholes wanna come, I thought, and hugged Mama tightly.

She slowly reached in the inside pocket of her jacket and handed me her badge. The badge read "*Equality King*", my old earth's first and last name.

"Take…this…and do well for Mama." She smiled crookedly, and her voice whispered off in the rain. Pain clutched my nerves when her body stopped shaking and began to wane. She stretched and rested in my arms with her blood easing down the sewer drain.

Hate filled my eyes and my lips quivered. My body was like an open wound swimming in an alcoholic river. I gripped the gun, as watching her life slip away hurt me. I heard one of the goons squirm from a distance with repentance of mercy.

"Please," he pleaded, still handcuffed facing the ground. "Somebody help me."

I grimaced and paced toward him. I kicked him over and fired raging eyes at him. Flashbacks of sitting near the holding cell earlier that evening hit my mind, but that didn't matter. Mama was gone, and my heart was shattered to pieces. Watching her die numbed any feelings inside me.

The goon closed his eyes and I aimed at his forehead. The gun shook in my hand, and I rested my index finger on the trigger. My legs wobbled, and my finger fell into a mild seizure. The light squeeze pressured the trigger to ease backwards, but the gun was lowered, and I walked away from him.

Rain pounded on my clothes as I walked toward the man dressed in black; the coward who killed my old earth. He slithered on the ground like a snake, but I had him. I had him good. I was a different person holding the gun with the power that no man could fathom.

He crawled helplessly on the wet concrete. My finger itched to give him a scholarship to hell. My mind screamed "No," but my heart yearned to rebel. I aimed the gun at the back of his head and my finger still rested on the trigger. My hands shook as his breathing shortened. Fighting off the urge to Newport him, I lowered the piece and seconds later dropped the gun in the mud. His body stopped moving after twitching violently as he choked on his own blood.

The rain ended with blue smearing over eve's darkness. I casually walked away and rested next to my old earth until the ambulance and police arrived. I've come with my mother expecting to shadow her, only to grieve over her lifeless body.

The passing of my old earth was like staring at my reflection through a cracked mirror. I loved her more than life itself, as she was the blood running through my veins. Staring at her motionless body broke me down and choked away hopes I had for the future. The pain of losing her robbed me cold as my feet locked on the concrete. I saw her more than just a mother, but a crutch when life had seemingly crippled me. And now with nothing to lean on, I was a baby running through a haunted castle with no one to protect me.

A cardinal floated on Mama's chest and stared at me. I marveled at the scarlet red coating the bird. New York wasn't known to have cardinals flying among the polluted sky, but I believed the bird was a blessing veiled in tragedy.

Viewing the negative as a positive was mildly therapeutic. At least Mama passed away on the job she loved. But while she died on the job she loved, I would later *live* with jobs I hated.

King Dhakir

10 YEARS LATER

Chapter 1: Not Your Ordinary Shower

"No! We're not selling the house." Felicia grilled the pale-skinned man sitting across from her on the couch.

"Miss Moreno, it would be better if you accept the $400,000 offer instead of fighting and possibly losing the brownstone altogether," Mr. Swine insisted.

"Over my dead body. You think you can just come here and pimp us by giving us crumbs?" Felicia huffed to catch her breath. "We *know* our worth, and this house is worth twice as much than what you're offering."

Mr. Swine adjusted his glasses in frustration through a cloud of cigar smoke. He shuffled through his real estate papers and cleared his throat.

"Are you sure you don't want to sell the house?" he asked, nasally.

"Why should I sell it? My family has been living in this house for over 50 years," Felicia retorted.

"Our realtor promises to relocate you and your family to a nicer neighborhood with better housing and an affordable mortgage."

"And where will you relocate us?"

"Westchester County," the man assured her, and Felicia's aunt, Josette, choked on her coffee.

"You must be insane to think we're leaving Fort Greene for Westchester County, Mr. Swine," Josette interjected after clearing her throat. She scowled at Mr. Swine through her black-framed glasses; her hawkish, brown eyes intimidating him.

"Do you have any children, ma'am?" Mr. Swine asked Josette.

"Yes, why?"

"Well, they have *better* schools in Westchester County. I'm sure your child will receive a better education there than here in Brooklyn." Mr. Swine fixed his collar, and Josette excused herself.

She strutted outside the living room and purposely switched her wide hips. Mr. Swine admired her coke bottle figure as his bottom lip quivered. Josette triggered his secret lust for her as he blushed and labored to swallow the glass of lemon iced-tea. He bottled his emotions and refocused on his sales pitch. His wife would shoot him dead and ditch him with no remorse if she found out the fantasies that lingered in his mind. He touched his wedding ring, but his glance at Josette's rotund rear-end was hard to hide. Finding out if Black women were sexually charged was like climbing on top of the highest mountain, and sleeping with Josette was the sweetest taboo.

Mr. Swine fumbled over questions in his head to ask them to prolong his visit. He wasn't too concerned about helping Felicia's staying at the brownstone as much as creeping inside their panties. He loosened his collar, and twirled a pen between his fingers.

"Once again, Mr. Swine," Felicia said, "thanks for the offer, but we're going to decline."

"But wait. I think you're making a big mistake by…not...a-a-accepting this offer." Mr. Swine flipped over his words. Felicia folded her arms in dissension and wanted him out.

"I'm not going to repeat myself. It was nice knowing you, and don't wake me at 9 o'clock in the morning for nonsense ever again." Felicia scolded him, and stood up from the love seat.

"But, miss…"

Mr. Swine paused; his eyes and mouth widened when Josette cut off his sentence. He jerked back onto the couch and damn near pissed his pants with a lump in the middle of his esophagus. His life winded in the cigar smoke from the ashtray after playing the role of gentrification's apologist. Meddling with the wrong family brought death scoffing in his face, as fear bled beneath his moonshine complexion.

"Leave before I do something I might regret." Josette clicked the double-barrel shotgun, ossified by Mr. Swine's persistence.

Mr. Swine slouched closer to the floor and stared at Josette. She aimed at him with cruel intentions. He held up his hands and jerked one knee away from Josette. His mind begged him to rush for the door, and his knees locked while shuffling papers in his briefcase. Josette held her aim with loath drawn on her face, and Mr. Swine stumbled as he scrambled out on the stoop.

While I heard Mr. Swine tumbling from the living room, I walked upstairs from my room in the basement. I paused when I caught Josette with the shotgun.

"I should aim this at *you*." Josette's menacing glare teased her intentions of *really* wanting to shoot me. "When are you getting a job so you can stop freeloading on my niece?"

"Oh, stop it, Jo. It's too early for that," Felicia pled.

"No, Fe Fe. As long as I'm breathing, I refuse to let any man sit up and mooch on my migenté."

I scratched my baby makers and relieved myself in the bathroom. After flushing the toilet, Josette met me in the kitchen. I'd walked into a sure conflict.

"I hoped you washed your hands." Josette jeered, and I brushed off her light insult.

"Remind me to shake ya' hand the next time I pee." I smiled, and fixed me a bowl of cereal. Josette fingered inside her designer purse almost the size of a book-bag and tossed me The New York Globe.

"Here, you should look for some jobs in the Classifieds."

"I already *got* a job," I responded.

"*That* job isn't paying nothing. You need a *better* job."

My mood swung from goofy to angry. Who was this broad to tell me I needed a better gig? I relaxed, poured me a glass of pink lemonade, and took a swig. She wasn't even living in the joint, and still had the nerve to dee-bo her way into my affairs.

"So I need a better job, huh?" I asked.

"Yes, you do, because making ten dollars an hour in retail is peanuts."

"Let me ask you a question, Josette." I was fuming; sick of her garbage. "You worked at retail before, right?"

"Yeah, but I've moved on."

"Yeah, by marrying a rich doctor. I bet you were born with a hard hat and shovel," I joaned on Josette, and she folded her arms with a devilish grin.

"Keep talking, Justice. So I can pee in your lemonade and put it in the 'fridge for you to drink it."

My face twisted in disgust. "You're sick. You know that, right? You're straight jacket, smearin' doo-doo on the padded wall sick."

"That's it. I'm out of here." Josette stood up and stormed out the house. Felicia shook her head. She was in the middle of a tug-of-war between Josette and me.

Josette stayed on my case about looking for a new job while her husband's salary soaked inside her designer purse. I stood my distance from her, but she always picked on me. I didn't know whether she liked me or carried some sick fascination by bothering me all the time. As a woman pushing 40, she acted juvenile by living in her second childhood.

Felicia's grandmother passed away a few years earlier, and she inherited the brownstone. Felicia and her old earth had taken over the spot, and I crashed there after my own grandmother had passed. I didn't *know* my father because he died from a weak heart. So living with Grandma had placed a roof over my head, but I stood aloof from the world by grieving over Mama's passing. Any cares I had for the world was gone, and I was happy with the "fuck the world" mentality.

After bouncing from homeless shelters, periodically resting at Casper's spot, and dorming on campus, Felicia had gratuitously welcomed me into her "Queendom" after I'd graduated from college. So I've been living there for a few years and always felt at home. The brownstone was close to Felicia's heart because her grandmother passed away in one of the bedrooms on the second floor. Felicia would wage war against anyone before losing the brownstone. Paranoia had bought her a shotgun that rested next to her bed, the same shotgun Josette used to aim at Mr. Swine.

"I'm tryin' the best I can to find a new gig, Fe Fe." I sighed.

"I know, baby, I know," Felicia exhaled. "But my aunt just wants the best for me."

"It's easy for her to get on my case since she married a trust fund baby. It's hard out here, man. I sent out 10 resumes, and jobs are frontin' on me because I don't got enough '*experience.*' What's the point of a college degree if I can't use it to get a decent job?" I blasted, but not to anyone in particular.

I stood up, kissed Felicia on the cheek, and headed for the first floor bathroom. "I'm takin' a shower. And think about what I'm gonna do next."

As I stepped in the tub, I twisted the knob to run the shower. The flood of water sprayed my body and thudded below my feet. Hemp-peppermint liquid soap meshed over my physique for a natural scent, and I never felt so fresh. Warm water trickled down and washed away the ugly scabs of yesterday's grind. Refined under the baptism of water, patches of silt circled and slid down the drain as the shower rained on me.

Soap covered my face and I fell deep in calmness 'til I heard the door creak. I reached for the face towel on the soap holder but only felt the wall. The water turned cold, then colder, and sprayed warmer again. The soap blinded me, and I wiped away the liquid with a whiff of the towel.

My sight cleared and I saw a shadowy figure lift its arm. The object dangling from the arm was shaped like a knife and the sight alarmed me. My nerves jumped with my stomach, squeezing like I was about to take a shit. As the figure grabbed the shower door and slid open the steam-fogged glass, I balled my hands into fists.

Immense heat flushed my body and my muscles tensed. I cringed as my lips quivered from the breeze of the slight opening. Soap suds re-coated my eye lids and I felt the warmth of the person stepping toward me. I smeared the suds away from my eyes and saw Felicia posing in front of me naked.

I caught a glimpse of her smooth bronze skin that was highlighted by the sun beaming from the window. My fingers outlined her hips as my lips pressed onto hers. Grabbing and caressing her waist, she laid the *candle* on the soap holder. The water splashed on the softness of her flesh, and she massaged away the tenseness in my shoulders. I rubbed soap over her body and the liquid clothed her with suds. Her nipples hardened and heated against my chest. I gently felt across her breasts, and a light moan echoed within our porcelain haven.

She turned with her back facing me, and I rubbed her down from the nape of her neck to the arch of her back with a wash cloth. Light kisses streaked down her spine and she pressed her thighs together in heat. I fingered her clit slowly in circles like hands on a clock. She held on to me like she was falling off a cliff. Stroking my yard stick that rose stiff, she squirmed, and felt my erection rubbing against her apple bottom. Licking the side of her neck, I massaged the fattened lips that wetted between her legs. She juiced across my fingertips that brushed up and down her bush as she came twice. She turned back around and madly tongue kissed me. I held her close as our lips eloped together.

The shine from the window outlined her curves and shone on her skin. She leaned away from me and turned off the shower. Water slipped down our bodies and rinsed away the liquor of passion from our pores. She stepped out the tub and opened her legs wide by sitting on the toilet, playing with her other set of lips.

"You know you're wrong for that, right?" I said, and she laughed as if she'd planned her tease all along.

She threw a towel at me, and we dried each other on our way to her bedroom. We cuddled on her bed like Adam and Eve, and she ran her fingers around my low haircut; following the circles of my waves. The kisses on my forehead triggered chills throughout my body, and I felt like the king of the world.

Felicia was six years older than me, and had befriended Mama years ago. Mama took a second job as a high school counselor and had worked with Felicia. Felicia was having guy problems, so Mama had tipped her off about how some dudes used women. The irony was that Mama had never taught Felicia about me. But I wasn't using Felicia, at least not intentionally.

"I'm hittin' up the library in Jamaica to e-mail my resume to some companies." I broke the silence.

"Why you going all the way to Queens?" Felicia asked.

"I wanna get away from Brooklyn for a minute to think about what I'm gonna do with my life." Silence filled the room for a few seconds while I contemplated. "Maybe I should join the military."

"Military?" she asked, very surprised.

"Nah, I'm just jokin'. But hell, if I can't find anything, then maybe I'll have no choice."

"Baby, don't talk like that. If you go hard at what you wanna do, you'll be able to fulfill anything you set your mind to."

"Yeah...I guess."

I got up from the bed and stretched. I stood in front of the mirror and posed like Mr. Universe, admiring my chiseled body from months of working out.

"I'm goin' to my room to get dressed. The longer I stay, the more you're tempting me not to leave." I leaned forward and kissed Felicia on the forehead.

Felicia wasn't my girlfriend, but a housemate with benefits. Her family owned the joint, so my word held no weight. Sometimes I'd brought other honeys over to the spot, at least when she wasn't there. Felicia brought home dudes she had dated to make a brother jealous. I didn't care. I always stashed a few cuties myself.

I slipped on a blue and gray collared shirt, blue suede loafers, and a pair of crisp, black slacks to match. Newsboy caps covered one side of my wall, and I chose the black with blue streaks joint. I dabbed some Egyptian musk on my neck and wrists, and was ready to flash my million-dollar smile to the world.

As I completed my circle of freshness, a cardinal flew out of nowhere and perched on my windowsill. The red bird glared at me while I made love to the mirror. I ignored the red bird and gawked at my handsome features.

"You one sexy brotha." I kissed the mirror and flicked my fingers across my collar. "You know I'm sexy, don't 'cha?" I winked at the red bird, and strutted upstairs from the basement.

Swaggering out the brownstone, I felt like I owned the block. I stopped at the bodega down the street to cop a bottle of pink lemonade to start my day. After dropping a dollar to the cashier, I carried on with a bop in my walk. I strolled down my block to the corner of Atlantic and Flatbush avenues to catch the train to Jamaica.

"Taxi, taxi…anyone want a taxi?" yelled a dark-skinned cab driver with a deep West African accent. A long scar running from the bottom of his ear to his chin gleamed in the sun, and he walked pigeon-toed toward me. I quietly turned him down, and he stalked everyone who walked near him for a ride.

Everyday commuters dodged food vendors and dashed to catch their train before leaving the station. Taxi cabs cluttered the Flatbush Avenue Long Island Rail Road stop, and car horns wailed throughout the block of traffic. The cry of honking horns and curses that swung from cab drivers' tongues annoyed me. Complete quietness was my ideal way of starting the day, but I had to settle for the soundtrack of New York traffic.

I shuddered from the commute when the swarming cold gripped my body. The day was cool, but I could've done without the hawk slapping my face. The sun blushed when the dawn's mist cooled the morning rush and left footprints in the sky. My body withdrew from the cold when I took my mind off the frigid temperature. I power walked to the station to hurry and catch my train. The train platform was packed with passengers, and I hurriedly purchased my train ticket. I ignored the clock and nearly dropped the ticket when I bumped into an elderly woman.

Damn! Just my luck. I stopped to say a quick "excuse me" and trucked my way to the train.

"Closing doors," the automated voice announced. I rushed to the last train car just in time. Commuters bulldozed their way inside, and luckily I found a seat. The body heat that filled the car erased the cold, and I unzipped my hooded sweater in relief.

The ticket taker marched down the aisle to punch the train passes. My eyes panned the aisles and caught a fly brown-skinned honey dressed in a green nursing uniform. The small beauty mark on the side of her lips turned me on, and I could see shorty peeking at me from the side of her glasses. She quickly looked forward when I caught her gaze. I chuckled at how slick she was, or at least tried to appear, so I brushed her off. *What an amateur,* I thought to myself and kept it moving.

I shifted my attention to the ticket taker. The tall, lanky man asked four college student types for their tickets. He stood over them, and impatience colored his face beet-red.

"Where you're going?" he asked.

"Mineola," a girl with a long nose answered.

"Thirteen dollars each."

"Thirteen dollars? Are you kidding me?" questioned a boy whose forehead creased.

"Yes, thirteen without a ticket. The ride with the ticket would've cost you six."

"Can you please let us go this time? Just once?" the boy pleaded.

"Sorry, I can't do that. You wouldn't want me to lose my job, now would you?" the ticket taker jokingly asked.

"My dad owns a jewelry store in Manhattan," the boy's friend sporting a Mohawk chimed in. "I bet he can pay you twice than what the L.I. double R is paying you."

The ticket taker smiled, and held out his hand. "Thanks, but no thanks. I'm happy with where I'm at."

"C'mon, bro. He can have you working by tomorrow." The boy pestered the ticket taker.

"I'm not going to repeat myself. The cost for the ride is thirteen, pal."

The geeks reluctantly gave the ticket taker $13 each. They grimaced as if they were down to their last. I laughed at their cheapness.

"If your dad's so rich, you shouldn't have a hard time paying the full amount." The ticket taker irritably counted the money and headed to the next car.

I left my seat and followed the ticket taker. I was tired of the crowdedness, and wanted more breathing room by sitting in the first train car. My eyes caught the college-types' when I squeezed past them. I opened my mouth slightly, but pride and the groups' emotionless faces silenced me. I killed the idea of asking them for a hook-up. I wasn't a dead-beat, and surely refused to shortcut my way on the road to success.

The first car of the train was loaded with empty seats, and I was starving to rest. Before the wool covered my eyes, loud noises snapped me out of the kin of death. I jumped from the ruckus. I caught the second part of the blaring clash of words from an argument between two men.

"...If I was white you'd let me go, right?" a chiseled face, brown-skinned brother lashed out. Let's name him "Skinny."

"I'm just asking you to pay the full fare," replied the same ticket taker from earlier.

"This is bullshit, man! Straight bullshit! I'm tellin' you, I lost my ticket," protested Skinny.

"Um, er...sir, you'll still have to pay for the full fare."

"I bought my ticket before, but I lost it!"

"Okay, that's fine. But you still have to pay for the ticket."

"Okay, okay. So you, you, you gonna make me give you all the money I got, huh? All I got is thirteen dollars." Skinny's anger triggered his stuttering, and he fumbled inside his army fatigue jacket pockets.

The ticket taker stood his ground as Skinny arose. His slim frame towered over the ticket taker and they faced each other, only a nose-length apart. Veins popped out of Skinny's neck as I walked by. I fixed my eyes on the two men and waited for Skinny to swing on the ticket guy.

"You ain't a good person," Skinny scolded the ticket taker.

"Okay, so I'm not a good person." The ticket taker's come-back was sarcastically funny.

"Yeah, and you's a fuckin' faggot, too. I'm a poor Black brotha, and you wanna take everything I got, right? You's a faggot, b. Straight homo."

The ticket taker angrily walked away and called for back-up. Two other ticket takers walked inside the car a few minutes later. One was brown-skinned, and the other was olive. The husky, olive-colored man grilled Skinny as he stood next to him. Let's name him "Chico."

"What's the problem?" Chico asked, looking up to Skinny.

"I lost my ticket, and *that* guy wants me to pay him full price," Skinny explained.

"Sir, you have to pay the thirteen dollar fare."

"Don't holla at me, man! Don't holla at me!" Skinny's mood drove off the cliff.

"Don't *you* holler at me." Chico stood on his square by not flinching. The train came to a sudden halt between the East New York and Jamaica stations. Travelers sat impatiently and bickered about the delay.

"Aye, you're making me late for work," one man yelled.

"I'm not moving the train until this guy pays or leaves," Chico announced.

"I lost my ticket to Huntington and I don't got no money to pay!" Skinny's patience hit the roof, and I had enough. I paced closer to the fuss and stood next to Skinny.

"Hey, brotha. I got the thirteen." I opened my wallet and fingered for a 10 and three singles. "I got you, man." I extended my arm to hand him the loot.

"I ain't takin' your money, Black man." Skinny waved off the olive branch and was too irate to calm down. He'd basically shitted on me. Skinny furiously followed Chico and the other ticket takers to the next car.

I felt embarrassed standing inside the train car filled with white people, but not because of what they would've thought about Blacks in general. I felt uneasy because they were probably the same ones who'll refuse to hire *me* based on someone else's actions. While Skinny foolishly played the race card, I wish I could've pulled a Houdini and disappear from my seat. Brothers like Skinny were the reason why people thought Black folk always cried wolf about racism blocking their progress. Yeah, racism still exists, but not in every instance, and definitely not the one I'd just witnessed.

The train was set in motion again and rolled into Jamaica station. I hopped off and saw cee-ciphers rush inside the train car to surround Skinny. I furiously turned away and focused on heading to the library.

An airplane sliced through the clouds, and I thought about quitting my job; daydreaming about flying aboard the joint. A brother with a college degree was in decent shape in America. So my mind ran down a list of options.

Military? Hmm…maybe.

Rapping? Nope, everybody and their mama are rappers.

Corrections officer? That's prison itself.

Club promoter? No.

Sell drugs? Hell no!

A sign outside the Jamaica Library read: "Help Wanted". But before I asked the desk receptionist about the gig, I logged-on to a computer to search for other jobs available. I e-mailed my resume to companies looking for data entry operators and law firm assistants. Uploading my resume on monster.com and careerbuilder.com also gave me a chance for a better gig.

After surfing the net, I stepped to a blonde-haired woman with thick, pop-bottled eyeglasses. She clicked away on a computer at the front desk and pretty much lived in her own bubble. Her wrinkled face looked like a road map, and looked as if she needed to wash for a few hours. She sat there quietly, picking her nose and flicking away boogers as she stared intensely at the screen. I felt sick to my stomach but still went about my business. I licked my lips before speaking.

"Excuse me, miss." I looked at her while hiding my disgust. "I would like more information about the library position posted outside."

"Uh…yes…we have….an…opening." She stuttered, pausing between words like she was thinking and talking at the same time. "Do you…have…any prior…experience?"

"I am knowledgeable about computers, and I know how to use a database to help patrons with any research they might need."

"Well…have you ever…worked…at…a library before?" She sounded like a robot.

"No, but I am a fast learner, and dedicated when it comes to working."

"This job…requires…hands-on…experience…with working…at a library."

"Okay, but I would appreciate if you would at least look at my resume and take me into consideration." I handed her a crisp resume from my book-bag. She didn't even bother to look at the paper. She stacked my joint on a graveyard of other resumes. Her rudeness boiled my mood.

"Aren't you at least gonna look at it?" I asked upsettingly.

"I will…give it…to…my manager…sir." She turned her head and robotically typed away.

"Whatever, man." I left the library vexed, and took the next train smoking to Penn Station. I headed to Harlem for work and anticipated even more nonsense.

Lord help me.

Chapter 2: What Happens in Harlem, Stays in Harlem

The Jamaica train stopped at Penn Station, and I took the "2" subway train from there to the world famous 125th Street, home of the Apollo Theatre. You know you're in Harlem once the fragrance of scented oils creeps inside your nostrils as you walk up the steps to the street.

Commonly known to many as 2-5th, the strip is flooded with a carnival of hustlers and vendors selling everything from scented oils to President Obama shirts from dawn to dusk. (Obama's image was EVERYWHERE: bath towels, bobble heads, pins, caps, cups, cut-off shirts, comic books, posters, condoms, underwear, etc.)

I copped some Egyptian Musk so I wouldn't have to spend an arm and leg on cologne at the mall. I wormed through the ant farm of folks shelling out dough to vendor tables lining the curbsides of the strip. I thought about copping a few self-help books from the African brothers, as I usually did on my leisure time, and noticed other joints most folks were eager to buy; half naked women on book covers with scandalous titles instead of Qu'rans and Bibles and Farrakhan recitals. Trifle dollars were also spent on bootlegged designer brands and other things folks got off on just to show out at the club and what not.

"I got socks! I got jeans! Half priced!" yelled a man holding up his merchandise on the corner of 125th and Lenox Avenue. I walked past a sea of vendors and checked out a photo wall of Black slaves burned and hung from trees. Chills flew over my flesh and my body shivered on its own. The wall stood near a group of men draped in white. One of them spoke with authority with words breezing out his mouth in a singing flow, weaving between noises from cars and people. I heard the sermon in fragments while curiously strolling by.

"The 12 tribes of Israel…we speak the gospel…the truth needs to be told…the original Egyptians were Black…We are the original Supermen."

I squeezed by the circle of people listening to the men who read scriptures from the Bible. A few onlookers stopped by to listen while others carried on with gossip about celebrities and the latest fashions. The circus of women scrambling to buy handbags nearly knocked me over. They danced and frantically swarmed around vendors, splurging their earnings that left their hands to fill the appetite for designer brands. The police beat stood attentively on Lenox Ave, frowning upon the fleet of cars packing the streets with rap blasting from speakers.

As I walked down Lenox, the row of coffee shops, big-name banks, and half-done condominium towers were newborns to Harlem. Blond hairs, blue eyes, and lighter shades sprinkled throughout the Black Mecca that undergone a nip-tuck over the past few years. Harlem reminded me of Fort Greene and Bed-Stuy with the rise of property taxes pushing long-time residents out the areas. As local hoodlums and hustlers fought over building blocks for whatever reason, realtors invested money and cleaned up neighborhoods that once drowned in bloodshed.

But who was to blame? I didn't have the answers. "Outsiders" were buying land when the have-nots who'd lived there for years shopped 'til exhaustion. They satisfied their thirst for imaginary status by spending $200 on brand-name shoes and high-priced clothes. Keeping up with the Joneses chained their pockets, as many looked and acted the part but weren't directing the play. The curtain closed when folks were spending their pain away, begging for the two weeks of pay to help them chase for happiness. The more I walked the streets, the less I felt I was moving forward since everything around me appeared backwards.

I squeezed through the busy street and finally reached the department store where I worked. The store was half empty when I scoped out the joint and walked through the automatic door.

"Hey, Justice," the female cashiers greeted me, one by one. I returned the greeting and swiped my name badge to clock in.

I didn't hate my job, at least at the time. I took it for what it was---a job. My life consisted of waking up, showering, eating, riding the train, going to work, leaving work, going to bed, showering, riding the train, going back to work…Oh, what the hell, you get the point. I was lucky to even find free time for myself to hit the gym, or shoot pool in Bed-Stuy without worrying about losing a few hours of rest.

Just to get through a day's work, I sometimes believed I wasn't slaving on the modern-day plantation. Lord knows I needed a Nat Turner in my life. I daydreamt about lamping on an island with fly honeys feeding me grapes and old wine with the wind breezing over us under a palm tree.

The pay at Shoe Fetish was okay, but I could take making fast-food cash for so long when I had dreams of filet-mignon money. If my job wasn't an excuse to meet women, I would've walked out a long time ago.

The joint sometimes looked like a photo shoot for one of those gentleman magazines you'll see on the newspaper stands. Damn never every female who shopped in Shoe Fetish were thick. I mean cornbread and collard greens thick. If you were into women with bodacious bodies, then you were in heaven. No joke, but sometimes I couldn't focus on work. My eyes were stuck on the large apple bottoms that wandered around the joint. Unbelievable I tell you; small waists, wide hips, and phat asses. I could've sworn they were strippers. Most of the girls I've met at work came from Harlem and the Bronx. I don't know what the city put in the water, but Uptown girls got it going on. I'd even caught some cats thirsting around the ladies side of shoes just to scope out the chicks shopping there. They were nuts, and I sometimes had to check some dudes for their disrespectful approaches to some of the women. Regardless of those minor problems, working retail did have its own perks.

"Justice, can you come here and help this lady?" hollered Clara, my supervisor.

I slumped over before responding to Clara. Understanding her through the thick West Indian accent was a chore. I had no choice but to figure out what she was saying. It sounded like a bunch of gibberish to me. Besides the accent, she was a pest. She was like the person on the block you ran from, but always found where you were hiding, or like a flu that could never go away.

"Justice, can you please help this lady while I go on break? She needs to know if other stores carry the same shoe in a different size." Clara limped away before I could even answer. I trucked over to the customer and flashed a fake, customer service smile.

"How can I help you, miss?" I lazily asked.

"Yes, I am looking for these shoes in a size 10," answered the woman with freckles. Shorty stood from the chair and was a straight up Amazon. Her long legs and wide hips served the jeans she was wearing justice, no pun intended. She made a brother uneasy by towering over me. I wasn't used to standing next to women who were taller than me. I felt awkward, even as I stood over 6 feet. Besides, I shouldn't have to use a ladder to kiss on dates anyway.

"Can you hurry up and find out because I'm in a rush?" she pressed me, triggering my 'I don't give a fuck' attitude that appeared more so than often at work.

I raised my eyebrows and paused for a moment. She looked in her pocket mirror and caked her face with makeup.

Okay, now you messed up

I thought, but said, "No problem. I'll call a nearby store to see if they have them."

The fakest Kool-Aid smile streaked across my face as I walked to the Receiving area.

"I shouldn't have to take this shit for $10 an hour," I mumbled, and helped myself to a drink at the water fountain.

The store's phone in the lingerie department was free, and I walked to the area, glanced at my watch, and stood there whistling to pass time. Ten seconds ticked by and signaled my cue to walk back to "Miss Can You Hurry Up," but not after about 10 minutes of walking aimlessly around the store; checking out mothers who could pass for my older sister. I gave mercy of ending every customer's nightmare by walking back to the Amazon.

"Sorry, miss, but the Brooklyn and Queens stores are out of the shoes you were looking for," I claimed, keeping a straight face. "You might wanna go to the closest Shoe Fetish in Jersey."

"Oh, no thank you. I'll just go to another store with better service," she angrily picked up her bags and almost knocked over a little boy while rushing out the store.

And you know what? I didn't give a rat's ass if she was mad at the service. Sometimes I found myself wanting to slap fire out of fast food workers for moving too slow with my order. Working at Shoe Fetish had changed my mind about them; I felt their pain. Coming across customers who thought I was a super-bionic robot irked me to the point of me not wanting to help them. I've realized over the years that the less I got paid, the more work was involved in a job.

I patrolled each aisle of the department and cleaned areas that looked as if a hurricane just hit the joint. Opening a box and finding used, worn out shoes tickled me. Why? Because managers and security guards working the camera booths watched employees more than they did customers.

Then they wondered why the store came up short in the audits at the end of each quarter.

As I threw away a dingy pair of shoes I found in the box, my head jerked away when I caught the eyes of a fox. Her light-brown eyes hypnotized me, and I fell under her spell. I cupped my hands over my mouth and blew into them to make sure a brother didn't have the dragon.

My legs numbed when the woman walked past me. Call me a pervert, but watching her rump jiggle was too right for me to pass up. Helping out attractive shorties was the only time I transformed into a model employee. So I voluntarily paced toward her to break the ice.

"May I help you with anything, miss?" I finessed the question.

"Do you work here?" she stood from the end-aisle seat and faced me.

"Yeah, why would you ask that?"

"Because you don't have a badge."

I chuckled at her observation. "Yeah, I do work here." I fingered inside my pocket and showed her my badge.

"I'm sorry, but guys usually pretend to work at the store just so they can get my number. Maybe you should pin your badge onto your shirt."

"Yeah, but that'll give someone a reason to stalk me," I joked, and she smiled. "The difference between me and the other guys tryna holla is I actually get paid for my time while they're doing what you said they do---pretend."

"Uh huh, check you out." she flicked her black micro-braids away from her face. She turned away from me and admired the purple open-toe dress shoes sitting on the display.

"So you like those shoes?" I asked to keep the conversation flowing.

"Yeah, they're fly. I'm thinking about getting those since purple is my favorite color."

"You should buy those and wear them when you see me perform."

"And what you do?" she asked with widened eyes.

"I strip." I held back laughter.

"Oh, I see. And where do you strip?"

"Why? You're comin' to see me?"

"I just might," she teased, and redness poked through her golden brown skin.

"You wouldn't know nothin' about that."

"You're right. I don't." she laughed, damn near turning red. "You better stop before your manager catches you flirting."

"Oh, please." I dismissed with a wave.

"Uh huh, she'll fire your butt for reckless behavior."

"My supervisor can learn a thing or two from me. She's the one who needs someone to clear those cobwebs."

"Boy, you're too much. You know that?" She leaned closer, and hit me with another question like a detective. "So where do you dance? C'mon, tell me."

"I dance privately. I don't allow anyone seein' me do my thing."

"Uh huh, whatever, so you telling me you're a gigolo?" her voice loudly squeaked.

"Shh, tone it down. I don't want everybody in a brotha's business. I just...you know...do my thing for a few lady friends."

"Okay, sure. Do you have sex with them?"

"Wow, now you're gettin' too personal."

"Well, we're grown, right?" She winked.

She placed her hands on the display shelf, and I noticed the purple diamond on the ring finger of the left hand. For some reason I slipped up, because every time I approached a woman in her late 20s to mid-30s, I always checked for evidence FIRST. The lady still had me under a spell, and I got caught with my pants down.

"Yeah…we're grown," I answered, and looked at my watch. I needed an excuse to cut the conversation short and leave her hanging. Not giving women too much at one time sparked more interest for them to get to know me even further. That philosophy of dating dried as an unwritten rule of mine.

"I'm about to go on break. I'm feelin' your style and would like to see that Kool-Aid smile again." I eased closer to her.

"I don't think my husband would like that."

"Okay, I respect that, but at least buy my CD and support a brotha." I smiled, and she held her hips in a "sista girl rolling her eyes and snaps her fingers in the air" kind of way.

"CD? I thought you were a stripper?"

"I strip and perform on the mic. I'm the king of all trades." I left to look in my book-bag for CDs to sell. I figured if I couldn't exchange numbers, at least I could pump some paper out of the deal.

After grabbing a CD, I returned to the lady and showed her the music.

"How you're gonna sell me something without giving me your name?" She pitched a slight attitude.

"I'm sorry. The name's Justice. What's yours?"

"My name is Sandra. Nice meeting you, Justice." We shook hands, and Sandra lowered her eyes, unsure about believing me. "Is that your real name?"

"Yeah."

"What's the name your mama gave you?"

"Justice," I sighed. I was tired of everyone questioning me about the realness of my name. "It is what it is. Take it or leave it."

"Uh huh, okay." She dropped her eyes to the CD case. "Wow, looks professional." Sandra reached inside her designer pocketbook. "How much?" she asked.

"Five bucks."

"Here." she handed me a Hamilton instead. "Never sell less than ten, suga'. I'll stop by again." Sandra blew me a kiss, and put a stain on my brain through the entire evening.

My shift ended, and I felt born again after leaving work. Working at Shoe Fetish drained the life out of me, especially on a slow night. I pulled together some change to take the M1 bus from 125th to 110th Street, and the "2" train from there.

The pain in my head thumped with a slow beat as hunger knotted my stomach. Either the "2" or "3" trains on 125th would've been an easier ride to Brooklyn. I wanted to check out the cuties on the bus instead. The honeys were the sole reward for standing on sore legs for eight hours, and I needed eye-candy to brush off my frustration.

The bus slowly crept near the sidewalk and stopped to pick up me and a few other passengers. I fingered inside my pocket and found a metro card.

"Damn," I whispered, and shook my head as the bus stopped in front of us. The joint was crowded as usual. Folks packed the rush hour buses like sardines with little to no room to move, nor breathe.

The lady bus driver with thick, round glasses nodded her head. I slid my metro card into the machine and squeezed through the aisle. I trucked to the back of the bus and saw a sea of rucked faces with reverse smiles and sleep in their eyes. Wrinkles tattooed the skin of folks riding the bus, lining years of struggles in the hustle of the city. I looked away from the facades that were bankrupt of joy while hoping to find an empty seat.

No luck. I stood next to a brown-skinned woman with locs, smelling like she'd showered in a combination of scented oils mixed with spoiled milk. The blend was agonizing as Chinese water torture. The foulness stung my nose and triggered a mild headache as if a heart was beating in my head. Luckily, a few cuties riding the bus took my mind off the orgy of odors. I copped a few peeks at their twins by standing over them. They never knew what was going on.

As the bus rocked down 5th Avenue, a teenaged-looking guy standing behind me rushed to claim the vacant seat I spotted. The beat from the iPod blared from his headphones. He mouthed off the lyrics to whatever song he was listening to, ignoring cold stares from the elderly standing.

"That guy got no courtesy of givin' up the seat," grunted a woman standing as she scratched her salt and pepper colored hair. The cool air from outside the bus seeped through cracked windows and erected goose bumps on me. The seat drama quickly took my mind off the weather.

"Yo, money." I stared down at the guy. "The lady wanna sit."

"Huh?" the guy responded, slowly removing his headphones.

"I said the lady wanna sit. Give up the seat, sun?" I retorted forcefully.

The redness glowing from the guy's face was eager to burst through his fair-skinned complexion. My cold facial expression gestured seriousness, and I wasn't in the mood for games. He sucked his teeth and placed the headphones back onto his ears.

"Sun, are you hard of hearin'? 'Cuz I can get that straightened out right now." I gritted my teeth and knocked the headphones away from money's ears.

"You ain't gonna do a damn thang," the guy barked back, baiting me to try him.

"Oh, I'm not?" I charged at him, but he didn't respond. A blond-bearded man sitting next to him sliced into the conversation.

"Aye, young blood, give the lady the seat," the bearded man said to the guy.

"Mind your business, old man." The guy shot at the bearded man.

"Well, I'm makin' it my business, and I'm tellin' you to be a gentleman and give the lady the seat."

"And what if I don't?"

"Stay sittin' there and find out." The bearded man turned his whole body to face the guy.

"Try me, and I'll beat the black off you," the guy promised. Half the bus passengers gasped. I laughed and turned my attention back to the guy.

"Brotha, I got this." I waved off the bearded man and faced the guy. "Yo, I'm not gonna tell you again. I'm givin' you five seconds to give up the seat for the lady."

"Please, stop the foolishness," the lady pleaded, but my ears blocked her words from reaching me.

Five seconds had passed by, and I grabbed the guy by the jacket. He lunged at me and we wrestled, knocking over standees.

"Oh, shit!" I heard someone shout during the commotion. The tires skidded and the force flung us forward. The guy and I stopped wrestling once the bus screeched to a halt. We stormed out the back door and jetted down 5th Ave, laughing mischievously. We never looked back as we ran.

"Hey, you! Stop!" A voice shouted from behind, and the words hit our backs with the blaze of wind. My lungs tightened and my chest shot with pain. Sweat moistened my skin and dampened my palms. Visions of jail bars and cop cars raced over me as we sped down to 110th Street. I gasped for air, and held on to the guy after we found a spot to rest in Central Park.

"Ayo, that shit was funny, sun. I love it when we play 'Joker' on the bus." I caught my breath, and was breathing normal again.

"Hell yeah, but yo', I didn't expect you to grab me so damn hard," said Casper, the guy I had wrestled on the bus.

"My bad, Caz, but I had to make it look real. That's what happens when you work out four days a week."

"Whatever, kid. You should've seen the look on homie with the beard's face. I swear to God, sun, I would've duffed money right in the mouth if he would've raised up on me."

"Yeah, man. I thought y'all was gonna scrap." I shrugged, and Casper laughed.

"Nah, man, money was too ugly for me to fight. Homeboy had a George Jefferson hairline, sun. I wasn't sure if I was lookin' at his scalp or forehead."

"Caz, you crazy. But yo', you think the bus driver is gonna chase after us?"

"Not her. The lady's thick ankles covered her feet; lookin' like she's glidin' every time she walks."

"You's a nut, sun." Amused from his comedy, I grabbed the pink lemonade from my book-bag and gulped from the bottle like it was cold even though it was warm. "Real talk, I'm in the mood to hustle and shoot some pool at Lucky's on Fulton Ave. I wanna make some of that old school paper. You down?" I asked.

"No doubt, that's whassup. I got nothin' else to do."

"Aight, cool, let's hurry up and reach the subway before cee-ciphers come and bag us."

Casper was my best friend since Mama had moved from Chicago to Brooklyn after I was born. He got his nickname because of his fair complexion; he could've passed for white if he wanted to cross over. Caz was my road dog, and we were each other's crutches whenever we fell on hard times.

"Hey! Police! Stop there!" We heard yells shoot down the street. I didn't know how the cops tracked us down so fast, but with two or three officers on every block in Harlem, it was easy to find and arrest people.

"Yo', Just, we should run near the Harlem Meer and get ghost," Casper panted as we jetted. We blazed deep inside the park near the north lake.

We ran and split a circle of pigeons feasting on bread crumbs. We even knocked over some health freaks on their evening run without mercy. My heart pounded to the beat of steps as I was losing my breath.

"We should hide somewhere." I looked around the park, searching for a good spot to ghost the cops.

"Aight, bet."

We found a stack of boxes next to a trash can. We covered ourselves and fronted like we were bums to hide from "the man." The night's darkness blinded the naked eye and gave us a trick to fool the cops.

"We'll wait here for a minute until the cee-ciphers leave," I whispered, and Casper nodded.

Shoes clacked on the concrete like door knocks and flashlights combed over trees and hills of rocks. I saw the feet of cops fly down the block after jetting from the street into the park. My mind roamed over the possibility of us not making our way home that night when they paced near.

"George, they went this way," yells from a fellow officer cooled the sweat flowing down my brow. He and his partner wandered around the park as if they had cracked light bulbs above their heads. They ran farther away from us, and I let out a sigh of relief. We flipped the boxes off us and went our way when the cops lost us. I crossed out riding the bus and tossed around ideas to ensure safety. After cee-ciphers trailed away from the area, I spotted a cab and alerted Casper.

"Caz, we should take a cab to the East Side and take the "6" train to Brooklyn," I suggested, and Casper nodded. We headed closer to the southern-most part of the park and lost them.

Running deep in Central Park for a better chance of safely hopping a cab, we looked over our shoulders every 10 seconds for more cee-ciphers. Sirens, batons, and handcuffs dined my hunger to escape the fate that touched many young males in the city. The bum trick was classic, and hiding from authorities was the only time I'd ever enjoy living the bum life.

Casper and I brushed off that run-in and later hopped the iron horse headed to Brooklyn. And while we thought of a good time, we sure weren't looking for the trouble that lied ahead.

Chapter 3: Can a Brother Get a Job?

"Rack the balls, sun," I hollered and powered the tip of the pool stick. I licked my index finger for good luck to duck any omens. Out hustling old timers for stacks of dollars was the climax to not so mundane nights. Winning major cash in the past had blessed my reputation as a pool shark; gambling on the green was my side hustle.

I wasn't the best pool player in Brooklyn, but I've hustled older dudes coming up as a shorty. Mama had taught me how to boogie on the green, and money came and went the more I played and got better. I used to jive cats by fronting about not knowing how to play pool. Spotting them a few balls boosted their confidence until I crushed their hopes by my dominance. Naïve players became victims, and I loved it; I needed clothes to rock, food to grub on, dough to spend, and school supplies. I hustled to avoid asking my old earth for bread. The birth of a pool shark was the start of the worst feeling for many who left with their pockets in the red.

"All you cats are leavin' broke tonight. So you might as well gimme your bread now," I taunted, and my eyes surfed around for the next victim.

Not a word sprang from the guys in the pool hall until a laugh rang out beside me.

"Look at *this* young blood." Old Man Willie blew smoke from his cigar. He sat next to his partners at a round table across from me. "Son, I've been hustlin' niggas like ya' before yur moms was born. I still smell baby formula on yur breath, grasshopper." He stood up and placed the white cue ball on the black circle of the pool table.

I twisted my lips at his comment. The immediate rush to pulverize him over the head with the pool peg tempted me. I hushed the voices in my head that egged me on.

"This ain't about my mama. This about me takin' your Viagra money, playa." I switched pool sticks, and he looked surprised at my boldness. "Maybe I'll let you win so you can take one of your dates to Chuck E Cheese."

His partners laughed, and redness shot throughout Willie's copper complexion. He walked around the pool table to my side. I clutched the pool stick, readying to swing.

"What did ya' say to me, boy?" Willie bubbled with fury.

"Go on and rack 'em up, Willie. I'll even spot you." I ignored his quarrel, and he backed away from me. Willie stamped each ball into the triangular rack and irritably grabbed a pool stick.

"Save that energy for the game, playa." I smiled, and stroked the pool stick in between my thumb and index finger.

Old Man Willie was notorious for sleeping with teenage girls. He sickened me. The diamonds he flaunted shined like stars and beckoned girls to flock to his cars. The rocks on each finger and designer brands that draped his body attracted young girls who aimlessly ran the streets. The plaid sweater vest and corduroy pants he wore at Lucky's were modest in contrast to his flamboyant style in the past. Old Man Willie was a "used to be"; someone well past his prime. He used to host big parties in Brooklyn and Manhattan in the 60's and 70's until crack hammered the gorilla on his back in the 80's.

As he sold girls caviar dreams by serving their minds with hopes of the good life, he was robbing them of their innocence. The sad part was hardly anyone cared. Older men dating girls young enough to be their daughters was normal around my way. Everyday I watched horny windbags and wild young girls hunger for 'hood celebrity. They ate from the same plate of greed as sex and money went together like bacon and eggs.

"How much ya' got on the game?" Old Man Willie asked me.

"Five bills."

Willie smirked, and burst out in his annoying trademarked laugh. "Aha cah cah cah cah. Young nigga, I piss $500."

"Well, you gonna have to do a lot of pissin' because you're losin' tonight. I'm goin' first."

I leaned over the pool table, angling to hit the cue ball. The force of the pool stick cracked the rack of balls and tapped a few strips into the pockets.

"Good lawd, I'm good!" I taunted Willie, not out of fun, but abhorrence. "My hands are itchin', Willie. You know what that means? That means I'm gettin' money, aha cha cha cha."

"Shut up, boy!" Willie was annoyed of me mocking his laugh. He positioned himself to hit the solids after I missed sinking a strip into a corner pocket. Pocketing a few balls and leading in the game, Willie pranced around the table. I took him from granted until he pocketed enough balls to make a brother panic.

"I guess ya' got nothin' to say now, huh? Young buck." Old Man Willie smoked his cigar and let out a hearty laugh.

Ain't no way I'm letting this old gizzard beat me.

I tapped a few stripes in the pockets after he'd missed. A stripe ball bounced off a corner pocket, and I slammed my hand onto the pool table.

"Damn!" The miss triggered my frustration. Willie smelled blood and went for the kill.

"It's over now, youngin'." He bent forward and sunk more solids into a few pockets. Those hits left him two balls away from winning. He hit one of the last two inside a pocket but missed the other. Beads of sweat dripped down his temple. He wiped his face with a napkin and nervously scratched his long beard. My shooting hand twitched with an itch to win.

I gained ground, and split two stripes that fell into pockets. The black ball was the only one left for me to hit.

"It's ooover now." I surveyed the table and envisioned how I planned to hit the black ball. "Black ball, right pocket," I called out.

The pool stick tapped the cue and pushed the ball toward the side pocket. The ball rolled in slow motion to the promise land. The beating from my heart sped with each roll of the ball. Floating across the table, the spinning of the ball spurred the feeling of me living $500 richer. Before the black ball fell into the pocket, Willie covered the hole with his hand. He held onto the ball and waved his index finger, signaling no.

"Aye, that was goin' in," I protested.

"No, it wasn't."

"Yeah, the hell it was, or you wouldn't have grabbed the ball. I want my money."

"Ya' ain't gettin' nothin'."

All eyes were stuck to Willie when he refused to chuck over the money I'd won. He shunned me by brushing off the bet, setting his mind on walking away unscathed. Shades of resentment stood over me; he robbed me without a fight.

Old Man Willie arrogantly strutted toward the door and carelessly blew cigar smoked in the air. I ran behind him, grabbed his shoulder, and turned him around. I pushed him against the wall with all my might.

"Nigga, I want my money!" I was exasperated, and he stumbled toward the exit.

"Don't ya' ever push me like that again, young blood." Willie lifted his sweater vest and clutched his pistol. He pulled the gun from his pants and my life clicked in slow motion. Gun shots burning through Mama's chest surfaced in the muzzle of Willie's gun. My tongue dried and my breathing stopped. I thought of lunging forward to tussle with him before he iced me. The gun rose between my forehead and nose. I stopped when he stepped to me with his weaponry for my curtain to close. Crazy enough to shoot what's left of me, his anger was hard for him to compose, with him itching to cut off my living like a vasectomy. Flushed with anger, Willie's eyes maddened and turned blood-shot red. Fury was burning inside him to leave me for dead.

"Hold on, Willie!" Lucky wrapped his tree-log arms around Willie, forcing him to lower his pistol. "This ain't goin' down in my place. Put the piece down and pay the man his money."

Old Man Willie's blood pressure drove back to normal. He reluctantly dug inside his pockets. He flashed the bankroll and stacked them in the palm of my hand.

"I'ma let you slide this time, young blood. But no one's gonna save ya' ass the next time if you don't watch yur mouth," he cautioned me through a thick Southern drawl, and walked off with a young girl by his side. I shrugged off Old Man Willie's threat and counted the hundreds from the bet I'd won. Running straight into a fire was suicide, but I was as good as dead if everybody found out Willie had punked me out of some paper. A strong reputation in the streets was a passport without flying.

"That was a close call, mah dude." Casper patted my shoulder, sipping on a tall glass of Long Island Iced Tea, his favorite drink.

"Fuck a Willie. He's just poli-talkin'," I said with my chest out. Deep down inside I was saving face. Old Man Willie lived pretty but shot ugly if baited. I hated Willie, and debated with myself about jumping him for trying to shoot me. But a one-way ticket to jail for beating on a dirt bag was a waste of time and energy.

Casper re-racked the balls and paused while looking behind me. His mouth dropped, and he stopped racking and pointed to the door.

"Yo, sun. Is that who I think it is?" he asked, and I turned. Shock lifted my eyebrows in awe. His designer boots knocked on the carpet as he popped the cork from a champagne bottle. New Yorking his way inside the joint, his swaggering spoke the pizzazz of a man who was king of the world.

"Scar-lo, what's good, homie?" I gave him a pound. He drank straight out the bottle like he was drinking water.

"I'm good, mah dude. I just came home last week," he said, as the red mink coat clothed his chubby frame with a 40-inch platinum chain dangling from his neck.

"Okay, okay. I see you comin' out the box lookin' fresh and all, playboy." Casper admired Scar-lo's style of dress. Scar-lo faced me as if Casper had never said a word.

"I'm doin' it big, Justice. My mans hooked me up. That's all. It ain't nothin'," Scar-lo bragged, and sipped from the bottle.

"I guess. So what you doing here?" I asked.

"I'm here to visit my man, Lucky. Then I'm gonna bounce back to East New York and get this money." Scar-lo gulped the bottle for a good five seconds and burped. "My bad, man. Everyday feels like Friday ever since I came home. But check it, come outside and check out this new ride I just copped."

Scar-lo led Casper and me outside Lucky's to check out his motorbike. He gawked at the joint and ran his fingers on the handle bars as if the ride was a woman.

"This my baby right here. I be doin' 10-block wheelies on this joint, kid." Scar-lo never broke his gaze from the bike.

"How'd you cop this, son?" I asked, shocked because he was fresh out of prison.

"Let's just say I'm enterprising now."

"Don't tell me you sellin' that cee-rule."

"Nah, man, crack is dead, b. I switched up the hustle. Ya' boy's changin' the game now." Scar-lo happily rubbed his hands together. I didn't trust his claim of "changing the game."

As he finished, two highly attractive dark-skinned girls stood at the sides of the bike. The daisy dukes they wore exposed their track lean legs, which couldn't hide the well-rounded rump they carried. Their long, black silky hair flowed in the night's breeze as they were close to perfect 10s under the street light's glow. Scar-lo sandwiched himself between their slim bodies, admiring his prizes. He stood there grinning, but his trophy was only an illusion in my eyes.

"Aight, money, I'm gonna bounce inside and hustle some of the old timers out their paper." I gave Scar-lo a pound and went my way. I rarely got a good vibe around him. His aura forced me back inside the pool hall.

Casper stayed outside with Scar-lo. He was a borderline groupie considering he was ignored throughout the whole conversation. Casper had a better chance with talking to a brick wall because Scar-lo's eyes were fixed on his bike the whole time. It was as if Casper was the wind, and Scar-lo was just hearing noises.

A cardinal flew past and brushed against me before I walked inside. I swatted the cardinal away before it landed on the ledge of a window above the pool hall. The red bird glared at me and suddenly flew away, vanishing in the sky. I felt on edge as if something bad was bound to happen after the red bird streaked off in the late night's mist. My instincts were talking to me, but I paid them no mind. I paced to the bar and was longing to drink away the worries.

As I called for the bartender, I spotted four model-types at the bar. The shorties snapped me out of vibes that held me back after leaving Scar-lo. I strolled to the bar and stood by a shorty who wasn't my intended target.

"You ladies are lookin' gorgeous tonight." I broke the ice and gave every one of them eye contact. "My name's Justice. Are you from around here? I haven't seen any of you before."

A light brown-skinned cutie wearing earrings the size of doorknockers turned her barstool toward me.

"No, we're from Queens. A friend of ours told us about the place, so we decided to come through and check it out." She reached out to shake my hand and introduced herself. "My name is Carmen, and these are my homegirls: Janice, Rashida, and Karen."

I shook hands with every last one of them, but yearned to speak with Janice, the brown-skinned woman with dark brown eyes who attracted me to the bar in the first place.

"We saw you and that old man get into it," Rashida interjected. "I'm glad he didn't shoot you or nothin'."

"Oh, it ain't nothin'. It's just an everyday thing."

"So that's how y'all get down in Brooklyn?" She whispered.

"Nah, there's knuckleheads everywhere." My eyes shifted from Rashida and caught Janice staring. "Do y'all always go out clubbin' a lot?" I asked the group while holding my gaze at Janice.

"Yeah, and other things and what not," Janice said. "We also like guys who buy us drinks." She hinted, and finished sipping her drink. She held in her burp and slurped on another glass resting next to her.

"Would you like to buy me and my homegirls a drink?" she finally drew up the courage to ask. That was when she messed up.

Strike one.

"Buy you a drink?" I looked at them like they were crazy.

"Yeah, buy us a drink. Don't you wanna put a smile on my face?" Janice played innocent, and I loved the reverse psychology. Janice and the other three friends stared at me and waited for an answer.

"I tell you what. Why don't I take you out, and buy you drinks while we're on our date," I said to Janice.

"Hmmm…I'll have to think about that," Janice responded.

"Do you have a cell so I can keep in touch with you?" I asked.

"Why don't I call *you*?"

Strike two.

"I don't have a problem with you calling me, but I don't see why there's a problem with us exchanging numbers."

"Well, I don't give guys my number. And is Justice your real name?"

"Yeah, Justice is my real name."

"So what's the name your mama gave you?"

"My birth name *is* Justice."

"Let me see some ID."

Strike three.

I casually walked away and headed to the restroom to relieve myself.

Two things I hated when meeting women at a lounge or any public place: her asking me for a drink without striking a conversation, and asking me if Justice was my real name. Maybe if my name was "Ray Ray" she would've believed me. And a shorty not giving me the math but asking for mine was comedy. I've always said if a woman was really interested, she'll have no problem with exchanging numbers. The chance of a breezy calling without giving up the number was like asking a monk for sex.

The '70s soul music blaring outside the restroom drowned the noises in the pool hall. Voices fell on deaf ears, which left me unaware of the happenings outside. I flushed the toilet, washed my hands, and hoped Casper had stepped back inside. The same vibes from speaking with Scar-lo earlier crept up and swept away any luck from beating Old Man Willie. I felt trapped inside the bathroom, only with the freedom to leave.

Stress grew small bags under my eyes as I looked in the mirror. The reflection was the theme song of my life---handsomely hopeless. A glow flared in my eyes and shined like crystals under flashing lights. It was just a phase until I got myself together to reach a higher plane in life.

As I snapped out of self-reflection and headed to the door, my hands fumbled with twisting the knob; I sensed static from the other side. My heart throbbed when the door creaked open. Warm air seeped inside and snatched away coldness from the restroom. I opened the door all the way and stood motionless; a gun was pointed at me. I knew it wasn't Willie because I would've been dead.

"Don't move! Police!" The officer flashed his badge and beckoned me to the wall. "Hands against the wall. This is a raid."

Miranda Rights? *No.* Asking me why was I there? *Nope.* Giving me liberty to explain my side of the story? *Never.* And cops wondered why anger towards them came from many so-called "minority" neighborhoods.

The cops spread my legs apart and patted me from head to toe. Violated and powerless, the moment isolated me from my own rights. I didn't know what to think because the scene felt unreal, almost as if I was floating in a dream.

The cee-ciphers ushered a stream of women outside Lucky's while lining us against the wall, almost poking their chests out and mocking our manhood. I was like a lion without his pride with my penis chopped off as I watched the frowns of the ladies standing outside. Cee-ciphers held on to their guns and sweated nervously, aiming to rock a fella and leave blood stains with our brains torn like shredded mozzarella. Known to pop Berettas at the blink of an eye, they held their aim. I feigned calmness to not give them a reason to shoot. They saw us as heathens lining against the front window pane of the joint. I felt reduced and stripped away, especially in front of a crowd of women who've viewed us as their strength.

"Aye, I ain't do shit, man. Let me go," a man protested, and others yelled their own complaints. The boys released us after they'd found nothing illegal and carelessly drove away after 5 minutes of patting us down.

"Fuck you, toy cops. Always tryna tear up shit," another man hollered, as he angrily tossed his arms in the air. I walked out the pool hall and spotted Casper. He grimaced while shaking off the police raid.

"Did you see that? Columbos had brothas hemmed up against the wall, feeling between they legs like some freaks," Casper described, with anger drawing across his face.

"It's open season on brothas, man."

"Hell yeah, sun. They had ya'll against the wall hard body. They did nothin' to me, though." he shrugged.

"No pat down or nothin'?" I asked.

"Nope. Nothin'. Nada. They just ran past me when I walked outside, sun."

Police not pushing up on Casper was strange. They usually hemmed up everyone during a raid. He was left unscathed, but was still fuming about me catching the shade end of the stick during the police lock-down.

I switched my mind from the raid to a bakery joint on Atlantic Avenue near downtown Brooklyn. The donut shop was calling my stomach, and I asked Casper to roll with me.

"Why you wanna go to downtown Brooklyn?" Casper asked with disdain rolling from his tongue.

"Why not?"

"Man, I don't wanna be around some yuppies. I wanna stay in the Stuy."

"It ain't that serious, g. They got some fire donuts on Atlantic. We should roll there and then jet back to your rest."

"That's out. Baby mom's trippin'. We gotta take the "G" train and head out to my grandma's spot in Ravenswood," he said, and unwillingly trudged with me to downtown BK.

Everything west of Flatbush Avenue sickened Casper. The "White Flight" from the Heights to Fort Greene angered many Brooklynites who disliked the sudden change of their borough. Similar to how Casper felt, folks didn't want Brooklyn to turn into Manhattan. Casper would've bulldozed every remodeled brownstone and condominium if given the chance to do it.

We hopped on the subway and trekked on the iron horse to downtown Brooklyn. We got off the "C" train and stopped by Henry's, a bakery I visited quite often. Casper and I walked a short distance before hitting the joint. A "Help Wanted" sign hung on the door, and we both looked at each other.

"I'm gonna ask them for a job," I said sarcastically. "Maybe they'll pay me more than Shoe Fetish."

"Stop playin', man. This side of BK gives me the creeps." Casper shuddered and hurried inside.

We stepped to the counter where two overweight women stood. Their menacing looks drew the impression that they didn't want us there, but what the hell, a brother was a sucker for their donuts.

"Henry Donuts, how can I help you?" one blond-haired lady asked, forcing kindness.

"Yeah, um, I would like five honey glazed donuts with the cream filling," I ordered and turned to Casper. "You sure you don't want nothin'? Those donuts are crack, sun."

"I'll pass. Just hurry up so we can bounce back to the Stuy." Casper rushed me, and glared at the other woman reading The New York Globe.

She stopped reading the newspaper and looked disturbed. She was breathing heavily as her nostrils flared. She glared through her thin, red framed glasses and looked at her partner. I tried to make sense of why the lady had stopped reading just to stare at me as if I was filth. She ignored us when we walked inside, but her neck jerked away from the paper as soon as I'd ordered some donuts.

"Excuse me, miss," Casper said properly. "Are you hiring?"

The blond-haired woman ignored him while wrapping the donuts. *I* asked the lady the same question and she responded, "No, we're not hiring."

"There's a help wanted sign on the door." Casper noted. The lady ignored him again as if he was a phantom. I felt Casper's temperature rise and so I stepped in before he snapped on the heifer.

"Miss, my man asked you a question. Are you hiring or not?" I danced on the border of annoyance and coolness.

"Well, er, um, we just hired someone last week."

"So why would you leave the sign on the door advertising for an opening?" I held myself from exploding.

"Listen, sir, we don't have any openings." The broad was irritated, and I lost my appetite.

Screw the donuts. I jetted without paying. Spending dead trees in their store was a thing of the past after they tried to play us like clowns.

"Casper, I got a plan." I stopped him as we walked down the block. He looked at me confusingly.

"What's good?"

"Just follow my lead."

Luckily for me, college students flooded Atlantic, which sat well with my plan. A young girl with reddish-orange hair and green eyes paced near us. I tapped her arm as she walked past.

"Excuse me, miss. I'm sorry to stop you from where you were going, but would you do me a quick favor?" I asked, and she smiled.

"Yes, sure."

"Can you go in that shop and ask for a job application? Tell them you want the job, and let me know what happened when you're done."

"Okay, cool."

The girl skipped inside, and Casper still wasn't hip to my plan. I sipped on a bottle of pink lemonade that was stashed in my book-bag and laughed at the scene unfolding. I tripped on the worst case scenario, even with a grip on reality.

We waited for a good five minutes until the girl slowly stepped out the door.

"So what happened?" I anticipated her answer.

"I asked for an application, and she gave me one."

"What!?" Even my ears jumped at her response.

"Yeah, she even said I could start today, but I told her I had to think about it."

Casper and I looked at each other; bewildered, frustrated, and indignant.

"Thank you, love," I said to the girl. She stood there and waited for me to say more.

"Why'd you want me to ask for an application?" her forehead creased. I wanted to tell her, but couldn't. The answer stormed around my mind, but deceit erased any explanation I could've mustered. Flooded with grief, I shook my head "no."

She read my facial expression and looked away, with evening winds drawing out coldness as the night kidnapped dawn. The sun sank behind the steel mountains and casted a shade over the block with the breeze blowing chills through my clothes. She stared me down for a few seconds and later walked away. I just couldn't answer her question for some reason.

Thinking about what happened in the donut shop, I saw we weren't human beings to them. I knew I was human, but didn't *feel* it ever since I was born. My college degree didn't mean shit; they didn't see it; they just saw an animal paying for their over-priced donuts. Crushing the walls of prejudice that sprawled my residence, I still moved to the beat of my own drum, even when rotten tongues flung messages of hate. My head spun like the exorcist from just thinking about it, but I got it off my mind after bigots crossed the line by name calling. The two suckfaces in the bakery store were no different. Their judging me by the wheat of my skin sent heat waves that left me puzzled. I was just as much a person as they were, but they still treated me as if I was an alien coming off the street. I knew why the geeks prejudged us, but the truth was too bittersweet to swallow.

***

Guzzling liquor on the rooftop of Casper's grandma's building in Ravenswood Houses flushed away the rage from earlier that night. The rare quietness of the projects soothed me, and I actually had time to think; a luxury among the city's rat race. I took another swig of the hard liquor from the plastic cup. The liquor burned my stomach, but later cooled me as I shivered from the effect.

I drifted from the liquor and wondered when luck was planning to stroke its magic wand upon me. The future was in the palm of my hands but I kept fumbling it. I looked over and saw Casper choking from the firewater. He got himself together and downed another drink with one swallow. The brotherly bond between Casper and me amid the daily trials of *creating* ourselves had strengthened our friendship. We stood together as each other's keeper.

"Aye, sun," Casper slurred between coughs. "What's good with you always drinkin' pink lemonade?"

"Pink lemonade is my joint, sun, chill." I sipped just to poke fun at his observation.

"But I'm just sayin'. I always see you sippin' on pink lemonade. You gonna have lemon headed kids, sun."

I laughed between sips and almost choked on the liquor. "Stop buggin' on my pink lemonade. Let me do me. At least I can hold my liquor, you 'I get drunk on fruit punch' face ass nigga," I joaned on him, and we laughed, guzzling our sorrows with tomorrows not guaranteed.

After 10 seconds of studying the stars, the laughter stopped, and the mood turned somber. Casper staggered on his feet and opened his arms like he was waiting for the world to hug him.

"Justice, do you see this?" Casper slowly turned with his arms still open. "I wanna feel like this, man---the feeling that sky's the limit and I'm flyin' with the birds," he said, and as he finished, a flock of cardinals flew gracefully over us.

I wondered if they were following me; the red birds appeared vague, but were very real. The red birds scattered in the air and formed a heart as they swarmed over the project building. Long Island City had never felt so calm.

"I don't know what to do..." Casper dropped his sentence to ponder. "I might roll with Scar-lo's crew."

I damn near choked from Casper's craziness. I spat out my drink and sat on the crate, not knowing what to think.

Scar-lo graduated from the school of hard knocks with a master's in criminology. He'd extorted everyone: rappers, stick-up kids, store owners and hustlers before cops bagged him on a gun charge. He ended up serving time in Rikers before bouncing from various prisons in upstate New York. Slicing inmates with razors had birthed his nickname, and before he went in, he'd built a major rep in Brooklyn and other boroughs. He'd also held down a solid rep behind bars. Recreating himself from stick-up kid to a flashy cat driving luxury cars with pretty girls by his side etched his name amongst ghetto stars.

"Are you crazy, man? You wanna roll with a cat like Scar-lo who's most likely to land his Black ass back in jail?" I charged at him, hoping what I was hearing was bluffing my ears.

"What else is there to do?" Casper tossed his hands in the air in defeat.

"Get a job," I responded.

"C'mon, sun. There's no jobs in New York that can pay me decent money to live. Makin' $8 an hour ain't shit. Why I gotta travel an hour and change to Long Island or Westchester County just for a damn job?"

"You gotta do what you gotta do."

"Yeah, and I'ma do just that. I'm not workin' for someone and fattenin' their pockets while my family starves." Casper turned away from me and stared over the ledge of the roof. "The workin' class nigga is broke."

"So you gonna sell drugs or stick up folks for money?" I asked. Casper didn't answer. He kept staring at the streets below.

"What about your daughter?" I asked him.

"What about my daughter?"

"She's not gonna have a father around when you're either dead or in jail."

"Justice, I'm *as* good as dead. I'm not around half the time anyway because I'm out lookin' for a job, or goin' hard with hustlin' clothes on the block. Those fat bastards across the bridge don't wanna hire me anyway."

"They don't wanna hire you because you only have a high school diploma."

"That's bullshit, man!" Casper faced me with coldness stiffening his face. "Goin' to college don't mean shit. It's who you know. I know brothas who went to college and still work in fast-food joints, payin' back loans that'll last them to their grave. You can read most of the shit you learn at college for free in a library anyway. But see, you was smart; you went to school to study law. And you need a license for that or somethin'. I don't need a damn degree to open a business…or become a writer…or some other artsy shit that people spend their lives away on."

Casper had a point, but I still drilled him. "So you just gonna fall in the trap and sell poison to your own people?"

"I gotta do what I gotta do, sun. I gotta feed my family, even if it kills me or someone else. It's a jungle out here, b. If I'm not gonna sell it, somebody else will. I gotta go for mines hard body." Casper shrugged his shoulders, and I shook my head in disbelief. He sensed my disappointment and sat next to me.

"Man, listen. Niggas who smoke that shit are weak anyways," he drunkenly reasoned.

"That's bullshit. You're giving the system a reason to lock you up and fill up prisons with brothas."

"Man, fuck that. Them peckerwoods wanna act holy when they're the ones bringin' dope in the country."

"Exactly! You talk about fattenin' someone's pockets, but whose pockets you knottin' when you pitch crack on the block? Who's gettin' money when they gotta bury your ass, or you slavin' in prison makin' peanuts?" I blazed the question, and Casper dropped his head to the ground. "Look at me, sun. You claim people smokin' crack and shootin' dope in their veins are weak, but you're givin' up and riskin' your life over bullshit."

Casper said, "I know what I'm thinkin' about doin' is wrong. But how can you live right when all you see is wrong?" He stood up and gulped a full cup of liquor with one swallow. "And it seems like you don't get rewarded when you do right. They only remember the bad guys. I'd rather die young and rich than old and broke."

Casper slumped against the ledge of the roof with his hands covering his face. He stood on top of the ledge again, and looked sober after staggering from the crate. The night casted a shadow over him as the glow from street lights below reflected off the surrounding buildings. He stretched his arms wide and his body was shaped like a cross. I thought he was crazy. I wasn't sure if he'd lost his mind by pretending he was a dare devil.

"You think I can fly with the birds?" He flapped his arms, and I was so lost for words. He laughed out loud. I hadn't seen Casper exuberant and madly insane at the same time; he clearly lost his mind. Funeralizing his emotions and baptizing his pain in liquor, Casper lived a broken man's dream; picking up pieces to scheme and make cream without staring at lady justice in his rearview. Sitting there not knowing whether he was itching to jump off the roof or step down, I stayed pinned onto the crate. He continued to laugh like a demonic clown.

He glanced at the sky and drunkenly fell backwards. I rushed over and held him before he *really* found himself dangling over the ledge on the other side of the roof.

"Your name's not Clark Kent, and you're not Superman." I held him straight against the ledge. Casper poured himself another full cup of that "get right" before carrying on.

"I always wanted to be a scientist. I remember looking at this poster with all the famous Black inventors and I wanted to be like them. But the school system is fucked up. Teachers never gave a shit about my dream, and the schools didn't have enough bread and no equipment for what I wanted to do. Do you know how I felt when those assholes told me I wasn't gone amount to shit? They pushed me away and never reached out to listen, but those are the same niggas sayin' I'm a threat to society when they *made* me this way; when a nigga like me rob them for shit they didn't wanna share. How can people talk bad about me without giving me choices to make it? I wasn't born with a silver spoon in my mouth, and I don't got shit to make it out. Yeah, some *do* make it out the 'hood, but not everyone makes it. It doesn't work that way. But you know what? I'm gonna do what I gotta do. And if that means riskin' everything I have, then so be it." Casper spilled his guts to the air and swallowed the last of his drink.

He handed me the bottle, and I poured more liquor into his cup and mine. I held my cup to the sky and gestured my head for him to do the same. Our eyes were locked onto the Manhattan skyline that looked like another country miles away.

"The only way to go *is* up. Let's toast to victory." I held my cup in the air and Casper hesitated. He smiled crookedly and styled a look of doubt. His arm slowly arose to the stars, and we toasted for success without the life behind bars.

Chapter 4: Drama at the Workplace

"Hey, Justice." Felicia hugged me when I walked inside the brownstone. She almost suffocated me with her 38DD's as my head pressed against her breasts.

"Is it bullets in your bra or are your nipples glad to see me?" I smirked, and she punched me softly on the arm.

"You got jokes, smart aleck." She walked back to the kitchen to stir what was cooking in the pot. The aroma snaking from the kitchen to my nose teased my stomach, strong enough for me to find out what Felicia was cooking for the night.

"Do you want any?" she asked.

"Maaaan, you don't even have to ask me twice."

I hung up my jacket and wet-kissed Felicia on the side of her neck. She moaned, and I held her closer to me. "What you cookin'?"

"I'm cooking squash, cornbread, red beans and rice, and barbeque salmon."

"Damn, you're hookin' it up tonight. What's the occasion?"

"Nothing, I was just in the mood to cook. A sista is going through some stress." She sighed, and her old earth strolled in the kitchen wearing a purple bathrobe. She straightened her brunette wig, turned her face away from me, and greeted Felicia in Spanish.

"Hey, Ms. Moreno. How are you?" I waved, but she never turned toward me. Ms. Moreno's bronze complexion reddened as she blasted Felicia. Her mom's knew how to speak English, but only spoke Spanish whenever I came around.

"Not now, Ma. Damn." Felicia brushed off Ms. Moreno. Ms. Moreno kept straightening her wig that kept falling lopsided. She quietly marched upstairs to her room, and I was glad the boogieman was gone.

"I think she needs a man." I laughed.

"She needs something." Felicia stirred the pot while I sat at the kitchen table.

Ms. Moreno never liked me ever since she caught Felicia and I "playing house" in the basement; the same basement where I rested my head. Chasing me out the brownstone with a machete, Ms. Moreno was dead on my heels with me wearing nothing but socks and boxer drawers. I didn't even care if people were watching me run the block half naked and out of breath with my heart pounding like a bass drum. I needed to get away from that crazy woman. I caught a gypsy cab and paid the man once I got back to my spot. Ms. Moreno put Felicia on punishment for the whole summer. Once Felicia became the bread winner and Ms. Moreno had aged, my staying there wasn't a problem…at least not for me.

While sitting at the table, I felt Felicia's eyes watching me, like a snake playing chess with a turtle before striking. The beat of her foot tapping the floor with grease popping, steam whistling from pots, and the clash of water banging on dishes was the symphony of friction. I listened to the prelude of Felicia and I colliding as my ears was glued to the downpour from the faucet. While she stared; studying, learning, and analyzing me, I ignored her by playing with a Rubik's cube.

"What you see yourself doing in five years, Justice?" she asked, shooting her hazels at me.

"What?" I looked at her confusingly.

"You heard me. Have you ever thought about doing something for yourself?"

I looked down at the counter and half-heartedly played with the Rubik's. "I never thought about it. Where is this coming from?" I was irritated at her angle towards me.

"I think you're wasting your life running the streets and not using your potential."

"How you figure that?"

"Because you have the ambition and motivation that's above what you're doing now. You can't work at Shoe Fetish forever." She sounded a lot like Josette. I still meddled with the cube and chuckled.

"What's so funny?" she asked.

"You're hilarious right now."

"Oh, so I'm a clown now?"

"I didn't say that. Stop being so melodramatic. You're trippin', ma." I twisted my face, clueless about her beef.

"You know what, Justice. You've being staying with me for a minute now, and I'm tired."

"What you mean you're tired?"

"I'm doing something with myself, Justice. I got a good paying job, I pay the bills around the house, and I take care of myself. I don't see you applying yourself. Your attitude about life isn't going anywhere, and this relationship isn't going anywhere."

I scratched my head, falling further in the depths of confusion. "Where is this all coming from?" I was out of it.

"Where is this all coming from?" she repeated.

"Yeah, what's good with you screamin' on me? And repeatin' the question means you're either thinkin' up a lie or an excuse."

Felicia laughed through her nose, not because she thought I was funny. "Law school fits you well. You always have a slick way of turning the conversation back to me." She sighed, and forcefully stacked some plates inside the cabinet. "I'm just ready to move on. I can't allow someone who doesn't give a damn about me in my life."

"Look, Fe Fe. I appreciate you for letting me stay at your rest until I get myself together."

"Yeah, but are you *really* trying?"

"I'm doin' me right now. Things are slow."

"Slow like how?"

"You know they ain't gonna give a brotha a good payin' job. A Black man is a white man with a felony. We're criminals before we walk in for an interview."

"Oh, please, Justice. You have a college degree. So don't give me that 'the white man don't wanna hire the Black man' shit. If you don't wanna work for the white man, then start your own business. Education is free, you know. Library cards don't cost a damn thing."

Heat seeping from the stove fueled my mood. Felicia was rubbing out any good temperament that lingered inside me. I was vexed, but hurt at the same time, especially when she clubbed me over the head with the truth.

"And what is this?" She swung a red thong in front of me. Excuses stormed around my head. I manned up instead. Well…not totally.

"It's a thong."

"No shit, Sherlock. But whose is it?"

"It's yours."

"No, it's not, Justice. Don't play me. My ass is too big for this anorexic broad you brought over here." She flung the underwear at me. "Next time you decide to bring some of your pigeons to the house, make sure you don't leave evidence."

"What the hell you doin' in my room, Felicia?" I snapped.

"I left my brush in there and stumbled across one of your jumpoff's sling shot."

"Okay, whatever."

"Whatever nothing. You're dirty, Justice. Stank… filthy…and dirty." She shook her head after hurling a barrage of unfavorable adjectives at me.

"Dirty? I don't see a ring on my finger."

The burner on the stove flared up, and warmth flooded the kitchen. The curtain of heat dampened my hands when quietness built up tension. I wasn't backing down. The staring match between us was a war to see who was first to break our gaze.

"See, that's why I shouldn't have allowed you to stay with me. I knew this was going to happen."

"What was gonna happen?" I was stumped.

"Me catching feelings for your ass even though we're not in a relationship."

"Oh, Lord have mercy. Are you serious?"

"Serious as you finding yourself a new job and not making chump change." Felicia chewed me out and punched below the belt. I flicked the Rubik's cube across the table and stood from my seat.

"Okay, you got me, but you know what, you gonna need me someday." I left the kitchen and stomped down the steps to the basement.

I flicked on the lights and found my room looking like a junkyard. Time never allowed me to clean my room with me always on the move. I searched for a broom after walking over a heap of pants, boxer drawers, and socks. Tiredness locked my body to sleep, and I climbed into my bed. I flipped over and stared at the ceiling, hearing Felicia's voice running through my head.

"What you see yourself doing in five years?"

"I think you're wasting your life running the streets and not using your potential."

"I don't see you applying yourself. Your attitude about life isn't going anywhere."

Not taking chances in life locked down my desires of wanting more. I wanted to do more, but didn't know how to solve the puzzle of doing so. Settling for breadcrumbs wasn't me, but deep down I was afraid of fighting for the loaf. I feared success even when I fought for it, dreamt about it, lost hours of sleep by thinking of ways to get it, and picturing myself in another world after I had it.

I smiled and closed my eyes. Resting in my bed felt like heaven, as waking up in the morning to go to work was hell on earth.

***

I walked down an aisle with a stack of boxes to unpack for the men's boots section. I juggled the boxes, and one opened and fell loose on the floor. The bottom box was stable in my hands, but the top half wobbled off balance. Snot nosed brats ran wild while some dashed next to me at the end of the aisle. Beads of sweat flew down my brow. The boxes swayed over the rug-rats and I swung left to keep them from falling.

Damn! Move out the way.

The stack of boxes blinded me as I stumbled across brats who circled me like sharks. The boxes scattered onto the floor with boots tumbling down the aisle. The crumb snatchers added to the stress by giggling, and I was a second away from ringing their necks. Something told me to look to my left to catch a man wearing a ski mask on the other side of the department. The man was hiding on the side of a pole and took off running after glancing at me.

"Aye! Aye, you!" I yelled, but the person jetted faster than a bank robber.

Oh, no. You ain't running away this time

I was moving in slow motion but inched closer to him. The goon tossed over a shopping cart filled with brooms in front of me. I flew on his tail and gained ground on him. Slipping on the wet floor in Receiving, the robber fell on his back and curled on the ground in a fetal position.

I towered over the man and snarled at him. The man lied motionless on the floor, and I yanked the mask off his head. The security alarm shrilled faintly inside the room while I gasped at the person behind the mask.

"Casper?" My hands shook, and I heard shoes from security clacking on the floor.

Security rushed to Receiving and scurried around Shoe Fetish to where I held him. My feet numbed with needles running through my blood stream. Screams of the alarm pounded my head and everything around me fell into a blur. The nerves in my hands collapsed when my body pinned Casper to the ground. His partner left him for dead as he fled from security toward a brown Caddy.

"Freeze," security yelled at the unknown man who still ran for his life. The alarm still shrieked, and the ringing slowly turned into my alarm clock. I snapped out of the dream and sprang from my bed breathing heavily. Coming back to my waking self, I caught my breath and wiped the sweat off my forehead.

The dream was a far cry from getting chased by giant sandals on a beach the night before. Shoe Fetish followed me everywhere, even in my rest. The alarm clock rang, and my mind pinned me onto the bed. The clock read 10:00 a.m., and I tapped the snooze button to add a good 10-minute rest. Those 10 minutes turned into 10 seconds when the alarm rang again.

Damn!!!

I was still pinned on the bed after another five minutes had past.

I'm getting up after I count to 10, I promised, and the temptation of calling in sick suffocated my energy to get up. I'd rather save those days off for more important reasons. So I slowly counted to ten and sprang to my feet. I wiped away the film of crust from my eyes and dried spit that lined the side of my mouth. I glanced at Mama's police badge sitting on the dresser. The badge gleamed in the sun as if it was made out of diamond. Waking up and looking at her badge kissed a smile on my face. Cleaning Mama's badge was an every day ritual of good luck, which also lifted my spirits.

The badge also gave me flashbacks of when Mama got killed, and it also pushed me to do something bigger in life.

I showered and got ready for a quick bite to eat in the kitchen. The heap of sausages I saw on a plate pulled me closer to the table. Before a brother got a chance to help himself, a voice sounded from behind my shoulder.

"Peace, king," an angelic voice greeted me from behind.

"Peace, princess. What's good with the sausages? Don't tell me that's swine on your plate," I teased.

"Yuck, I don't mess with the pig. I don't want worms crawlin' in my brain. These are turkey sausages. Help yourself." Caprice handed me a plate from the cabinet. I stared at the sausages like I hadn't eaten in years.

"Now, that's what I'm talkin' about. Good lookin' out, because a brotha's starvin'." I rubbed my stomach and prepared for the morning grub. Caprice poured me a glass of orange juice and sat next to me as we feasted.

Caprice was Josette's daughter and Felicia's niece. She stayed over sometimes during the week to attend school. The girl was nothing like her mother, thank God, and I kept her under my wing. I swept away the bullshit that most young girls picked up during their teenage years; falling for sweet talk and spreading eagle for any guy who walked by. She took heed to the wisdom I brought forth about the streets, but sometimes the glamour of fast cash called her to rebel against what I strived to teach her.

"I saw you on Fulton yesterday with Casper," Caprice said in between bites.

"What did I tell you about hangin' on Fulton?" I charged at her.

"I was with my homegirls. We were just chillin' at the arcades."

"I better not see you hangin' around Fulton. I'll break your tail in half, you hear?" I threatened.

"What's wrong with me hangin' around Fulton?"

"I don't want you around there. You're too young for the wolves out there."

"Oh, please. I'm about to go to high school. I'm old enough to hold my own."

"Old enough? Girl, you ain't old enough to know your elbow from ya' ass," I said, and she rolled her eyes. "See, that's what's wrong with you young girls nowadays, actin' too fast for your own good."

"I'm not worried about any wolves." She reached inside her book-bag and whipped out a switch blade. "I got *this* to handle it."

I swiped my hand to snatch the switch blade from her, but she was too quick. "Cappie, where you get that from?"

"One of my homegirls gave me it to me."

"Oh, so now y'all murder mamis, huh? Goin' around stabbin' folks with shanks?"

"Look, Justice, I'm a pretty girl." She flicked her curly, brunette hair with high confidence, tipping on arrogance. "And I know how some of these dudes get down."

Laughter bellowed out my mouth. I slapped the table from Caprice's comedy even though she was serious.

"So you're a gorilla killa now, huh?" I laughed through my nose.

"I'm serious, Justice. I gots tah regulate if any one of these niggas violate."

"Okay, killa. Just make sure the school doesn't catch you with razors in your book-bag. And I told you about that 'nigga' shit."

Caprice huffed with a slight smirk. "I know, I know. 'We ain't niggas. We come from kings and queens,'" she repeated my constant reminders. "My bad, it slips sometimes. And don't worry. I know where to stash my razor." She got up from the table and hugged me. "I gotta go. Don't wanna be late for school."

She ran and breezed out the door. My laughter shrunk to worry as I feared for Caprice's safety. She was my heart, and anyone who dared to violate Caprice was falling asleep to some sweet chin music courtesy of my fist.

The last of the pink lemonade from the jug washed down the turkey sausages. I made my way outside and headed to work. Catching a slender pale-skinned man dressed in a black suit snapping pictures of the brownstone, I felt disrespected to the utmost.

"Get the fuck outta here!" I threw a glass bottle but missed his head. The guy stumbled across the street and almost fell on his face. The fools who pressed Felicia to sell the brownstone refused to quit; they wanted her to give up the brownstone so they could turn the joint into a condo. Realtors were known for outsmarting dumb negroes who sold their homes, which were then resold for triple the price. That was cool and all, but we weren't giving up without a fight.

The two-story brownstone was a beauty. I couldn't blame the ass wipes for wanting Felicia to sell the joint. Green ivy coated one half of the rusted colored bricks with a gray silted stoop leading down to the sidewalk. If I didn't want to be bothered with Felicia and her old earth, I'd open the front gate to smooth my way to the side door for the basement. The place was sight to see, and Felicia always kept the spot clean.

As I took a stroll down my block, fumes from engine pipes outlined the sky with trees starving for water. Shades of gray colored the sky and answered the leaves prayers by crying rain. A drop never touched me when I rushed toward the bus stop and scrambled for cover. As the sky would later brush off gray clouds, the sun poked through the blanket of darkness and embraced me with warmth as I walked into the corner bodega.

"Aye, hermano," I greeted the cashier. "I wanna play the Mega Millions."

He glanced at me with his lazy eye and smiled. "Okay, hermano. I got you."

I handed him a dollar, and he printed out my paper of hope from the lottery machine.

"How's the chicas treating you?" he asked.

"They're fine. Too much for me to handle." I glanced down, and placed the lottery ticket in my back pocket. "Aight, hermano, luego."

Daydreaming about winning the lottery, I walked down the block in my own bubble. My blessings were on a long shot. I played for the jackpot and walked on quicksand by relying on a gamble to bail me out. I've spent major cash playing the lottery with Lady Luck laughing in my face with her hand enslaving my pockets.

I took the "A" train to work and saw my man, Prince, standing outside the department store glancing down at his cell. The rain stopped, and the sunshine locked on his low-cut hair, fashioned with 360-degree waves. He looked up and gazed at a short, curvy woman strolling pass. While damn near drooling at the woman, his cell flopped from his hands and dropped on the ground.

"Damn," he shrieked, and I crept beside him.

"Peace, king. That shorty made you drop your phone, g." I laughed.

"Peace, king. Yeah, man. Honey was hot. I had to check her out." Prince picked up his cell and checked his text messages. "Ayo, check out what this girl sent me."

He flicked through his picture mail and I was taken aback.

"Damn, sun! Who's that?" I asked in awe, feasting my eyes on a naked honey with an ass that could've eclipsed the sun.

"Man, this shorty I met out in Pelan."

"Pelan? Wow, I need to hit up the Bronx more often. They got some bad freaks out there, sun. I peep them everyday shopping in Shoe Fetish."

"You ain't said nothin' but a word." Prince closed his cell after showing me more naked photos of other females. "There's more where that came from. So what's good with you and Felicia?"

"She's trippin', g. Actin' like she's my damn mama."

"See, Justice. I told you that was gonna happen. That's why I always have a place of my own instead of stayin' with someone because they wanna monopolize my cipher."

I scratched my head and glanced down. "It's okay. I'm workin' on gettin' my own place."

"I hear that. I bet you're tired of her gettin' on you, ain't you?"

"Man, am I? She's just mad I'm seein' other women."

"You should've expected that, king. It's not good to see other women while she's lettin' you stay with her. It's a slap in the face. If you wanna see other shorties, you need to get your own rest."

"Yeah, I hear you."

"Because think about it: she's cooking for you, lettin' you stay rent-free, and I know you hittin' the power u."

"Yeah, she's a good woman, and I appreciate her lookin' out for a brotha," I confessed.

"So take her out sometimes. She probably thinks you're no good by taking advantage of her."

"I hear you. She cooked last night, too."

"And I bet the food was righteous, wasn't it?"

"Yeah, she cooked cornbread from scratch, squash, red beans and rice, and barbeque salmon," I remembered, still salivating from the grub the night before. "No swine, sun. Shorty doesn't even eat the pig."

"See, man, not a lot of sistas would do that for brothas nowadays. I think you should surprise Felicia with somethin' nice."

"Yeah, you right." I nodded, and Prince paused to catch a group of honeys walking inside.

"I don't know about you, but I'll see you inside." He laughed, and followed the flock of women inside the joint.

I followed suit and walked past the registers to clock in. I was glad I worked in Shoe Fetish because the check-out lines were mad crazy. The last thing I needed was blacking out on an unruly customer. Working retail was hard, especially with impatient shoppers.

Yells flew near the registers when an elderly woman was spazzing out at one of the cashiers.

"I want my refund!" the woman with patches of gray hair snapped.

"Ms., do you have your receipt?" asked the plus-sized cashier.

"I lost it, but I wanna bring this back."

"I'm not allowed to give you a refund without a receipt."

"What! Why do I need a receipt?" The old lady blew her lid.

"Because you need proof of purchase. You can't replace the dress with another one without a receipt."

"I don't wanna replace the dress! I want my money back!" The woman stomped. I looked on and wished I had popcorn and Ju-Ju Bees.

"Lady, please calm down." The cashier was ostensibly vexed.

"Don't tell me to calm down. I wanna speak to your manager."

A swarm of eyes from the lines stared at the exchange. Front store arguments always entertained me. The department store always carried its share of drama. It was ignorant as hell, but watching a trashy reality show for free beats cable any day.

The cashier lifted the store's phone and called the manager to the front. "Adam to register 2! Adam to register 2!" The cashier turned and mumbled to the cashier next her.

"This bitch better calm down before I slap the Medicaid out of her."

Adam rushed toward the registers and faced the woman. "What's the problem, ma'am?" he asked nervously.

"This lady won't give me back my money."

"Do you have a receipt?"

"No, but is there a way I can get my money back?"

"Yes, ma'am, but you'll need a receipt."

The lady's anger grew from a spark to a blaze in a millisecond. "I want my damn money back. This is bullshit!"

"Ma'am. I won't help you unless you calm down."

"What?" she blasted.

"Calm down."

"Don't tell me to call down you freckled-faced, red headed devil."

Small laughter rang from the lines as Adam's face turned tomato. "I don't have to take this. I'm going to call security." Adam phoned security, and they later escorted the lady out the store.

I left the front area to Shoe Fetish with tiredness overwhelming me. I wasn't even there for 10 minutes, and the urge to go home had already sunk in. I needed some time off, which meant I had to go through the iron curtain of Clara and Adam.

I took a deep breath and dodged Clara in between aisles. Her constant complaints about workers not placing shoe size stickers on the left side of the boxes incarcerated my time. I could never escape her nagging.

"I'm sick and tired of them not putting the stickers on right," Clara complained to herself. "I teach them over and over and over again so they can get it right."

She turned, and her eyes got me. Damn! I was caught.

"Justice! Did you place the stickers on incorrectly?"

"No, Clara. I didn't," I lazily responded.

"I try to tell you guys to put on the stickers right. You don't listen. I tried to tell you guys to snake the shelves."

"I have been snaking the shelves," I contested.

"Lemme see. Lemme see you snake." Clara challenged me. I couldn't believe she was testing me when I've been working there for three years. She practically spat on my intelligence.

"Snaking" was stacking boxes of the same shoe at the top of the shelf and working my way down and up until finishing with the next brand of shoes. Shoe Fetish was Clara's second home and snaking was a way of organizing her domain.

I showed her my famous snake, and she was speechless. Clara was a trip sometimes. My patience carried me whenever I worked with her.

"Clara, I want to put in for vacation." I wasted no time with my request. "I have 14 days of vacation hours to use, and I want to use them at the end of the month."

"Okay, I don't mind, Justice. Make sure you let Adam know."

Adam was the manager of the entire department store. He worked like he was always high on dope. I wasn't sure how the company had promoted him. The guy didn't know the meaning of common sense.

Adam was separating bed sheets from the blankets and pillows in the Linens department. Sweat greased his face, and a giant stain spotted the front of his white dress shirt. He looked like he'd finished running a marathon on the hottest day of the summer. I got sick from just looking at him.

"Adam, do you have a minute?" I asked, and he stopped stacking blankets on the shelves.

"Sure, what's up?"

"I have two weeks of vacation time and I want to put in for days off," I requested, and he paused; contemplating.

"I don't think I can do that, Justice."

"Why not?" My mouth dropped like an anvil.

"You'd already taken a week off earlier in the year when you sprained your ankle."

Is this dude serious?

"Adam, I had no control over that situation." I caught myself from fuming. "Clara approved my days off and doesn't seem bothered by it."

"Well, she's not the boss. I am. You're allowed to take your vacation days later during the year, but not now."

Adam was foul for using my ankle sprain as an excuse to hold my vacation days for hostage. Twisting my ankle in a basketball game had forced me to miss a week. He could've at least compromised instead of flat out turning me down.

I sulked back to my department, and the joint was a total wreck with shoes scattered across the floor. Spending an hour reorganizing shoes onto the racks and sweeping, I was a millisecond away from quitting. My heart was begging me to walk out, but my mind was chained to the department.

As I whistled while sweeping the floor, a person crept behind me and tapped my shoulder. I turned and caught her eyes. She smiled, and I greeted her with the same gesture.

"Can I help you with anything, miss?" I gazed from her sandals that exposed colorful pedicure toes to the long, red dress skirt hugging her body.

"Yes, I'm looking for some sandals."

"Okay, come follow me."

She followed me to the shelves that stored all our sandals. The girl's presence struck a nerve, and touched me with uneasiness as she walked behind me. It was something about her that yelled trouble; I was too deaf to listen. Shorty gave me bad vibes but I let her slide because she was a cutie.

"So where you're from?" I broke the ice.

"Long Island."

"Damn, you came all the way to Harlem from L.I.?"

"Well…um…they didn't have the sandals I liked out there." She combed through her long, black hair with her fingers. I knew she was suspect. I just couldn't put my finger on it.

As my eyes surfed around the children's department, the girl stepped in front of me, bent over to check out another pair of sandals, and flaunted her allure; tricking my mind to follow the flash of underwear peeking from her hiked up skirt. She wiggled her ass and cobra clutched my attention. Her roundness damn jerked me away from everything, like the two guys standing on the other side of the aisle with black garbage bags. But damn! She was too fine to pass up. I'd fallen victim to the rhythm of lust; teasing, flirting, and pleasing my foolish eyes.

She stood upright and smiled.

"I would like these." She pointed to the sandals at the bottom of the shelf.

"They'll look fine on you." I said, and turned away from the children's department.

"Thank you. Would you like for me to wear these for you?" She brushed her hand across my arm.

"Wear them for me?"

"Yeah, I'll wear them with a brown dress."

"I wouldn't mind that, love. I wanna get to know you first."

"We can get to know each other when we go out, handsome." She winked, and an alarm from what I thought was a toy gun sounded in the Children's department. My eyes switched to the noise and caught one of the goons tossing children's clothes into black garbage bags. His pants sagged damn near to his knees, and he lifted them to run. The girl stepped in front of me, but I flung her to the side.

"Hey," I hollered. "Stop!"

I knocked over a shopping cart and dodged clothes racks. I weaved through crumb snatchers playing with toys in the aisles and jumped over them like a hurdler. The goon knocked over a shopping cart and a clothes rack to block my path.

Damn!

He rammed through the Receiving door. I took the long way to the other side to cut him off. The door burst open, and I frantically hurdled over boxes. My leg caught the top of the box and I stumbled on the floor. My hands smacked onto the ground and broke my fall. Pain shot through my hands and I lost him. He got away by jetting inside a car.

Exhaust fumes from the car fanned my face when I limped outside. The fumes brushed off my arms when I rushed to the car once I regained sight. The car sped and almost ran over pedestrians, zooming through red lights and hauling fast down the street.

Rich, the store's so-called security guard, trucked his way to Receiving. He panted and showed signs of a man who needed to chain himself to a treadmill, looking like a low-budget Cap 'N Crunch.

"Justice, are you okay?" He caught his breath and noticed the stream of blood leaking from my elbow.

"Does it look like I'm all right? Nobody was here to have my back." My frustration slapped his pride. "What took you so long?" I asked.

"Well, I didn't know what was going on."

"You wasn't lookin' at the cameras? Those guys were in the store for a hot minute."

"Justice, please, not now. I'm doing the best I can." He pulled out a pen and notepad like a news reporter. "So what did you see?"

"I saw two Spanish lookin' cats; both ugly with acne on their faces. They hopped in a rusted brown Cadillac."

"Did you get the license plate number?"

"No, I didn't have time."

Rich handed me a handkerchief to wipe away the blood leaking down my arm. "Wait here. I'm gonna give you some alcohol and bandage from the security booth."

He skipped off while I held the cloth to my arm. At least Rich was good for something, which was nothing, and I wondered why I was busting my tail for these imbeciles.

Adam power-walked to Receiving; his appearance alone annoyed me.

"Justice, wha-what happened?" he asked frantically.

"Ask Rich. He has all the details."

"Well, can *you* tell me?"

"Whatever I know, Rich knows." I walked away from him and headed to the bathroom.

Adam and Rich always showed up after the damage had been done. They were the type who'll watch you get your ass beat from the window and ask if you needed help when the fight was over. I got the vibe that they didn't care about me and other employees. So I just worked for a paycheck like they did, and never showed an ounce of attachment to the department.

Mama had once told me about the difference between the slave and the 9-to-5 worker. The slave had no rights, and worked in the harshest conditions without pay. The slave had no choice but to work back-breaking hours without the liberty to remain free. The 9-to-5 worker was like the slave, but had a few rights to go along with pay. The worker was told when to clock-in, how long they were to stay in a certain area, and sometimes worked past their regular hours just to finish an assignment. They *could* leave for another job, only to find themselves in a better plantation that fitted their needs.

Thinking about Mama's words angered me even more, but I laughed at the word "paycheck," as folks were paid to be put in check. Everybody needed a job, and not everyone can be owners, managers, etc. Every tribe needs a

Chief to lead the Indians, and two hustlers living under the same roof would lead to confusion. So I understood the need for a pecking order. I didn't mind working at the department store. I just hated the heads pulling the strings. The managers sometimes sat back without lifting a finger and gave orders instructed from Corporate.

Working in the store had opened my eyes to see that people were paid not based on how *much* they've worked, but rather their position of power. Most supervisors didn't know how to run the joint better than some of the workers and me, especially Adam. I knew when, where, and how security made their routine checks, how to speak with customers, the kind of shoes we carried, how to organize tasks to avoid late completion, and which shoes to place on certain shelves without the help of Clara. Adam didn't know where to place products on sale day to make it easier for customers to spot them. *I* was the one who gave him knowledge about the importance of product placement. He didn't know how to sell anything in the store. I did! I bet he couldn't even sell his soul to the devil for half price.

My spirits were high even when they never showed appreciation of my work. Adam ruling the store with an iron fist and not giving me vacation time was the tip of the feather that broke the donkey's back.

Chapter 5: Working My Magic

My cell vibrated inside the phone holder attached to my belt. Felicia's name sprang on the text message ID, and a smile streaked across my face.

Hey, baby. What u doin? She texted.

I'm livin large…pissed off at the guards who r just…well…large

LOL. U funny. I'm about to get off and head to the gym. Just lettin u noe I won't be home til late.

I'll be home... I reached a dead end when I thought of the conversation Prince and I had in front of the store…*I wanna take u out to an Indian joint 2nite.* I resumed the text.

2nite?

Yeah, 2nite

I'm goin' to the gym 2nite

A night off from gettin' your sweat on is not gonna hurt. You got the rest of the week.

5 minutes past until she responded. *Okay, where?*

On 32nd street...Midtown

Okay, meet me in front of Penn Station

Bet

***

Sparks flew when Felicia walked inside the Taj restaurant; she lit up the joint from dimness. I fought off lusting, but she pushed me forward like a yo-yo string. A hunger for desire tattooed a rush in my pulse to take her home and comb my magic inside her Garden of Eden. Felicia switched down the aisle between tables and smiled as she walked toward me. I handed her a purple rose and kissed her softly.

"Hey, mami." I hugged her closer to me. "How was work?"

"Oh, God. Mad stressful. We got to think of a marketing plan for a hot new product coming out," she said excitedly.

"What kind of product?"

"Facial cream."

"Facial cream?" I was disgusted.

"Yeah, why are you so cynical?

"You know how I feel about sistas bleaching their skin to look white."

"Oh, stop, Justice. I don't want to hear anymore of your Pro-Black malarkey." She giggled, and her taking my comments for a joke soured my mood.

"I'm serious. It's another form of self-hate. White folks tan their skin to look like us and we bleach our skin to look like them."

"Calm down, mah brotha. No one is trying to take away someone's Blackness. The cream is to help people clear their skin, not bleach it. So let's not talk about this. I wanna order some food without you turning Huey P on me, okay?" She mockingly pumped a fist in the air as if she was Tommie Smith and John Carlos at the '68 Olympics.

She rested her legs between my thighs while sitting across from me. Moans fluttered from her mouth when I unstrapped her open toe shoes and gently massaged her foot. She shuddered from my hypnosis, struggling to utter words from her mouth.

"Y-y-you better stop." She stuttered.

"Okay, okay." I released her foot and her eyes slowly reopened. "I wouldn't want you to get arrested for public orgasms," I said, and she derisively sucked her teeth.

Before Felicia could respond, the waiter strolled by and handed us menus.

"Do you like any water or bread before you order?" The tall, cocoa-complexioned man asked with a heavy Indian accent.

"I'm good," I answered.

"Yes, I would like a glass of water, please." The waiter jotted down Felicia's request. I caught him peeking at her breasts.

No tip for him.

"You look nice tonight, miss," the waiter flirted; his mustache looking like a black worm was above his lips.

"Oh, thank you, sir." Felicia blushed, and the waiter turned to me and smiled.

"Sir, please give us a minute to look over the menu," I asserted, and the waiter nodded before walking off.

"It's a wrap." I was steaming mad.

"What?" Felicia confusingly looked at me.

"I caught dude lookin' at your breasts."

"Okay…so."

"Okay, so? 'You look nice tonight, miss,'" I mocked the waiter. Felicia was amused by my jealousy.

"Yeah, whatever, he might want a lil' bit of soul food in his life." She laughed, but I saw nothing funny.

Felicia opened the menu and seemed lost on the dishes. "I don't know what the hell to get."

"What do you like?" I asked.

"Some chicken and vegetables are fine, but I don't understand the Indian words."

"Let a brotha hook it up." I turned and looked for the waiter. I signaled him over to take our order. The man hastily walked to the table.

"Are you ready to order now?" he asked.

"Yeah, we're ready. We would like to order Chana, Dalchini Palu, Chicken Tikka Masala, and Palak Paneer. Please make the food not too spicy. She has virgin lungs."

"Anything to drink?"

"Is white Zinfandel cool with you?" I asked Felicia, and she nodded for the go ahead. "Zinfandel is cool."

The $25 bottle of white Zinfandel didn't burn a hole in my wallet. I was tired of drinking soda every time I went out. The waiter jotted down the order and left for the kitchen. Felicia was baffled at the order I had given.

"What'd you just order?"

"Chana is spicy chick peas, Dalchini Palau is cinnamon fried rice, Palak Paneer is spinach curry with cheese, and Tikka Masala is chicken chucks in a tomato curry sauce."

"Humph. That better be worth me skipping my workout class."

"Trust me. It's worth it."

We chomped down on the ethnic dish once the food arrived. We drank the Zinfandel to wash down the grub and grooved to Indian jazz blaring from the speakers. Her foot tapped my shin and snapped me out of my vibe with the tunes, licking her lips with her eyes widened as if she'd seen a ghost.

"The food is great, baby. Let me find out you think outside the 'hood," she said with food cuffed in her mouth. "I got plans for us."

She caught me off guard. "What you had in mind?" I asked.

"I know of a spot out in Jersey."

"What spot?" I looked at her quizzically.

"You'll see when you get there. Let's roll out of here." She grabbed her jacket and purse while I flagged the waiter.

"Check, please!"

***

"Wow, this...place...is...funky." I marveled at the luxurious hotel room with a Jacuzzi lamping in front of the windows. A bottle of champagne rested deep inside a bucket of ice on the dresser, and red silk sheets covered a perfectly made bed.

"How'd you find this joint?" I asked, still looking around like I was on a different planet.

"My job gives us discounts to the hotel. We hold seminars and conventions here."

"Damn, and all I get is 10 percent discounts."

I stooped down and opened a chest filled with liquor and snacks. "Sooky, sooky, now. I'm about to get my drink on."

"Come bring the liqs and join me in the Jacuzzi." Felicia's business skirt fell around her ankles. The sight of her legs pushed blood to rush where the sun didn't shine. She stripped completely naked and bent over to tease me, showing off the grass that called me to play ball.

"You gonna stand there like a little boy or handle this like a man?" She played naughty, and tempted me by licking her lips. She slowly stepped inside the bubbling water with her hand stroking her clit. Her finger beckoned me to follow her, and I was naked in a blink of an eye.

I stepped inside the warm water and popped the cork of the champagne bottle. I tipped the bottle over her breasts and licked each drop. A road of wine guided my tongue to caress her hardened nipples while my fingers played with the pearl between her legs. Her eyes rolled in the back of her head; she shrieked, shivered, and exhaled. My tongue ran circles under her breasts with warm water cupped inside my mouth. She wrapped her legs around my waist while stroking me back and forth.

I pushed up and studied her movements; the way she wormed and breathed after each touch. I was the master teacher drawing over every spot that sent shockwaves with each kiss. I lifted her on the edge of the tub and spread her legs to rest them on my shoulders. My tongue worked its magic and curved around the juices of her pink walls. Sucking on the crease between her legs, I swallowed every drop of her nectar. She snaked around and pressed her hand onto my head, unable to take the washing between her hay stack. Shivering from the touches on her other lips, loud moans seeped from her mouth with moisture springing between her legs that ran faster than ice cream melting under heat. She climaxed and shook her hips back and forth as if she was shocked with a taser tongue.

I wasn't finished with the lesson. I splashed above water to recess my ruler inside her. Wrapping her legs around me, she caught every inch that measured the wettest crease of her ebony. Writing my name in cursive with licks over her neck, I felt her blowing deep breaths. She tightly held me in; relishing the kisses that stood the hairs on her skin. Wetness soaked my unprotected love as her tight caramel walls hugged my hunger between her thighs.

"Oh, yes, daddy…" she whispered, and her voice trailed away in bliss. A kiss to the forehead mixed with the scent of Egyptian musk got her open. Water splashed loudly with bubbles simmering when I grinded faster. She begged me to push deeper. Her lips squeezed my neck and intensified my yearning to pour all of me inside her rawness that gripped me.

Her sweetness felt too good for me to pull out and hold on. Switching my position with me behind her, our breathing blew louder, and my muscles tensed. Sweat dripped down my forehead without end as we matched breaths. I sped faster with my hips bouncing off her ass. Slaps of my hips banging her ass bounced off walls with me feeling out of my skin. As I grew weak from thrusting, I gave into her good and plenty and emptied all my strength inside her. Kissing the side of her face, I collapsed on top of her and stared at the Manhattan skyline, out of breath like we'd just finished a race.

Bubbles in the Jacuzzi fizzled, and we cuddled on the king-sized bed. I blew out the candles and kissed her on the forehead. As the sun crept and arose east, we sweated through another round of the mo' better and later rested on the wet spot…just like the good ol' days.

***

Customers crowded Shoe Fetish the next day and annoyed me with a thousand questions:

"Do you have these shoes?"

"Can you call another store to see if they have blah blah blah?"

"Where are these shoes?"

"How much do these shoes cost?

After a while, customers started sounding like the teacher from Charlie Brown: *"Wha wha wha…wha wha wha."* I signed up for the job, so I had to sleep in the bed I made.

Shoppers crammed the lines in the front of the store and cashiers were empty of baggers. Adam rushed back to the shoe department and signaled me to come to the front.

"Justice, come to the front and help the cashiers. They don't have baggers."

"Excuse me." I stood firm in my department.

"The lines are long and we need help in the front."

"Adam, could you at least *ask* me if you would like something done?" I waited before moving an inch forward.

Adam's face flushed red. "Okay, okay, Justice. Can you *please* come to the front and help the cashiers with bagging?" He mustered the request, and a fake smile buttered my face.

"No problem. See what happens when you ask?" I walked around him and headed toward the area where I hated working the most.

A lot of managers in the joint had lacked serious social skills. Every store manager in the country should take an interpersonal communications class as a job requirement. The work etiquettes of most supervisors in the store sucked horribly. The joint was flooded with poo-puts who shouldn't be labeled "supervisor" anymore than a girl on the street is called a singer just because she knew how to carry a note.

I got behind Essence and bagged merchandise while she scanned the prices. I panned over the long faces of shoppers waiting in line. I couldn't wait to head back to the shoe department. Attitudes from the customers were off the hook, and I didn't have the patience for it.

"Hey, Justice." Essence smiled while scanning.

"What's good?

"Ain't nothin'. I heard you was chasin' dudes out the store."

"Yeah, Rich ain't doing his damn job. All he does is eat. I can *see* him gettin' fat."

"You crazy." Essence laughed, and swung her long, silky hair away from her face. "Let's do somethin' this weekend."

"I'm busy."

"Uh huh, with your little girlfriends?"

"Not even. I'm findin' ways to get out this joint," I said, and Essence sucked her teeth.

"I hope it's not anything illegal."

"Why it gotta be illegal?"

"I'm just sayin'. Don't do anything stupid."

Essence was my workplace girlfriend, on the down low, and was a good sister to speak with. She liked me and never gossiped about our affairs at work. Fantasies of us doing the mo' better on company time flooded my mind.

Daydreams of her lying on top of me filled my time as blood rushed between my legs from just thinking about it. I fell into an addiction that hit me with the force of cocaine in the course of standing next to her. I maintained my composure and kept bagging.

"Essence, I heard you slept with that nigga, Ben," Jemima, another cashier, said loudly at her register. Essence kept bagging; ignoring her. "That nigga told me about it last night." Jemima carried on.

"Yeah, whatever." Essence tried blocking out Jemima, but the pigeon kept going.

"The nigga drove me home last night and told me about it."

"Stop lyin', Jemima," Ben interjected on the other side of Essence. "Stop spreadin' rumors about niggas."

"Nigga, you didn't tell me you and Essence boned in her house after work?" Jemima asked, and held her hips. "Tell the truth, nigga."

"No, a nigga didn't. You talkin' crazy. You just mad 'cuz a nigga don't wanna get with your ugly ass."

"Whatever, nigga. You always tryna holla and I keep turnin' you down."

"Please, you let lame niggas at your school bag that. I know about you sleepin' with half the football team, and one of my niggas." Ben laughed while working his register. Customers couldn't help but snicker at the clownery that was going down in front of me.

"You ain't got nothin' to say to a nigga now, huh?" Ben taunted Jemima. All she could do was shoot a barrage of "whatever" as her comeback. I got tired of the nonsense and spoke up.

"Chill with that. We got customers here." I budged into their conversation.

"Mind your business, Justice," Jemima bellowed at me. I was disgusted to the 5th power.

"If you wanna make yourself look like fools in public then be my guest," I said, and Jemima sucked her teeth. Jemima and Ben's bickering was like listening to the song you hated through a 10-hour drive with the MP3 on repeat. All they needed was black paint on their faces with red coloring around their mouths to cap off their buffoonery.

Adam walked by, and his presence alone crushed the tongue lashing from the two clowns. My peers couldn't shut their mouths when I'd warned them, but hushed once the manager strolled by. Amazing.

"Now ya'll wanna shut up when Adam comes by, huh?" I blasted them. Ben and Jemima worked quietly. "Yessuh, massuh, I will git back tah werk 'n finis, massuh," I spoke like an ignorant slave, and Jemima shot me the middle finger. I blew Jemima a kiss and Essence bumped into me.

"What was that for?" I looked at her like she'd gone mad.

"Don't blow that heifer a kiss. You might catch the House In Vegas."

"What's the 'House In Vegas'?" I asked.

"H.I.V., man. Get with the times." She giggled. I thought the phrase was corny.

"That was type lame. But I was just thinkin'. Let's go to the Black History Museum next weekend," I suggested.

"Black History Museum?"

"Yeah, I haven't been there in a minute. They have a Marcus Garvey exhibit I wanna check out."

"I wanna go to the UniverSoul Circus at Madison Square Garden on Saturday."

"Circus?"

"Yeah, the circus. I wanna see the animals and clowns."

"You see clowns here for free every day."

"No, silly, I wanna see the acrobats jump through rings of fire with the clowns jugglin' fire on their hands. Not that off the wall 'Back to Africa' shit."

As Essence put down the Motherland, an elderly woman donning a West African garb with her head wrapped in a purple kente cloth huffed at the remark. Essence glanced at the woman and rolled her eyes at the lady's scowl. She brushed off the lady by turning to me.

"Anyway, what you're doin' tonight?" Essence asked me.

"I dunno…might head out to Lucky's in Bed-Stuy."

"Lucky's? What you know about Lucky's?" Essence was surprised.

"No, what *you* know about Lucky's, Miss Harlem? There's nothin' but old, thirsty men tryna holla at young girls."

"And what you doin' there?" she asked.

"Don't worry about it. I do my thing."

"Ha, okay. Don't let me catch you huggin' up on grandma. I know you like older women and all," Essence teased.

"Oh, please. I love women like wine; mature and fine. But that's beside the point. I don't want you around there."

"Why not?"

"You're too classy for Lucky's. That joint is a 'hood spot."

"Aw, ain't that sweet. You care about me," she mocked me.

"Aight, don't say nothin' when those old windbags try harassing you with mirrors under your skirt."

"Don't worry. You might see me roll in there tonight with my girls."

"Yeah, and come to work the next day smellin' like dentures."

I knew Essence was too flashy for the grittiness of Lucky's. I wasn't sure if she could fend off the wolves begging to chew her for breakfast and spit her out for lunch. I urged her not to go, but she was hard-headed.

Her shift ended before mine, and it was time for me to split from bagging.

"I'm goin' back to my department. The lines don't look as bad." I walked off, and Essence held my arm. I jerked away and went on about my business. Before I could sniff the brand newness of shoes from the department, a voice hollered behind me. "Aye, Justice! Wait up, playa."

I turned and gave Ben a menacing look. "What you doing screamin' out my government like that, b?" I berated him as if he was my son.

"My bad, man, but I wanna holla at you for a minute."

I looked at him from head to toe and hesitated. "What's good?" I asked.

The shuffling of Ben's feet showed me he was nervous. He stuttered before letting it off his mind. "I wanted to know if you was seeing Essence."

"What?" I grimaced.

"Well, um, I like Essence. I wanna see if *that* was yours before a nigga…I'm sorry, before a *brotha* stepped to her." He corrected himself, and I laughed under my breath. Essence would rather drink piss poured from the devil before dating Ben.

"I'm good, man. Handle your business."

"Are you sure?" Ben asked excitedly. "'Cuz I know y'all supposed to be goin' out and all."

"Ben, are you kiddin' me?" He was getting on my nerves. "Do ya' thing, money."

"Okay, cool. I just wanna know what was good."

"Uh huh, aight. You should holla at her."

"Aight, cool. Peace, brotha." Ben skipped off and was setting himself up for failure. I wasn't the one to shatter a man dreams. So I played the role of a fool.

I turned and heard sounds of pain. Loud groans from Shoe Fetish alarmed me to head to the department. I thought someone had felt down or something. But nope, it was Clara, limping back and forth as normal. Struggling to stand, her face cringed with pain. Stiffness drained her from moving any faster as groans were muffled from her mouth.

"Let me help you put those shoes on the rack." I lifted a box from a stack of shipments and opened it with a cutter.

"Thanks, Justice. I'm tired, tired, tired," Clara panted, and I understood her feelings. The shoe numbers and security fasteners sat next to me. I began to help since Clara closed for the night.

"Clara, how long you've been working at this store?" I asked, wondering what had driven her to work at a boring place for so long.

"For twenty years."

"Twenty years!"

"Yep, twenty years I've been working here. That's why I want this place to look nice and neat when the regional store manager comes. I always come, and the store looks messy. Customers tear up the place, leaving shoes on the floor, and they teef the shoes. No one cares anymore and I don't like it. This is my life!" She tossed her hands to the air and caught herself from losing her breath after a long-winded account.

"When are you retiring?" I asked.

"Six years from now."

"Six years will be here before you know it. I think you need a vacation."

"No, no, no. I need to work as long as I can."

"How long can you walk around here limpin' without surgery? Your health is more important than breakin' your back for the store," I reasoned. She quieted while stocking the shelves.

"Yeah, I went to the doctor and I might have my surgery soon, but I dunno." She stopped stamping prices on the shoes and stretched. "I'm taking a break, Justice. Make sure no one teef in this department."

"I got you," I assured, tickled about how she said "thief" as "teef."

Clara walked on her last leg for the company. She was disposable, easily replaced. The belt of a steady paycheck whipped her crippled and tied her down for 20 years. I showed no sympathy after watching her limp helplessly around; kissing up to the "higher-ups" and the rest of her peers. After listening to Clara's story, I disliked her even more.

Time slowly past by, and three women caught my attention during the evening. Picking up shoe boxes scattered on the floor kept me busy until I came across "Baby Phat," a plus-sized cutie with a coke bottle shape. She was frantically searching the aisles until I stepped to her.

"Good evening, miss. How may I help you?" I smiled, and she returned her own.

"I'm looking for some high heels." She looked around the aisle. "I look sexy in heels. Do you have any?"

"Yeah, we have some, but shoes don't make the woman. The woman makes the shoes. And I know exactly what you're looking for."

I led her to the aisle with many styles of flats. She sat down and waited for me. "These joints are perfect for you. Cinderella's glass slippers ain't got nothin' on you, ma."

She smiled crookedly. "Why don't you want me to wear heels? You think I'm too fat?" She frowned.

"No, no, no. Heels are going out of style. Guys don't check for shorties with heels. And why would you wanna walk around with heels anyway?"

"Well…I don't know…I just thought they looked good on me." She looked down at her shoes. I rubbed my chin, thinking.

"Hmm, can you take off your shoes, please?" I asked, and she slipped off her sneakers. "See, the shape of your feet is better suited for a 'U' shaped toe box. The heels that we have are 'V' shaped. It'll benefit you if you take the U-shaped flats with padding on the bottom."

Words flew out my mouth like water. Even I was amazed at myself for breaking down shoes to a science. "Baby Phat" grabbed two boxes of flats and went on her way.

"Cinna-bunz" caught my attention when she was weaving up and down the aisles. Her long, teal dress pressed against her body. Her rump jiggled and stood out, as if two cantaloupes were poking out below her back.

"Do you need any help?" My eyes shot at hers. She ignored me like I was the invisible man. She shook her head "no." I smirked because she wasn't getting away that easy.

"C'mon, girl, you gonna ask me for help anyway. So what you're looking for?"

"Well…um…I'm lookin' for some high heels." She licked on a rainbow-colored lollipop with stilettos on her red and black painted toes. She smelled like she'd taken a bath in a tub of perfume; her strong scent stung my nose.

"Aight, cool. I got some joints for you."

"Cinna-bunz" followed me to the rack, and her body swallowed my attention span. I lost my train of thought, but picked up where I left off. I pointed out some high heels, not wanting to repeat the same mistake as I did with shorty who claimed she came all the way from Long Island to shop.

"Okay, these shoes are *you*."

She twisted her lips and was unsure about the shoes. "Um, they're okay."

I toned down the playfulness and pitched harder. "Look, sis. The caramel color of the high heels matches your complexion. It's about coordination, baby." I grabbed the high heels and placed them next to her feet. "Sparks will fly when you walk down the street." I measured her face and body, and smiled. "A gorgeous young thang like you would wanna glide down the street lookin' pretty. You'll have the females hushin' and dudes rushin', ma."

After my sales pitch, "Cinna-bunz" bought the caramel colored high-heels along with a matching dress skirt from the ladies' room.

Then "Chocolate Tai" bumped into me. I needed to inject myself with insulin for every drop of her sweetness.

"Excuse me, sir." She tapped my shoulders, and I towered over her petite 5'4" frame. "Do you have any open-toe shoes?"

"Yeah, over here." I led her to the area before deciding to show her what we had. "Your toes better be on point." I joked.

"What?" She looked like she was about to spaz out on me.

"I'm just playin', ma. Shorties walkin' around with pimples on their toes always ask for those shoes."

"Boy, you're crazy." She laughed, and I shrugged.

"It is what is it. Peep our selection of shoes and let me know what you like."

She glanced around, and my eyes whisked over her top-heavy figure. Protruding deliciously out her tank top, her nipples looked like they were squeezing to burst through and kiss me. I dropped my eyes so she wouldn't catch me staring at her breasts. Her upper body roped my mind like a lasso and stroked away any good intentions I thought of.

"I want these." She clutched the black and blue open-toe shoes. "And my toes *are* on point, thank you."

"Is that so? Lemme see you try on the shoes then," I challenged her, and the sneakers popped off her feet. "I'm kickin' you out the store if your feet smell like toe cheese." I clowned, and "Chocolate Tai" removed her socks. I was amazed that she had no corns hilling on her toes.

"Okay, okay, not bad." I rubbed my hands together and was impressed.

"You can't front on my toes."

"You right, I can't. But I would've passed out if your toes looked like the back of a Crunch bar." She laughed, bought the shoes, and exchanged numbers with me.

Most of the customers were women who loved shoes. I went the extra mile for the sale and cell number. I always got my rocks off days later after a few calls. Some cats went club hopping to bag a few shorties, or even tried talking to them on the street. I didn't need to do any of that. I worked at a spot where women loved to shop. I had it made by getting paid and bagging phone numbers at the same time. Even though it seemed like a good pastime, skirt chasing on the job would later wound up as the story of my life, and the beginning of my downfall.

Chapter 6: Trouble is My Middle Name

I needed a drink, and I needed it bad. So the first place I thought of was Lucky's. My stomach cringed at the thought of a late-night binge of alcohol because drinking firewater wasn't my thing. I thought otherwise since I needed a drink of that "get right" in the worst way.

I hopped on the iron horse after work and got off the train onto the stomping grounds of Bedford-Stuyvesant, commonly known as "Bed-Stuy." Fulton looked dead with steel gated stores lining the streets marking their close, but hopefully Lucky's would beat life into my night. I craved for some smooth R&B tunes after work as Lucky hosted open mic slow jams every week. Roy, the bouncer, blocked the door before I had a chance to step inside.

"Hey, Just, where have you been, baby boy?" Roy gave me a pound.

"Man, I've been workin'. You still work at the high school in the Oasis?"

"Yeah, I'm still out in Queens. Those kids are drivin' me crazy. Shouldn't you be out sellin' shoes and sniffin' old ladies' feet?" He joaned on me.

"Funny guy, but I'ma be nice, because I'm diggin' the extra-medium shirt you're wearin' tonight." I got him back. Three ladies standing in line in front of the joint snickered. Embarrassment struck Roy's face.

"Raise your hands before I won't let your ass in." Roy searched me, and I swaggered inside the joint after the pat down.

Bright lights from the ceiling blinded me along with the plume of cigar smoke filling the room. I choked and sliced my way through the pool hall. A hand tapped me on the shoulder as I breezed through. The smoke burned my eyes and blew sleep into them. A sheet of haze hung in front of me. I waved off the smoke to see the person behind me.

"What's good, mah dude?" Scar-lo gave me a pound.

"I'm good, man, just maintainin' from work."

"I hear that, but yo', I wanna holla at you for a minute, if you don't mind."

"Cool." Uncomfortable with whatever Scar-lo wanted to speak with me about, I half-heartedly agreed; ambivalent about him finding sudden interest in me.

Uncertainty traced over me while I followed Scar-lo to a darkened area of the pool hall. We sat down at a table, and he closed the curtain that draped from a metal pole around the booth. He cleared his throat and rested his chubby arms on the wooden table.

"Listen. We've known each other since we chased girls around the sandbox, right?" He asked in a gruff tone.

"Yeah." I shrugged.

"And you know how I do. I make money. Lots of money."

"Okay, so?"

"You saw the honeys rollin' in with me when I walked in? Well, they with me. The cars, jewels, mini-mansion in New Jeruz is all mine." Scar-lo poured us a glass of champagne that spilled from the rim. "I got money galore, and I keeps my paper right. I blow my nose with 20's and wipe my ass with 50's, b. Money ain't shit to me because I'm gettin' it, and…"

The more Scar-lo went on, the more I thought he had the intelligence of a cucumber.

"Get to the point, Scars," I charged, abruptly cutting him off.

"I want you down with my team."

"What team?"

"My extortion crew." He pulled out a large bankroll from his pockets. Hundreds slipped from his hands as his fingers peeled each Benjamin. "This sure beats makin' cupcake money at a shoe store."

"I thought you said you were *'enterprising.'*" I brought up the jargon he'd used on the night he showed me and Casper his bike.

"I am, baby paw. I got the grips on a few rappers gettin' money. They rappin' about my life on a record, so it's only right for ya' boy Scars to get his cut. Nah-mean?"

As a burst of heat seeped through the pool hall's coolness, the sudden warmth charged me to find Scar-lo disgustingly silly. Scar-lo wasn't discreet about his street earnings and splurging on mirages, and the burning of anger choked my calmness the more he bragged. There was no reason to talk some sense into him because money and power was the only language he understood. As I saw dollar signs in his eyes, the "prize" of thick thighs, breasts and faces of women fizzled in champagne bubbles, flowing over the oversized glass and slipping off the edge of the wooden table. The offer to join his crew past my mind, but freedom and breathing were far more important than any amount of money.

"No, thank you. I'll pass."

"Oh, okay, I see." Scar-lo counted the hundreds flipping off his fingers. "You don't wanna leave that bullshit job, huh? You wanna go home smellin' like toe jam and corn chips, I see."

"Why you disrespectin' me?" I leaned forward with my arms also resting on the table.

"Disrespect! Nigga, I'm tryna help you out. See, that's what's wrong with our people. A brotha turns down another brotha who wants to help."

"Scar-lo, if you were my brotha, you wouldn't pull me into your shit. I don't need your help."

I pulled back the curtain and trekked to the stage area. Scar-lo pissed me off and basically spat in my face. Money was glamorous, but not enough when prison, death and the wheelchair lay as possible outcomes. I blocked out Scar-lo and faced the stage to catch a woman singing.

The stage lights beamed on the woman, and her harmony kissed my eardrums; a sponge that soaked her dreamy vocals, kinda like a Billie Holiday song. I lunged closer and saw the darkness that was textured over her as if her skin was the fire of the sun. The wind from outside, as the entrance door opened, sent chills down my spine and rippled goose-bumps that erected on my skin.

"Damn, honey is hot," a voice from behind me admired. And yes, I agreed.

The band complemented the voice that carried the room into heaven. My eyes zoomed even closer, checking out how well she worked the black stockings covering her toned legs that were built like a track runner. She pranced across the stage and excited the crowd as the purple dress skirt slid toward her thighs. Sticks banged on the drums, the keyboardist meddled with the keys, and the guitarist combed his fingers across the strings with her voice weaving in and out with the rhythm.

"Ayo, what's her name?" Another man beside me asked.

"I don't know. I haven't seen her before." I shrugged.

"She must not be from here," he replied, and I wondered where she'd come from.

Her black, silk locs floated in the air with each twist and spin. Lucky's was known as a 'hood spot, but the singer took over the joint for the night by sprinkling her elegance. The song lasted for a few minutes, and I was impressed by the fast paced, Afro-jazz melody. After her song ended, a thunderous applause erupted from the audience as she walked off stage.

"Give it up for the group, 'Amor'," announced Big Bear, the night's host and resident MC. Every dude fixed their eyes on her like hungry wolves after she walked past them. After walking through a sea of handshakes and pounds, the mystery woman headed toward the bar. My eyes spoke to hers by inviting me to get at her.

I headed toward the bar and greeted her. "Peace, my name's Justice. What's yours?" I asked as we shook hands.

"Nandi."

"Nandi? Sounds pretty. Does your name mean anything?"

"Yeah, it means 'a woman of high esteem' in Zulu."

I cracked a smile. "High esteem it is because you and your band went hard on stage," I said, and Nandi's cheeks reddened, even through her dark-brown complexion.

"Oh, thank you. I wasn't sure how the audience was going to respond." We released our grip. Her hands felt smooth as silk.

"Where you're from?" I asked.

"Chicago."

"Wow, I was born in the Chi, too. What side you're from?"

"The Wild Hunnids."

"Uh huh, what you know about the Southside?" I joked.

"What do *you* know about the Southside?"

"Not much. I was born on the Northside and was raised in Brooklyn almost all my life."

"Yeah, and you got the nerve to tell me I didn't know about anything."

Nandi's band members approached us and I greeted them. They seemed cool, and reminded me of Black hippies from the '60s. I laughed inside while shaking hands with the male band members who sported thin, orange gloves that were cut off at the fingers; suspect were written all over them.

"I'm sorry to cut your conversation short, Nandi," said a tall, slender brown-skinned man with a short Mohawk. "The owner of the club wants to toast with us."

Nandi glanced back at me and stroked her fingers on the back of my hand. "Excuse me, Justice. I have to run with my crew. I'll be back." She stood from the stool, and the band escorted her to the bar.

I stared in awe. She stood out from the rest of the women in the joint. She possessed a flow about her. Figuring out her 'glow' puzzled me because she had "IT." You knew when someone was destined for greatness just by looking at them, and superstar was written all over her.

While Nandi toasted with Lucky, I hungered to hustle on the pool table. I won a couple of games but lost my last that left me broke. The mix of cigar smoke, overhearing broke pimps gossip about their past glories, and losing bread pushed me to the brink of smashing the pool stick in half. Scar-lo walked by, and my eyes followed him. Payback for him disrespecting me was slapping me over the head with karma; beating him was the perfect cure for my woes.

"Aye, Scars," I yelled, and he turned to me. "Grab a stick so I can take away that stack you showed me."

"I don't wanna take your lunch money, baby boy." He waved me off.

"Put your money where your mouth is, millionaire," I challenged, and he contemplated; pondering about whether he should play or leave the joint. "Let's play little bank take big bank," I taunted, and he smiled crookedly.

Scar-lo walked over to the wall and grabbed a stick. A stack of hundreds slammed onto the green surface of the pool table and he winked.

"You ain't said nothin' but a word. I put a G on it."

"I don't have a thousand on me. But I'll take yours."

"You crazy. I wanna see if you got a G."

"I tell you what. If I win I get that thousand, but if you win, I'll double what I owe you," I offered, and the high stakes tempted Scar-lo to the point of him agreeing with the bet. He didn't waiver, so I racked the balls to crack the triangle to start the game.

Scar-lo jumped to an early lead and danced around the table, thinking two thousand was in the bank. He sank five striped balls into the pockets and rolled his way two shy of knocking in the black ball.

I played possum by spotting him. I knew he had a weakness for taking whoever challenged him for granted. His lead shrunk when I sunk enough solid balls to edge him one away from the black. The last ball dropped into a corner pocket, and I mapped out how I wanted the game to end.

"Black ball, side pocket…game over." I tapped the cue ball into the black and the game-winner sank into the hole. I blew the tip of the pool stick, pretending I was blowing off smoke from a gun that'd just fired. Scar-lo was tight about losing. His feelings were irrelevant to me. All I wanted him to do was un-ass my money.

Two thousand dollars peeled off Scar-lo's finger tips and he paced to me. He smiled forcefully, but shook my hand with the money clutched inside my palm.

"This probably the most money you'll ever see at one time, playboy." Losing the two grand erased the brief smile on his face. The smart remark was love taps compared to me walking away two stacks richer. A river of sweat crept from his temple down to his neck as heat from the vents added to the strain of him losing. Two attractive, plus-sized girls saw his frustration and stood next to him, each holding an arm.

"C'mon, baby. Let's motivate out of here." One woman grabbed his arm while the other kissed the side of his neck. The kiss eased his fury, and the girls followed him out the door like sheep.

The stack of 20s and 50s fiddled in my hand. The greenbacks rolled off my fingers and payback couldn't have been so sweet. My guard was lowered until I felt a hand touching my shoulder. I jumped, but turned around to a face I loved to see.

"You need to be easy, brotha. I see New York got you tensed." Nandi laughed, and lightly tapped my shoulder for a second time. "Maybe you can use some of your winnings to take a sista out."

"Yeah, I wouldn't mind taking you out. What's your math?" I asked.

"What's my what?" She grimaced.

"What's your math?"

"Justice…baby…honey. I'm from the Chi. You can't throw that NY slang at me and expect me to know what you mean."

"It ain't slang. Math is the righteous way of saying 'number.' It has nothin' to do with slang, ma. Mathematics is the key to life."

She replied, "Thanks for the explanation. I see I can learn from you. That's a good thing."

I gave her my cell, and she punched in her name and number.

"I see you're not a knuckleheaded brotha, either."

"That's not my style," I said, and she called the number so I could have hers and handed me my cell.

"When is it good to call you?" I asked.

"Any time. I gotta roll with my band. So use that number wisely, Mr. Math."

"No doubt, queen. Peace."

As Nandi left, my worst nightmare walked in. Steaming mad when she showed up inside a place like Lucky's, her stubbornness burned a hole in my heart. The joint fell dark, with only the ceiling lights illuminating her circle.

"What you doing here?" I flared, and she didn't answer. "Didn't I tell you to stay away from here?" She shied away, and I glanced at her friends, daring them to interfere.

"You ain't my daddy, Justice," she countered and finally facing me.

"I am now. C'mon, you about to go." I grabbed her arm and pulled her to the door. She pulled away and glared at me.

"Who the hell you think you are, Justice? You think you can run my life?"

"I told you, this 'hood ain't for you. Leave before I drag you outside."

"I'm not movin' a muscle. I'm a *grown* woman, man."

Old Man Willie stood beside Caprice and held her waist. I was taken aback by the bold move of him. I clutched my fist to crack his nose in half. He laughed under his breath and held on to Caprice.

"Aha cah cah cah cah, young blood." Old Man Willie smirked after his infectious cackle. "She's with me."

"Willie, this ain't none of your business."

"She *is* my business."

"Stay out of this, Willie."

"What is it to you?"

"That's family, and she's *way* too young for you."

"Aha cah cah cah cah, you know the game, young blood. Don't hate the player, hate the flavor."

"Let her go before I strap you to a chair and cut those dried up curls off your head."

Laughter from the pool hall forced Willie to let go of Caprice. He patted his poor excuse of a Jheri curl and straightened his collar.

"Okay, suit yourself," Willie stepped away from Caprice and headed to the pool tables. I grabbed Caprice's arm and she pulled to free herself from my grip. She tripped over her high heels and her dress lifted.

"Get up, girl." I lifted Caprice to carry her outside. As I carried her, a large thump hit me and I dropped to the floor. The sharp pain throbbed inside my back. I saw nothing but whiteness. The pool stick cracked as I blacked out for a split second. I backed away from Willie to gain footing. The pain felt as if a pile of bricks had dropped on me and I slipped away to grab a chair for support. I staggered while holding the chair and lost focus. Willie towered over me and repeatedly kicked my ribs with his sharp-toed dress shoes. He knelt down and punched my sides with his thick gold rings. The impact hurt so bad that the adrenaline numbed the sting.

The old man got up and kicked again but I caught his foot. He hobbled on one leg and hopped to keep his balance. I swung my leg and swept him on the ground. He plummeted to the floor like an anchor.

The razor I hid in the inseam of my newsboy cap slipped out. I pressed the blade onto his cheek with rancor. He shrieked with fear tinting his eyes.

"Stay away from Caprice or I'll kill you. Ya' hear? I'll kill you," I madly whispered, and suddenly gunshots from Mama's death blared around Willie's face. I couldn't recognize my voice with me wrapped around the Hyde of snuffing him out. Deep breaths flew out my mouth with his life singing with doubt. Flashbacks of Willie pulling his gun on me deepened my fuse to thresh him out. The energy of fear turned into hate as the blade cracked his flesh.

"You're food the next time I see you breathe near Caprice." I threatened with the itch to violate his face.

The blade scratched his cheek and broke his skin. Blood leaked down his beard. His eyelids squeezed together from the moment he feared. I wasn't about to carve him, but rather the guy who pumped lead in my old earth on the night she passed. His likeness suddenly appeared in place of Willie, and violently pushed me to carve him. Before slicing his grill like a Jack-O-Lantern, the smoke that lingered in the lounge mopped away the guy's image. Willie appeared to be Willie again, and my heart pumped back to normal. I stood over him and gave him a taste of his own medicine by pimp-slapping him across the face before I decided he'd suffered enough.

As I got up from back-slapping Willie, the scene moved in slow motion with everyone facing me; hawking, frowning, smiling, gazing…as if I was a freak show in front of a plastic audience. An older man approved my actions by nodded his head "yes," but I wasn't moved. They were nothing but bitches to me on the strength of them waiting for someone to finally stand up to Willie. So much time had past with no one ever confronting him about sleeping with under-aged girls. I guess I was the one to play hero.

The bouncers grabbed Old Man Willie and showed him the door. Caprice's eyes flooded with tears as she looked on. Her sobs robbed my night's joy, but I was glad Nandi had left instead of her getting the first impression of me as a mad man.

The house lights rained down and blurred my sight. I squinted from the burst of light and found Caprice fixing her skirt. Her eyes glossed, and I wiped away tears of grief from her cheeks. I wrapped my arms around her shoulders and we exited Lucky's in one piece.

Chapter 7: TGIM (Thank God It's Monday)

I loved Mondays. There was nothing like walking inside the store and finding the joint empty. Customers flooded the floor after Wednesdays like clockwork as they geared for the weekend. I started off the week by vacuuming the carpet and stocking new shipments on shelves.

As I stocked boxes of ladies' flats, Coffey strolled by the shoe department and hugged me. She was another reason why I loved starting off the week working the morning shift.

"Hey, handsome." Coffey smiled, and nudged me on the ribs. "How are you this morning?"

"I'm fine, queen. Just chillin' and striving for perfection," I said.

"Ain't nothing wrong with that." She grabbed a box of purple flats from the shelf. "I better get these before someone else takes them. Do you wanna walk with me to the front?"

I nodded, and walked with her to the Customer Service booth.

I've known Coffey years before we worked at the department store. She managed Customer Service and was one of the few key holders who had some sense. Attending night school for her PhD, she worked the morning shift and I rarely saw her. She was a light-brown skinned sister with natural short-cropped hair without make-up smothering her pores. She always wore different button-up blouses, loose slacks cuffed at the bottom, and matching flats for her daily fashion. Her dress code looked average, but waves of men were drawn to her like the moon pulling the ocean.

"Have you've been good lately, Justice?" she asked. I grinned while glancing away.

"Why wouldn't I be?"

"I wasn't born yesterday, Justice. I see you acting bad with them young gals in the shoe department."

"I'm not a bad boy. I'm a good boy with bad habits."

Coffey cheesed. "You always start my day with a smile."

"Yeah? So when you gonna let a brotha take you out?" I asked half seriously.

"Honey, I'm old enough to be your mother. You know I'm happily married." She raised her left hand and flashed the rock on the ring.

"I respect that, love."

"Thank you, honey. We need more respectable men like you in the world. I can't say the same for Adam, that's for sure." She cringed and carried on. "I had to complain to Corporate about him."

"I know he has a thing for high-yella sistas, but damn. What happened?"

"To make a long story short, the fool made passes at me and hinted about wanting to sleep with me without coming all the way out with it."

"I see he's not fired." I cringed.

"Oh, please. They just gave him a warning and called it a day. I'm about to leave in a few months after I graduate from school anyway." She exhaled with a sigh of relief and activated her register. "When are you out of here?"

"I don't know."

"Why not?" she asked. I shrugged and stood in front of her clueless. "You're an educated brotha who went to school to make good use of yourself. I'm gonna get my doctorate. You should go on to law school and do the damn thing. *It's easier to trick a fool than someone who's intelligent.*"

As she finished, a cardinal flew inside the store and perched on a pipe that stretched across the building below the ceiling. The red bird flapped its wings and lapped around in circles before swooping past Coffey and I. She shooed the red bird away and stumbled against the booth. The red bird tumbled, circled over me like a halo before changing colors from red to purple, and flew back to the ceiling.

"They need to do something with those damn birds flying around the store." Coffey brushed herself off as the cardinal hawked down at us.

Not taking my eyes off the purple bird, all my senses withered away and slept in the coffin of my past; the past I wanted to forget. Every so often when I saw the bird, my right hand itched; the same hand that licked off shots on that memorable evening. The purple sheathing its feathers glossed as a faint wind blew by. Silencing the unwelcoming gun blasts that haunted me, the cardinal slurred a whistle that erased those dreadful thoughts and sung a melody before exiting out the small opening in the roof.

The bird left, and Adam shuffled by the booth in a panic. He slowly stepped to the booth when he saw Coffey and stopped short of reaching me. Tension was thick, and she ignored him when he stood beside me.

"Justice…Justice." Adam swayed back and forth like he had ants in his pants. "I need you to stand in the front of the store and help us get rid of the cooling fans by the end of the day."

I was annoyed and asked, "Why me?"

"Why not?" He patted me on the shoulder like we'd been close friends. "You're the best seller we got in the store."

Adam smiled. I was too swift to fall for the con game.

"Do I at least get commission?" I asked.

"Well…not exactly. But I *will* give you those vacation days you wanted."

Cha-ching

Music to my ears; he hit me in the heart by giving me the early vacation days that shouldn't have been negotiated in the first place. I agreed, but still had a score to settle.

"Adam, I heard about what happened between you and Coffey," I lightly remarked, as me mentioning her name slapped surprise across his face.

"What are you're talkin' about, Justice?" He peeked over my shoulders to glance at Coffey who stood a few yards away from us.

"I don't know what happened because I wasn't there. But if I hear anything about you're disrespecting her again, there's gonna be problems."

His eyebrows arched. "Are you threatening me, Justice?"

"No, it's a promise." My icy response chilled him, and I walked away with everything that needed to be said.

Snapping my thoughts back to work, I sold the fans like they were Bibles. The persuasive tricks I'd learned in law classes paid off. Adam would later treat me as if he'd always liked me, even after confronting him about the Coffey incident.

Casper strolled inside the store wearing a karate jacket with Chinese symbols plastered on the sleeves. He strutted like he was on to something fresh.

"Sun, you're Bruce Leroy now?" I asked, amazed at his latest hustle.

"I'm sellin' karate jackets…with a 'hood twist." Casper twirled in a circle and popped his collar. "I've been sellin' these joints hard body, sun; makin' money hands over fists."

"What do the Chinese words mean?"

"I don't know…eh, beef and broccoli?" Casper shrugged, and gave me 'the hell if I know' kind of look. "I don't know one word. I'm just sellin' 'em."

"You's a funny cat, Caz." I laughed and marveled at his merchandise covered in plastic. "I don't see folks in China walkin' around with English sayings on their bodies."

Casper sighed deeply and frowned. "Black man, listen. I didn't invent the wheel, but got-dammit, I'ma put some gold rims on it," he said, and I thought he was a functional crazy. "Speakin' of food, I'm starvin'. I just came to check you out. How's the plantation, oops, I mean, job treatin' you?"

"Carrot top got me up here sellin' fans. I went from public enemy number one to the store's poster child. You need one?" I modeled the cooling fan, and Casper brushed me off.

"I'll pass. Flippin' over the pillow every hour is good enough for me. I'll catch you later. I'ma ride the train to Medina and hit up Lucky's tonight. Peace."

We gave each other pounds and Casper went about his business.

I glanced at my watch and wished for time to speed by. The hands on the store's clock moved at a snail's pace. Boredom shot through my body even when I placed new shoe boxes on shelves. The store was starving for customers, which dashed my hopes of passing time by flirting with cuties shopping for shoes. Mondays were usually slow, and I wrote rhymes near stacks of boxes by the shoe racks to keep me going. Music usually brushed the dust off my brain and stopped me from going insane with nothing to do. I kicked a freestyle and rhymed in front of a mirror at the end of an aisle.

"I'm stuck and trapped, working a nine to five blues,
Makin' minimum wage, I can quit if I choose,
To lose, in the struggle stay away from gettin' fed up,
A smile on my face, as I still keep my head up..."

I left the mirror and saw a pile of open shoe boxes in the middle of an aisle. Customers showed no mercy. They rarely cleaned up after themselves. I picked up the loose shoes in a hurry and matched them with the correct boxes.

"Tired for a while cleanin' up dirty aisles,
Children runnin' wild from their mothers cryin' loud,
I left the area after sweeping like the wind,
Came back minutes later, saw it dirty again..."

I tiredly walked to organize the other shoe racks. Matching shoes on the racks was a pain in the ass, especially when customers scattered them around. Customers acted as if they had savage in their blood. Some shoes even ended up in other departments of the store.

"I'm tryin' to chill, time is movin' like a turtle,
Standin' on my feet 'til my ankles turn purple,
I rather chase dreams, like dancin' on the stage,
Rockin' to the beat instead of minimum wage..."

Sweeping and rhyming through the aisle between the shoe and Children's departments was therapeutic. I danced and pretended that the broom was a microphone.

"Goin' through a phase where I'm lookin' for the glory,
I know you could relate 'cause we share the same story,
Need this job, but don't want it 'cause it bores me,
I respect the grind, but the grind isn't for me..."

I stopped rhyming and stared at the time. It took an eternity for the store to close. Freedom ticked on the clock and teased me to bounce out the joint. A short, brown-skinned woman was surfing her hands around discounted shoes on the racks. I slowly stepped to her, and she cautiously turned her head.

"Excuse me, miss. Please place the shoes back on the rack when you're done," I referred to the open boxes of shoes scattered around her feet.

"Excuse me?" She expressed an attitude by tugging on the scarf that snaked around her neck.

Confusingly, I said, "We're almost closed. I would appreciate if you could re-rack the shoes when you're finished."

After I politely spoke to the woman, her senses when AWOL, and she snapped at me. "I know how to re-rack shoes. I'm not dirty."

"I'm not sayin' you were dirty. I would like to leave early. Customers have a habit of makin' a mess, you know." The gloves were off. I was pissed that the heifer just fucked up my high of leaving work early.

"Mister, I've worked in retail before, and I *know* everything is not gonna look fine after you leave."

"Okay, so you've worked retail before, want a cookie?" My wise crack triggered her frustration. The lady spun her head around and brushed away the thick, long braids that dangled in front of her face.

"What's your boss's name?" she asked.

"Boss? I *am* a boss. My *manager* is up front if you're looking for him." I gunned back.

"Thank you. I'm reporting you since you wanna be a smart guy."

She stormed out the department, and I went about my business. I treated the situation like killing a flea with a sledge hammer. Arguing with females wasn't my thing. I paid her no mind and re-racked the shoes she'd left on the ground. Minutes later I saw Adam rushing toward the department with me not thinking anything of it. I honestly forgot about shorty until pepperoni face panted in front of me as if lions were chasing him.

"Justice, I just got a complaint from a customer about you harassing her."

"I didn't harass that woman." I was so angry about the baseless complaint that I wanted to laugh. "I politely asked her to place the shoes back on the racks because the store was closing."

"Yeah, I know, but I want to make sure the store is customer friendly."

"Adam, how can I do my job when my own manager doesn't have my back?" I heatedly bolted at him. "I gave her a reminder. Ninety-eight percent of my day consists of me cleaning up after customers."

"Trust me. I understand where you're coming from, but customers are always right."

"That's not fair. Who are you catering to, your employees, or customers who treat the store like the city dump?"

"Both, but I gotta make sure there isn't a problem. She could've been a mystery shopper. I don't want Corporate coming down on *me*." He pointed to himself, and I had enough.

"Okay, that's cool. So do I need to walk around this place with a long poster hanging in front of me telling shoppers they can do anything they want because my manager says so?"

His face reddened after my brief tirade. He stopped himself for laying out whatever was drawn inside that pea brain of his, opting for a more calm response.

"The next time you have a problem with a customer, call me, or another supervisor that's around," he instructed, and I wanted to break his face for being so fucking weak.

Adam skipped off and left me for dead. I wanted to quit on the spot, but the reason was a coward's death; leaving on my terms was the load off my breath. My "manager" showed his true colors, but strangely as it may had looked, I felt rejuvenated; I saw the store as what it was, a job and nothing more. Maybe I was too down on myself like a man with more hang-ups than a prank call. Fantasies of leaving the store without a back-up plan were a blind man's paradise. Cold as ice and twice as bold, a *plan* inside me was bubbling. I just wasn't pushed over the edge…yet.

The ringtone from my cell shortened my reflections. Felicia's named popped up on the Caller ID. I thought about ignoring the call. As the music went on, I fought the urge and answered.

"Peace." I heard sobs.

"Hello…Justice?"

"Hey, what's good?"

"Come home when you get a chance." Felicia's voice cracked in between her sniffling.

"Why, what happened?" I asked.

"I don't wanna talk about it now. But, please, when you get a chance…come see me."

Confusion played tricks on me. I sat on a chair at the end of an aisle, thinking. Terror squeezed my stomach and my knees weakened. Shuffling over words, I gripped the bottom of the cell with my thumb. Struggling to swallow, my mind raced like the wind and my legs went numb.

"What happened?" I finally asked.

"I-I don't wanna talk about it. Come home when you get a chance."

"Aight, I'm on my way." The call ended, and I was petrified. Two thoughts wreaked havoc on my mind: *Was she pregnant? Did a family member die?*

Leaving without consulting key holders would've been a dumb move. I grudgingly walked over to Clara and didn't know what to expect.

"Clara, I need to go home because of a family emergency," I said, facing her back. She stopped piling shoe boxes in the middle of the aisle. Clara turned around and paused for a few seconds, cleaning her glasses with a cloth.

"Okay, Justice. The department looks clean, so you *can* clock out."

"Thanks," I said, but planned on leaving even if she would've said "no."

I grabbed my jacket from the lunchroom and rushed to clock out. I headed out the door with loose screws in my head.

"Where you're going?" asked Suzie, one of the store's head managers who reminded me of a black scarecrow.

"I'm goin' home."

"You can't go home without helping us recover the store."

"Clara said I can leave early," I countered.

"I'm a key holder and I make the decisions."

"I got permission to leave." I eased closer to the exit.

"You can't leave, Justice, and that's final."

"Bet. So fire me if you're not satisfied with that."

I never looked back as I stormed out the joint.

Chapter 8: Kismet

Tears soaked Felicia's cheeks and washed away her eye liner. The mascara smeared, and I held her as we sat on the bed.

"What happened?" I asked.

"Those bastards might finally get what they want."

"What 'chu mean?"

She turned to face me. "I got laid off at the marketing firm this morning. The company wasn't doing well, so they let me go."

"They didn't give you a notice?"

"Well, kinda…sorta. They announced the layoffs, but I didn't know I was one of those people."

"Okay, have you tried finding another job?"

"That's not the problem. The problem is I need steady income until I find a new gig so we won't lose the house."

"That's right…damn."

Felicia collapsed from my arms and stared at the ceiling. I stood from the bed and leaned back on an incliner chair, staring at the ceiling, thinking.

"I'll lose my mind if I have to give up the brownstone. Damn near everyone in my family was raised here." Felicia sulked and pressed on her forehead like she had a fever.

"I'll do anything. Anything I can do to help. Even if that means gettin' another job," I swore.

"No, Justice. You don't have to do that."

"Why not?" I asked upsettingly.

"It's my problem. Mi familia. I'm not putting the burden on you to help our situation." Felicia stopped crying as the tears dried. I was crushed by what she'd said.

"I'm not gonna live under your roof and let leeches like Mr. Swine get his way. I'ma think of somethin'," I protested. Felicia huffed and flopped backwards on her bed.

Felicia's mild break-down was painful to watch even though I'd heard the same story before. My grandmother was forced to move into a "mixed-income" apartment after the city bulldozed her building. The city tearing down her housing project didn't hurt me, but watching Grandma having to move against her will did.

Felicia curled in a fetal position and buried herself under blankets. I rocked on the chair and thought of every possible way of helping her with the problem.

"I'll figure something out for sure," I thought out loud, and sipped on a glass of pink lemonade sitting on the nightstand next to me. I left the room because I needed to think alone.

The park down the street from the house was my place of meditation, my personal church. After countless arguments between Felicia and me, the park cleared my thoughts.

Clouds blanketed the sunshine and cued in the night. The sight of birds taking flight from rooftops was the height of my emotional healing. I appreciated the outdoors. Shouting fights and broken lead pipes used to keep me awake. I'd learned to ignore the trademarks of the city by accepting it. The park was my Noah's Arc when the city's overcrowding drowned me from thinking. I rarely had time to enjoy the scenery and bob my head to the screeches of trains and car engines passing by with no one around me.

The "drummer man" banging his hands on bongos in the park entertained residents around the way. I always saw the dark-brown skinned brother playing his tunes near the benches of lovers kissing and holding hands. He collected money from folks shooting the breeze; smiling, dancing, and bobbing their heads while Drummer Man's long, thick locs swung in the air as he jammed. He never spoke a lick of English. He spoke Swahili. How did I know? I recognized some words because I took a Swahili class in college. I'm ashamed to say I forgot about 95 percent of what I'd learned in that course.

A slew of cardinals squawked over me and camped out in trees. Scar-lo drove by and parked his sports car beside me. He got out, slammed his car door, and zoomed past me as he rushed near a row of swings.

Drummer Man quickly banged his hands on the bongos...
"ba doom ba doom ba doom doom doom"

Stopping in front of a short, stocky guy standing near a row of swings, Scar-lo knocked him out cold with a mouth shot. He stood over the guy, spat on him, and angrily slammed a stack of candy bars on the face of the poor guy. Scar-lo turned around and faced me. Money strutted to my direction as if nothing happened.

"What's good, baby paw?" Scar-lo hugged me. I looked over his shoulder and saw a woman passing for a supermodel sitting in the passenger side of his luxury car.

"Ain't nothin'. Just came home from work," I said, even though I wasn't in the mood to speak with him. "What's good with you slammin' candy bars on dude over there?"

"That what happens when cats don't pay up." Scar-lo opened a PayDay candy bar and chewed on it. "I snatch what I'm owed."

"I see." I nodded, still disturbed about what I'd seen.

"I heard about what happened. Sorry about the news." Scar-lo sarcastically shook his head as if he was grieving.

"What news?" I asked with my eyes slanted, studying him.

"The news about Fe Fe losin' her job and possibly the brownstone."

I was paralyzed by his words. "How did you know about that?"

"C'mon, sun. This Scars you talkin' to, baby. I always keep my ear to the street." He pulled out a wad of money and patted the stack of hundreds on my shoulder. "I feel your temperature, Just. You're sick 'cuz you can't support your girl. But *this* the cure for the common cold, baby." He smirked with the stack in his hand. I didn't find him humorous.

The elections had past, but Scar-lo was campaigning strong by flashing dead presidents in my face. He politicked hard with fast cars and women as my college tuition swung from his neck. I wasn't casting my vote anytime soon.

Drummer Man's hands switched speeds and drummed slowly on the bongos...

"Ba dum...dum...dum ba dum...dum...dum"

"Thanks, but no thanks. I'm gettin' mine *my* way. Not Yours." I stood on my square, and heatedly walked off. Scar-lo persisted by waving blood money with murder soaking the creases of his palms.

"My way *is* the way, baby. Wake up or go to sleep broke, mah nigga," he yelled when I walked further away from him.

With Scar-lo fresh out of prison living the good life, I wondered if he *was* the way to make it. While I toiled to pay off college loans, Scar-lo lived like a king as a convicted felon and high school dropout. The more I saw him flaunt his jewels, the more I hated my education.

I walked with my head high and needed an escape. So I took the "A" train and headed off to Manhattan.

***

"Brotha man, I got DVDs: new movies and wet flicks. Two for $5."

"No, thank you." I walked past and brushed off the hustle man.

"May God bless you, brethren," he walked away to the beat of his hustle to pitch deals to others on the street.

The "A" train trekked me to downtown Manhattan, my getaway from Brooklyn. The Village in Manhattan reminded me of the "New Brooklyn": tattoo parlors, clothing boutiques, pizza spots, café lounges, and bistros with not a liquor store in sight.

A porn shop on Avenue of the Americas between 3rd and 4th streets pulled me across the crowded block. I really didn't watch porn, but if I needed to learn a new trick or two, then a wet flick was the perfect teacher.

A tall brown-skinned man stood outside his SUV looking nervous. He stared at the store and hesitated with going inside. I slowly stepped inside the joint and laughed at some of the DVD titles as I browsed the aisles.

"Sexy Teachers Vol. 5"

"Black Cock on White Chicks"

"Big Girls Gone Wild"

"Pretty School Girls"

"Big Wet Butts Galore Vol. 13"

I guess there was a market for everything.

The store bored me after about ten minutes of looking around at pornos, sex toys, lubricants, whips, and dominatrix outfits. As I headed to the exit, a group of brothers dressed in construction boots, baggy jeans, and du-rags under their fitted hats rushed down a flight of steps inside the shop. Moans and screams blaring from booth monitors rang below. I shook off the idea of finding out what was going on and trudged past the counter.

"Excuse me." I grabbed the attention of the clerk with a unibrow. "What's downstairs over there?" I asked.

"Oh, that's the gay section, my friend," he answered with a thick Middle Eastern accent.

I left the store speechless.

Strolling down 3rd Street toward Washington Square Park, I spotted a precious jewel. Walking past the long lines in front of the Village Underground, I fell in a dream-like state. I was hypnotized from the locs bouncing from the switch of her walk. My body twitched and pulled me closer to her as if my senses had a mind of their own. I power walked and damn near got hit by a taxi just to speak with shorty. Noises spewed out the mouth of the driver, but my ears shielded me from hearing.

"Excuse me, miss." I walked beside her and she turned. Her chocolate skin tone sent a rush through my body.

"Hey, how are you?" she responded. Shorty looked mad familiar, kinda like dreaming of someone and meeting them later in life.

"I thought you looked stunning. That's why I walked over here to speak with you," I managed to say, still held captive by her beauty of darkness.

"Oh, so you don't remember who I am?" She held her hips and flicked the long strands of locs away from her face. I stood speechless as the long, purple dress she wore outlined her curves.

"Of course, I know." I ran through a collage of names and faces I've met over the past few weeks. "We met at Lucky's in Brooklyn." I recovered with the wild guess and her eyes lit up. Who said you couldn't hit a bulls-eye in the dark.

"Uh huh, you better not get me confused with all those jump-offs you talk to," she said, and her voice reminded me of my favorite love song.

"It's not even like that. I remembered you by the voice that sang the roof off the building. It's been awhile since I've seen you...*Nandi.*"

She smiled and reached for a hug. "I'm glad you remembered my name. A lot of folks think it's too hard to pronounce. So where you headed?"

"Just walkin'. I wanna get away from my block for a minute."

"Yeah, I hear you. I was headed to the Brooklyn Promenade to check out the Manhattan skyline. You wanna roll?"

"Yeah, I'm down with that. You must be a tourist because half of Brooklyn never heard of the Promenade," I said. She rolled her eyes and playfully muffed my arm.

I was king of NY walking with Nandi. She was the finest woman in the city to me. She wrapped her arms under mine and triggered sensual thoughts; I pictured us resting together in nothing besides our birthday suits. Her eyes crystallized a clear imagination that took me to a secret fantasy that traveled beyond the animal in man. The sheer allure of her presence took me to an unknown land of getting to know her mentally. I feared falling for the woman. She was dangerously attractive with a touch of inno***sin***ce.

A line of bums marched past us and the wind of foulness stung my nose. My sense of smell halted when we hurried past the walking toilets. A bum resting on the ground tapped me on the leg and I glared at him.

"Hey, brethren. Can you spare some change?" he asked, toothless with dirty dread-locs.

"Hold on, playa," I said, and left Nandi with him.

I walked inside a crowded Mickey D's and grabbed a stack of papers. The papers would serve him and his buddies well. I rushed outside before they thought about trying anything with Nandi.

"Here." I handed the bum the stack of papers. "Give those to you and your homies."

The bum stared at them with a stupid look on his face. Nandi and I dipped off to the train station on 4th Street that stood just a few feet from us.

"What did you give him?" Nandi asked.

"I gave him some job applications. If he can say, 'Can I have some money,' I'm sure he has the sense to say, 'Can I take your order?'"

***

The Brooklyn Promenade lied next to the East River facing downtown Manhattan. The river waves clashed against the docks as flocks of pigeons bobbed around an elderly man tossing bread crumbs on the concrete. As cars drove under the Promenade, locals walked their dogs while lovers massaged each other's lips. Unlike in Midtown, car pollution and restaurant garbage cluttering the curbs wasn't a problem around those parts.

"This is nice." I stared at the boxes of lights beaming from the Manhattan skyline.

The Brooklyn Bridge towered over the ocean walk, and I was in awe. I'd never walked on the Promenade even though I lived in Brooklyn most of my life. Most New Yorkers stayed in their comfort zone and rarely roamed outside their neighborhoods. Why should we when everything was on our block?

"Yeah, this place is hella cool. I head down here to relax when I want to get away from everybody," Nandi said, and wrapped her arms under mine.

We strolled back and forth across the joint and caught the scenes. She glanced at me and clutched tightly around my arm. Her eyes gazed back at the skyline and she seemed at peace.

We sat on the park bench because my feet screamed for rest. My eyes caught hers, and I sought to bring out the mystery by looking at her browns.

"What brings you to NY from the Chi?" I sparked the conversation.

"Music. I don't stay here, but my band's family does. We travel a lot and make money doing shows across the country."

"Wow, that's good. At least you're doin' somethin' you enjoy."

"Yeah, it pays the bills and what not." Her hands played with her locs and her body shifted toward me. "So, Mr. Man. What you do?"

I thought for a second. "I'm an exotic dancer."

"No, you're not. Stop playin'. What you do for real?"

Damn! She didn't go for the "I'm a stripper" joke. So far, so good.

"I work retail in Harlem. I sell shoes and hold my breath from the invasion of funky feet."

She laughed. "That's funny. Folks need to keep their feet on point."

"I guess they don't make odor eaters like they used to." I turned away from her, thinking of another subject to build on. "Are you with someone right now?" I asked.

"Nah, I'm just doing me."

My lips twisted in disbelief when I faced her again. "Uh huh, I know you got mad dudes wanna get with you."

"Yeah, but I want a good man, not some guy who just wanna sniff my panties. And what about you, Mr. Player?"

"Why a brotha gotta be a player?" I asked with a smirk on my face.

"You give off that vibe. You're probably used to breaking hearts and dodging girls when they call you. You nearly pee'd your pants when you *almost* forgot who I was."

This girl is good.

"Doesn't matter." I inched closer to her. "'Cuz I'm with the flyest shorty in NY right now."

"Is that so?"

"Damn right. Why should a king court a peasant when I have you as a queen?"

"*Have* me?" She asked with raised eyebrows.

"What's wrong with me saying that?"

"That's *if* you have me."

"Put the G in front of the I and an F before the T, and I'll have you."

"And what does that supposed to mean?"

"That means I'll have you for a *gift*."

She laughed and slapped my knee. "That was lame. Not only are you a player, but also a charmer."

"No, I just like what I see."

We sat silent for a few seconds. Our eyes met, and our lips stood an inch from each other. Lights from the poles over the Promenade shined on her face when I tilted my lips to kiss her. She blocked the kiss and leaned back. I sat still, but leaned forward again.

"Not so fast." She waved her finger like Mutombo after blocking a shot. She sensed my disappointment but stayed solid. Burning for a kiss scorched my want for a silent "yes." So I leaned in again, only to land in rejection.

She leaned forward and softly stroked my low-cut, wavy hair. Her lips pressed onto my forehead and nose. The mix between her kiss and the wind chilled me. She blew a light breath on the wetness coating my eyelids and pushed my mind to skid into a quick blackout.

"*That's* how you supposed to do it." She giggled, and glanced down at her watch. "Oh, damn. Gotta go. Call me."

The scene ran from zero to sixty as she stood and gave me her card that listed her upcoming shows. My brainwaves ran in a maze of confusion. I hungered for more. Nevertheless, I wasn't a sucker for a cute face, even when watching her walk away was hard to digest. My eyes were pressed on to her as she switched off into the night until she disappeared. I sat lonely and defeated.

***

Ambulance sirens screamed from afar, and a crowd of cop cars blocked Fulton Ave. I stopped to check out the scene and locked my eyes down the block facing Lucky's. A large crowd surrounded the front entrance with two officers carrying a woman crying viciously.

"No, no, no!" she bellowed. I stood puzzled, wondering what had happened. The worst case scenario crept in my mind.

I know Casper said he was gonna chill at the spot tonight, I thought, but still drew doubts.

It couldn't be him. I hope it's not him. It can't be him.

As I slowly walked down the ave, my eyes were fixed on the ambulance crew struggling to roll the stretcher out the door. My heart throbbed when I switched my focus to girls wiping away tears as they mobbed outside the joint. Stepping closer to the scene, I leaned forward and saw a lake of dry maroon spotting the white sheet draped over the victim.

The person's face wasn't covered, so I eased closer for a better view. As yellow and white lights from the ambulance twirled around the block like a carnival, the emergency crew backed away onlookers from the stretcher and hurriedly pushed it onto the truck.

The ring finger of the body hung off the stretcher and glistened from the street light. I caught a glimpse of the person's face, and a slanted smile was planted on his mug.

"Well, if it isn't Old Man Willie," I said under my breath. He was arrogant even when he was maimed. Dried blood painted the dollar bills that scattered the sidewalks, and crack heads picked up the dough with no shame. Street lights were on him for his last second of fame as karma closed the curtain and took him out the game. The fat lady sang while his aficionados grieved, and the streets showed no mercy as dead was what he became. I never wished ill on anyone, but old flames were the blame when I didn't care too much about him as I had Caprice in mind. My mood changed from the sadness of murder, to the pleasure of imagining him rotting in hell with gasoline drawers.

The reaper got to him before I did.

Chapter 9: Hate O'clock

Casper stopped by Shoe Fetish donned in a dashiki, thick black and gold beads roped as a chain, black combat boots, and a Muslim beanie. He swaggered his way to my department with confidence flowing from his strut. Even as I snickered at his unique style of gear, shoppers walked past Casper as if he wasn't there.

"What's hap'nin, captain?" Casper gave me a pound, and I stared at him confusingly.

"As-Salāmu `alaykum, my brotha," I teased Casper and measured him from head to toe. "You look like a 24-karat Muslim, sun. What's good with the new look?"

"Man, I'm bringin' back African medallions, dookie rope chains, and dashikis, sun. Brothas ain't even up on this." He spun around like he was modeling. "They laugh at me now, but it only takes one brave soul to start a movement."

"Whatever happened to the Chinese gear you had?" I asked.

"I still go hard with those. I'm an equal opportunist, baby."

"Yeah, whatever, man. You buggin'. I bet you don't even know what the colors on the flag mean." I pointed to the red, black, and green flag that Casper held in his hand.

"Like I give a damn. The shit's sellin' and that's all that matters. Those revolutionary, 'Back to Africa' cats are beastin' for these joints hard body." He playfully swung the flag in the air.

"Funny dude. Let me put you on in case someone asks you about the flag." I grabbed the flag from him and pointed at each color. "The 'red' is the blood, the 'black' is the people, and the 'green' is the land we walk on. Read a book, playboy." I shook my head and was disappointed in Casper. I grabbed the submarine sandwich I stashed on a shelf.

"We just had a small party upstairs," I said between bites.

"They let ya'll eat on the sales floor?"

"Nope, I don't feel like being bothered with gossip folk. I'm grubbin' down here." I took another bite and wiped my hands with a towel. I shuffled through a few men's boots from a new shipment and placed them on the floor. Casper checked out new arrivals on the aisles and reminded me of what I had wanted to tell him.

"Oh yeah, I went out with shorty last night," I said.

"Who? The porno chick you met at the club awhile back?" Casper's eyes were ebullient as he smiled.

"Nope, I deaded her a minute ago. Her breath stunk so hard that I smelled the plaque through her jaws, sun."

"Oh, damn. I wonder why. So if it's not her, then who?"

"The shorty I met at Lucky's."

"The dark-skinned honey?" he asked, and I nodded. "Where did ya'll go?"

"To the Promenade."

"The Promenade?" Casper looked stunned. "I would've took shorty to the rooftop of my building and called it a day."

"She's not that type of girl. She's a cool sista, ya' know."

"Whatever. Every chick got a lil' freak in 'em. I don't care if she's a nun. It takes one man to bring out the inner beast," Casper yelled like George of the Jungle a bit after his "schooling." I was amazed to see no one turning to him as he made such a scene.

"She's cool and all, but she fronted on me and didn't kiss a brotha," I added, and he laughed.

"She's just frontin'. You know how shorties love to put up a defensive wall until a real cat like me bulldozes his way into them panties. They make love to the good shit I tell them in their ear." Casper dropped a jewel on me, and everything he said made sense.

"True dat. But yo', I'm about to head out to lunch. Walk with me outside right quick."

Casper and I stepped outside the store and he lit a cigarette. While walking out, I thought of what Casper had said about Nandi possibly playing a game of possum. He tickled me, as I'd never called a woman a hoe even if she slept with me on the first date.

You see, sleeping on the first *date* and *night* are two separate things. If a shorty was willing to give me the pum pum on the first night we met, I might look at her suspect. The *first date* meant we had talked on the phone, internet, or whatever the case, and got familiar with each other. The *first night* meant I met shorty at the club, and she let me slide between her thighs without knowing my full name.

Casper whistled between drags of the cigarette while I watched two bums fighting across the street from us. They looked like two slaves scrapping over bones in the field with their worn out gear. I stared at them with a bottle of pink lemonade in my hand and blurted, "I need to get outta here. The pay and stress of this job ain't worth it."

Casper's lips hugged the cancer stick that fumed from his mouth. "At least you got a job. I'm out here hustlin' Chinese and African clothes tryna convince folks dashikis are coming back." He blew out toxins and ripped away the freshness of air in my circle. "Ayo, I spoke to Scar-lo the other day," he said.

"About what?" I feared hearing the worst.

"You know, about makin' that paper."

"That fool tried to politic with me about gettin' money. What did he say to you?"

"Hustlin' and doin' my thing."

"You're losin' your mind if you wanna hustle for a psychopath like him. He doesn't even pay you any attention." I grimaced.

"I'm not losin' my mind. It's better than working for peanuts and living day to day while the family starves."

"That's short-term hustlin', sun. You get caught and become nothin' but a nigga behind bars slavin' for 25 cents an hour makin' license plates and road signs," I threw at him, and he hit the nicotine even harder in frustration. "At least I can front like I have money, get girls, and grind for somethin' instead of worryin' about gettin' stabbed and killed in the beast."

Casper was too much in a funk to hear me out. "So what I'm gonna do? Hustlin' is all I know. Look where we at." His arms panned 125th Street to make a point. "You lookin' at generations of poverty. Everybody in my family slaved at 9 to 5s, and we *still* live in the projects. So what's the point of workin' and not worryin' about prison when I feel like a prisoner in my own 'hood? I'm not a peanut nigga. I want cashews."

Casper dragged on the cigarette, and I stood silent for a moment. His point slapped away the words that brewed in my mind. I stood firm on the issue.

"I don't know about you, but I'm not gonna sling drugs and fall in the trap, and watch them swallow the key," I said, and while he puffed, I thought of my next move.

Keeping my hands clean juggled around the fabric of my brain as rebellious thoughts bubbled against Shoe Fetish. I relished for the day I become rich and laugh straight to the bank. As the underworld was the easiest way down the road to riches, a dead-end was the cliff with death breaking the fall.

The spiritual unrest that pressed against me shot hunger pains to my brain and begged me to solve the puzzle of finding my way in life's maze. I asked my elders for answers with no avail. They were busy bathing their sins in collection plates while trying to bribe their way to heaven and save themselves from hell. As the glamour of fast money and champagne cheers flirted with me, pride steered me away from illusions that swallowed many young males. Having someone telling me when to clock in, take lunch, and work was like jail, as I felt like an indentured servant. Sleepless nights kept me awake with me thinking about attending law school while staring at the Johnnie Cochran poster hanging on my wall. Life was a battle, and I fought hard to soldier my way to victory.

"Justice!" Suzie snapped me out of thought. "Did you clock out for lunch?"

"What?" Her question surprised me because I didn't have to report to her.

"I *said* did you clock out?"

"Yes, I did."

"But didn't Adam give you lunch?"

"No, and why would *Adam* give me lunch?"

"Justice, didn't Adam buy submarine sandwiches and salad for everyone? When this is done, it's a working lunch hour. We have deadlines to meet, but you're available for overtime on it. If you take a lunch, then OT is not available."

Warm winds blew over me as my temperature boiled in August numbers.

"Suzie, no one told me about deadlines," I shot back. She folded her arms and tapped her foot. "You or any other supervisor should talk to me about issues with lunch and deadlines in the future," I called her out, and Suzie stormed back inside the store. Casper turned to me and busted out laughing.

"Shhh-sphhh," he sounded a whipping noise and laughed even harder, almost sounding like a hyena. "Damn, sun, they got you like Kunta Kinté in this piece."

"She's psycho, real talk. You can tell she's missin' a few sandwiches at the picnic."

"Man, forget all that, what you doin' tonight?"

"I dunno, man. I think I'm about to fall out at the rest and take it easy."

"What time you get off work?"

"Around...10-ish."

"Aight, cool. I'ma head up to the BX to holla at this fly African honey I met at the club last week. Then come back so me and you can roll to Medina together."

"Aight, bet. I'll catch you on the rebound, king. Peace."

We gave each other pounds, and I headed back inside the store. Pressing my hands together as if I was praying, I needed a hundred Hail Marys to keep my cool.

"Please, don't let me hurt somebody today." I prayed to myself, and broke back to the shoe department with my mood on edge.

Clara limped away from the shoe boxes and sat down on a chair before acknowledging me. She panted with one of the meanest gas faces known to man. For a minute I thought she'd swallowed piss, until she turned to me and smirked.

"Justice, Suzie just told me what happened."

"What did she say?" I rolled my eyes.

"She told me you went to lunch without permission, but I told her Adam didn't give us a deadline to finish the shoes."

"Good, because I'm tired of her breathin' down my neck."

"Yeah, yeah...she wants every-ting her way, ya' know."

I stacked new arrivals on the shelves to pass time. Exhausted from finishing the seven-hour shoe project alone, a crook in my neck pained me. I twirled my head to get rid of the stiffness. I thought about leaving early when Suzie had pissed me off. I dismissed her rant as child's play.

Suzie was a nutcase. Maybe hating her was too strong of a feeling, but I thought she was a waste of semen.

She stood as part of the reason why I disliked work. She had a habit of loving to breath down my neck. "What a jerk," I said. But instead of getting upset, I'd sometimes kill her with kindness; smiling without shucking and jiving by complimenting her on the cheap nylon dresses she rocked. The fashion police would've arrested her for public ugliness. I wasn't kissing up to get on her good side. I showered her with praises just to throw water on hot grease whenever she'd expected me to cop an attitude since she came across as a rude supervisor.

I cooled off after awhile and alleviated my frustration. When the store closed, employees recovered their departments, and Adam let us out earlier than expected. I checked out and met Casper on 125th to catch the "3" train to Brooklyn.

The train stormed down the tunnel, thundering like echoes of a baseline blasting through speakers with head-lights flashing through steel beams. Water leaking from cracks of the ceiling dripped on the platform as rats danced on the puddle. They weaved between tracks as the train clacked its way to the stop, surging on the rails with the rhythm of a step team. Silts of dirt blanketed the once white walls as ceiling lights reflected the grind; the fatigue, the hustle, the glory, the hell; as I scraped my way to the top with dirt under my nails.

We trooped inside a car once the train arrived. The stench of bum funk pinched our noses and we trucked to another car, far from foulness as possible.

"They need to do something about these bums stinkin' up the train, sun," Casper complained, and we sat opposite of each other. The train skidded on the tracks and wailed in the subway tunnel. Screeches from the train's iron pressing against the tracks led me to think of Adam harassing Coffey and Suzie's nagging for some odd reason.

Suzie's rant shot down the last bit of patience I had for the store. I've had it up to my neck and lost my stream of consciousness. A stir of emotions boiled over, and I blacked out; mentally drained and emotionally exhausted. I worked hard at a job that treated me like a bowl of pennies and I had nowhere to go besides striking back.

"I got an idea." I tossed to Casper about what I had in mind. "I can hook you up at Shoe Fetish."

"Man, I ain't tryna sniff shoes all day, mah dude," he sneered, and I laughed at his assumption.

"Nah, man, I can hook up a plan where you and your crew can get some gear. I know when security makes their routine checks around the store."

"Explain." Casper leaned forward as the train screeched on the tracks.

"Aight, the security guards don't do jack besides eat and sleep on the job. They usually walk around the store every 15 minutes past the hour, doin' nothin' but harassin' high school chicks. Not only that, but each department only has one person workin' the area, two at the most, and all they do is gossip about men they'll never have," I said carelessly, and went on once I knew Casper was drawn to me. "The departments are so big, that it's impossible to know what's goin' on, especially when there's a rush of customers inside the store on weekends."

"So what you sayin'?" he asked.

"I'm sayin' I got a plan to hit up the store for some gear."

"You think this plan will work?"

"Man, they steal shoes even when security guards are alert, and with two workers in the same department. I check the aisles every other minute, and some fools *still* jack us for shoes."

The train stopped and a few passengers exited the car. A short, light-brown skinned woman sporting a mini-skirt stepped inside and sat a few seats down from us. I would've sat next to her and broke her off with some Grade-A game, but I drifted away from that temptation.

"What you want me to do with the clothes?" Casper asked.

"Sell them and take some for you and your fam."

"Yeah, and I know dudes around the way who'll buy some joints from me, too" he said, and shook his head. "Why you buggin' out on the store all of a sudden?"

"I got my reasons. I'm just tired of the bullshit, ya' know?"

"Yeah, I hear you. I guess playin' the 'Mister Goody Two Shoes' role was tiresome, huh?" Casper leaned back on his seat. Pressing his hands together, he leaned forward again and his eyes shot a "hell yeah" before moving his mouth.

"Let's do this," he said with a devilish smirk.

I was comfortable with going over the plan when a couple of old ladies were the only ones besides us inside the car after a few stops. They smiled when I waved to them. Casper waved as well, but they exhaled and looked forward without greeting him.

The train horns cried out as the cars thumping on the rails muffled our tactics. The anger I held in finally erupted and got the best of me. Outsmarting security was the recipe to ease my pain of working there. The agony of living underpaid enslaved my state of being. I pushed myself to let out steam, even if that meant risking everything I had. Resentment packed my heart and sparked the idea that stood in the dark for months. And the more I worked, the more built up rage exploded and came to light.

Intermission #1: Smiles on My Face

Sweeping the B.S. of customers and their mess,
And the stress of waking up and dragging to work,
I still have smiles on my face,

I'm blessed to see a steady paycheck,
Yet I'm severely underpaid,
I still have smiles on my face,

Taking control of my life is a dream,
Even when it seems like I'm waking up to nightmares,
I still have smiles on my face,

I wanna scream, yell, and lash out at everyone in my way,
As I wonder if I'd failed to live up to my potential,
I still have smiles on my face.

Monday, July 7th, 2008 10:42am

I HATE MY JOB
BOOK 2:
(The Inferno)

King Dhakir

Chapter 10: Brooklyn: The "New" Manhattan?

The "new" Brooklyn is a maze broken apart like a puzzle. I tried coping with the reshaping of my home that looked different each year that past by. I missed the "old" BK, the borough known for its heavy hustle with the wolves and foxes. Music blaring from boom boxes, screaming ambulances and honking horns was the soundtrack to my youth. Fire hydrants shot water and cooled us in the hottest summers while police sirens chasing gun runners served as background music.

Games of "catch a girl, kiss a girl" and hide-and-seek on streets of the concrete jungle kept our minds off poverty. Amist the smiles and laughter amongst my crew, I also hated the nervous conditions that coupled with the good times: looking over my shoulder for stick-up kids lurking for a come up, and different hoods beefing with each other like slaves battling over who had the best plantation.

Finding crack vials with different colored tops styled the playground concrete. My crew carried on with shooting dice away from the sight of truant cops. We ran wild at night by jetting through blocks as they fought hard to catch us for curfew. Even in our youth, we knew the streets better than algebra; hustlers teaching us nickel and dime bags before we learned basic mathematics in class.

Flashbacks of my childhood marked my brain while walking down Fulton with Felicia. Signs of "Condos for Rent" were plastered on windows of buildings that once stood as warehouses and crack spots. The remix of Fort Greene and Bed-Stuy silenced gun shots a little, but killed the spirits of mom and pop stores that once serviced the community. Yeah, Brooklyn was a lot safer than the 80's and 90's, but a lot of us wouldn't enjoy the rebirth of our beloved borough.

Felicia and I carried groceries down memory lane and observed the change that seized Brooklyn over the years. A bike messenger sped close against parked cars on Fulton and brushed on Felicia.

"Watch where you're going, fucker," she flared, as hearing her use vulgarities was rare. "They're tryna turn Brooklyn into Manhattan." She turned to me and exhaled.

"You ain't lyin'," I said, and felt lost while surfing my eyes across the half done buildings that took the place of open air lots. It seemed like the city hated open air at the highest degree. Vacant lots were either parking spots or advertisements on gates that promoted an affordable view of Manhattan, whatever that meant.

I lounged in Brooklyn for years, and never really paid close attention to the sudden change. Skeletons of new towers shadowed the streets and blocked the sun before the shine retired west. My mind locked to a beat thudding from a condo above us, and I briefly escaped within the "boom bap" of the drums.

"What are you thinkin' about?" I asked Felicia, snapping away from the beat that hypnotized me.

"Well…thinking about getting a new job and not losing the brownstone."

"I don't mind chippin' in for the mortgage," I said.

"You don't have to do that, Justice. I saved enough money to last us for the year until I find a new gig."

I looked at her like she'd lost her noodles. "I've been living with you for a hot minute now. A brotha gotta help a sista out somehow."

She didn't respond. Freeloading was beneath me. I just couldn't see myself looking in the mirror every day without helping Felicia with her troubles. I doubled my hours at Shoe Fetish to chip in with the mortgage in case she changed her mind.

We walked silently a few blocks closer to the brownstone and spotted a moving van with people carrying furniture. Walking closer to a graystone that was across the street from us, a familiar face stepped out his door. He waved and blew out smoke from his Cuban cigar; the smoke snaked in the air while he limped toward us.

"Sak Pase!" the man crept with a cane supporting his dead leg. "Long time, no see."

"What's good, Felix?" Felicia hugged West Indian Felix and kissed him on the cheek.

"We're moving out of Brooklyn," Felix replied.

"To where?" I asked.

"Virginia, my friend. Me and my wife just bought a home out there. The taxes in New York are too much for my island blood."

"Do you have a job out there?" Felicia cut in.

"You damn skippy. My job transferred me to the Richmond branch, and my wife is finding a new job." Felix turned to his home and repeatedly tapped the cane on the concrete. "I'll sure miss the graystone. But having a five bedroom mini-mansion cost way less than that right there."

"Wow, I think I might have to move down South." I said, but deep down I knew Brooklyn was home.

"Felix! Honey. I need you to sign some papers." Felix's wife yelled from the front door and waved to us.

"Okay, my friends. I'll see you folks later. We have to get going before traffic hits that doggone I-95. Take care."

We parted after goodbyes, hugs, and handshakes, and trudged our way home. As we paced closer to the brownstone, an idea clicked. Maybe the "new" Brooklyn wasn't for me, and I tripped over the thought of moving down south.

BK's face-lift suffocated my love for staying there, and I needed air to breathe. The cost of living squeezed my pockets dry like crumpled leaves and I needed to get away for awhile, if not forever. As the sky swallowed intoxicants from exhaust pipes that stung my nose, dust from construction sites sometimes gorilla gripped my lungs. I felt like I was drowning; struggling to swim and stay afloat as I walked through a foreign place. And while I disliked the smog and hustle of the city, I was like Dorothy wandering around clueless with no yellow brick road.

"Peace, brotha and sista," a tall, light skinned woman with cropped, brown hair stopped and greeted us. She interrupted my train of thought, but shorty was fly, so I didn't care. "Would you mind if I give you flyers for the rally my organization is throwing two months from now?"

"Sure." I reached for the flyer and so did Felicia. "What's your organization about?" My ears were wide open.

"The organization is called H.O.P.E, it means H-elping O-ur P-eople E-veryday. We're rallying in front of Capital Hall in downtown against the city moving residents out their homes for condos."

"Interesting. My name's Felicia, and I'm the president of WISDOM. It's an organization fighting for women's rights. I'm sure my organization will show interest in your movement."

"Right on! My name is Fatima, and my contact info is on the flyer. We should link up and build. We're based out in Bed-Stuy."

"No doubt, I'll be sure to contact you. I'm going through the same problem by fighting to keep my brownstone."

"Wow, that's crazy. I think you should most definitely come to the rally so our voices can be heard and stop injustices plaguing our community."

"Okay, cool. I'll do that."

"Catch you later, family. Peace." Fatima went on her way and brought hope to Felicia's housing situated. I wasn't moved. Negroes had a way with talking a good game without fight for back-up. So I shrugged off the flyer.

Felicia and I reached the brownstone and sat the bag of groceries on the stoop. I tossed her a question I'd always pondered ever since I saw the *Eyes on the Prize* documentaries.

"What you think about rallies?" I sat on the stoop with her.

"I think a rally is what we need. I'm down for anything positive. What you think?"

"It's a waste of time," I replied coldly.

"Why you say that?"

"What has rallies and marchin' done for us? It's just a buncha folks yellin' and screamin' and makin' noises."

"That's not true. It depends on the cause, and rallies show that people can stick together."

"Stick together? Niggas only stick together when it's time to have sex and go to funerals."

"Boy, you crazy." She laughed.

"Real talk. What happens after marchin'? Everybody wanna be righteous for a few hours but go back to the same shit before they got there. Nothin' is gonna change unless *we* do somethin' about it and not rely on a handout."

A wail of winds flew over our heads and calmed me from blowing up. Clouds hugged the sky and hinted hail storms. The skies brushed off the grays and cleared with stars peppering the background. Frustrated and thinking about what I've just said, Felicia scrambled for a comeback while bracing herself from the evening cool.

"Yeah, you're right, Justice. But things don't change overnight. Our people need to take a stand on something instead of dying for nothing."

"Things don't change overnight, you right, but it's all about green, Felicia; those dead politicians. Being broke and marchin' don't mean shit without money. We're the only race who'll march for damn near everything under the sun and still pass down poverty without the history of our culture."

"But here me out," she sighed. "This is a problem in Brooklyn and every other neighborhood in America, and *you* know that. It's better to fight instead of tucking our tails like cowards."

Felicia was right, but I lost faith in the community coming together. Rallying for a day and going back to the same ol' blahzay blahzay had hurt me far worse than us not taking action at all. The truth was that no one really cared about the 'hood until a tragedy struck them. I wanted to fight, but not with my head sticking out the window waiting for it to get chopped off.

"So riddle me this, what's the difference between now and the Civil Rights days?" I tested her.

"We got more rights."

"Yeah, but we still don't own anything in *our* 'hood. Every ethnic group got stores, food spots, and bodegas in our 'hood except for us. And what you want *them* to do? Give us crumbs so they can hush us up?"

"Look, I'm not gonna go back and forth with you. Yeah, we should've invested in our communities a long time ago, but we can't think about that now. It's time to ride or die, and I got nothing to lose."

Felicia grabbed the grocery bags and heatedly carried them inside the house. I brushed off the gesture and spotted another moving van sitting across the street from the brownstone. A girl stepped out the vehicle and fumbled inside her purse. Curiosity pushed me to check out the new neighbors and give them a piece of my mind. I knew they were out-of-towners, which meant easy food.

Two guys were carrying large speakers up their stoop while the girl wheeled an amp out of the moving van. The girl stopped and used her fingers to comb her blond hair. She smiled and walked toward me. The two tall, lanky guys rested the speakers on top of the steps and slowly walked down the stoop. I clutched my hands into a fist as Emmitt Till's smashed face flared in my mind.

I stared at the two men cautiously walking toward me. They stopped once they stood a few yards close to the girl. She extended a hand, still smiling from ear to ear, all the while inviting peace from her end.

"Hey, my name is Jess. We just moved here from Ohio." She shook my hand, and the guys didn't move a muscle.

"Cool, cool. I was born in the Midwest, too," I said, releasing her grip.

"Where from?"

"Chicago."

"Chi-town! The windy city. I love that place." She looked over her shoulder and gestured the guys to move closer to us. "These are my bands mates, Rob and Pete."

We exchanged hand-shakes, and their stiffness gave off nervousness.

"Don't worry. The wolves ain't out yet. So you won't get robbed around here…at least not tonight," I joked, and they let out nervous laughter. "I'm just kiddin'. This a nice spot. I'm Justice, and I stay across the street.

"Justice? That's a cool name," said Pete, standing tall with black glasses and tattoos covering both arms.

"Thanks. So what brings you to Brooklyn?"

"We go to the university in downtown Brooklyn during the day, and we perform in Manhattan at night." Rob answered while combing his black, fuzzy hair-do with his fingers.

"Aight, that's gravy. Well, New York is a lot different than the Midwest."

"Yeah, I see. The people here are rude."

I laughed lightly and was amused at their rude awakening. "You'll get used to it. Folks out here just missed a few hugs in their childhood. That's all."

"Well…I guess." Jess fingered inside her handbag and handed me a flyer. "Justice, maybe you and some friends can show us some New York hospitality. Our band is rocking at this place named 'Libra' a few weeks from now. I mean, that's if you like rock music."

"I love anything that sounds good."

"Okay, awesome. We would appreciate the support. We're gonna shut that place down."

I stared at the flyer while the evening's winds slapped me across the cheek. "I'll let you know if I'm gonna roll."

"Cool, just holler if you need anything, dude."

We shook hands and they went about their business. As I walked back to the brownstone, I was bent on the past. The words "Fort Greene" had rarely, if ever, spewed out the mouths of someone other than Black and Latino, let alone a thought.

"So where you're from?" I had had asked a few cool white dudes who went to high school with me in Fort Greene.

Bensonhurst

Howard Beach

Sunset Park

Bay Ridge

They would say, as none of them were natives. Learning different cultures was cool, but I guess gentrification was the receipt for the price of us holding hands and singing, "We Are the World."

The flyer from Jess sparked my interest and I quickly thought about taking Nandi to their show. Nandi was into music, and maybe she could network with some folks at the spot.

While walking across the street, a car skidded and damn near crashed into me. The car horn shrieked, and the vehicle swooped passed me to the brownstone. All of them looked like young models, and Caprice waved and stepped out posing like one.

"What you think, Just?" She posed in a long, purple dress that drew out her juvenile curves that begged to mature.

"You look kinda fly there, young buck," I said to Caprice.

"I know, I know. I try. We're on our way to the spring dance."

"That's right. But why'd you come here?"

"Mama left Felicia some money for me to pick up. I gotta hurry and jet outta here," she hastily worked the high heels gracefully up the stoop. The switch in her strut caught my eyes for a second. I shamelessly turned away from looking at her twin onions.

What are they feeding kids these days?

I snapped away from her youthful curves that perverted my sight and turned to her friends. They looked attractive for their age, but that didn't matter. The forbidden fruit held me back from dirtying the water that has yet been tainted. As police handcuffs clacked and blacked out shameless lust to thrust in my mental camera, the girls blushed and stole peeks that spoke an undercover crush. Principles flushed down the filth from clogging my mind, as only a weak man would've fell victim to their youthful beauty.

"You must be Caprice's uncle." A dark skinned girl with braces smiled.

"Yeah, something like that."

"I like your name, Justice. It's pretty. What does it mean?"

"Google it. And how'd you know my name?"

"Word gets around," cut in a light, brown skinned girl sitting in the backseat. Awkwardness crept in when the girls said they knew my name. Words spread, but I never hung out with girls Caprice's age. I guessed she'd told them about me during their usual gossip. Those girls were young enough to be my little sisters. No amount of good looks was breaking me. I never went after jail bait.

"Uh huh, don't get into trouble tonight." I injected, and they laughed.

"Yeah, but we wish *you* could come. Niggas these days don't got no mojo." A heavy set girl blew laughter out of me. Her spunk was hilarious.

"I'm flattered, but I'm too old for you."

Caprice saved me by jetting out the brownstone to the car. "Oh, I forgot to tell you. I'm trying out for the school's spelling bee," Caprice said as she hugged me.

"Word?"

"Yeah, man. I'm gonna kill it. I've been practicing all month for it."

"I'm proud of you, girl. Keep doin' ya' thing, and be safe, ya' hear?"

"Don't worry, Justice. We got razors." She tip-toed to the passenger side before skating off with her cronies.

The clouds sung lullabies of chills that shrilled coldness and masked the sun's fever. The day started out cool with the breaths of wind that never hit me. Caprice was warmth for the winter of my heart that sparked the affection I had for her. Splintered off from the darkness of the world that made me cold and heartless, I protected her with the ribs that sheltered her from the Eve of ignorance in the Rotten Apple. I prayed she wouldn't fall in the depths of salivating for bootlegged brands and the hands of wannabe ballers with their own dreams on lay-a-way. She was my reason for breathing, and watching her fail was like me shedding blood from my own hands.

Overwhelmed with joy, I called Nandi to see if she was down to jet with me to Lucky's to shoot a few games of pool. I later changed my mind since I wasn't in the mood to chin check some clown for making passes at Nandi. So I chose Harlem Lanes.

Bowling at Harlem Lanes off 126th street was a sexy choice. I hit Nandi on the horn and she was down to bowl. We met in front of the joint as we smelled blunt smoke seeping from a Jeep blasting music across the street. Dude must've been smoking on some strong Mary Jane because the rain of funk stung my nose.

The police sirens rang aloud and stopped behind the vehicle. Instead of being nosey, we decided to take the elevator inside the building to the bowling alley.

"Have you ever bowled before?" I asked Nandi while riding the elevator.

"Yeah, I'm okay."

"Aight, I'ma take it easy on you."

"Mmhm." She laughed lightly to herself before the elevator doors opened.

I automatically felt my pockets and thought of how much money I'd spent during the week. A cheapskate was I not, but facing embarrassment by coming up short in front of a lady of Nandi's caliber would've been humiliating.

I spent 25 dollars yesterday...10 today...and 100 for the whole week.

Calculating the total in my head was a bootleg version of an ATM. I couldn't jet to the ATM next to the building while purchasing shoes and two games of bowling. I took the risk anyway. Nandi shivered from the brisk chill of the bowling alley and I gave her my hooded sweater. Thinking of how much money I *really* had while handing her my hoody, I dug in my pockets and pulled out a twenty and five.

Yes!!!

I handed the woman working the register the money and our alley lit up.

"I don't know, Nandi. I think you need the bumpers."

"Ha, ha. Very funny."

"Funny? You wanna put money on this?" I dared.

"I don't want to take your lunch money, Justice."

"Let's put 20 on it?"

"Fine."

The machine racked the bowling pins while I rubbed my hands together with a grin. Hustling the older heads at pool tables was my thing, but bowling was another. Regardless, there was no way in hell I was letting Nandi hustle me out of a twenty.

She went first and bowled a strike. That might've been a jinx because she was hitting strikes left and right. Her smooth release was butter while the balls I rolled kept finding themselves in the gutter.

"That's, aight. This only a warm up." I stretched my arms over my head. "I haven't played in a minute."

She rolled her eyes and would later win the first game.

While I was sitting, a familiar face walked towards us. She ignored Nandi and sat next to me. Seeing her was bad timing. So I played cool.

"Hey, Justice," Essence threw a fake greeting to me. "What brings you around here?"

"Bowling with me and my lady."

"Oh, okay." Essence stood and walked over to Nandi to shake her hand. "Nice to meet you. I'm Essence."

"Nandi, and likewise." Nandi reached to shake Essence's hand. Essence turned to me with bad intentions flaring in her eyes.

"Nandi's a pretty name. Justice *never* told me about you." Essence lowered her eyes at me. I wanted to bowl her face into the pins. "You two look like a nice couple. I guess Justice was ready to hang up his *player* jersey."

Furious wasn't even the word when Essence tried to cock block. I wasn't talking to her again if she'd ruined my chances with Nandi. She playfully waved her hands "goodbye" after the smart remark and left for the other side of the bowling alley. Nandi's laughter only increased my jumpiness.

"What's so funny?" I asked.

"Oh, nothing. That must've been your exes or somethin'?"

"Somethin' like that, but she's not important. What's important is that we finish our game so you can hand over those greenbacks."

The second game began, and to make a long story short, she whopped my tail again. The game was like a re-run of the first because she was striking like it was going out of style. I went to the ATM machine next to the bowling alley and withdrew $20. I shamefully handed her the money and had no choice but to gracefully bow out.

"Gracias." she grinned.

"You knew how to play all along." I looked at her suspect.

"Justice, I never told you I was a pro. I said I was 'okay.'" She winked, and I smacked my forehead, not believing I fell for the hustler's okey doke.

Nandi had to trek downtown for a meeting with her band members. Planning a tour across the Northeast, I knew I wouldn't see her for at least two weeks; two weeks that I'd wished was a day.

"I'll call you when I get back." She promised before her stop on 34th Street. The train scratched the tracks and the scream of the stop cued in my move.

"Gimme some sugar." I playfully puckered my lips expecting a kiss. Nandi poked my dimple and kissed my cheek before stepping off the train. I sat there mad shell shocked because she wasn't giving me what I wanted. Her constant tease wasn't cool, but I wanted to read more into her. I just didn't know what page I was on. Drawn by her mystery, she was a book that read like a page-turner. My curiosity searched for more.

She blew me a kiss and carried on to switch trains. Uncontrollably horny, I called up a shorty from Flatbush and made a late night creep to her brownstone. A brother always had "emergency booty" whenever a date fronted on me. Strangely as it may have seemed, I missed Nandi even before she went on tour regardless of getting my rocks off by another woman.

Chapter 11: Casual (Sex) Day

Thank God for Fridays.

I breezed down Lenox Ave. a minute past the hour I was supposed to clock in. The automatic doors locked me out, and I saw no one walking around the first floor in the department store. I waited for a few minutes until Adam caught me outside. His mouth puckered with distain while he slowly turned the key.

"Justice, you're late," he grumbled, and I brushed him off. His words tumbled from one ear through the other.

"Aight," I said, walking off.

"You need to clock in and be ready when you're scheduled to work," He sighed, and I shot straight to the time clock. "Oh, one more thing, Justice, we're having a store meeting next week about the ongoing problem with theft. So be on time, alright?"

"Got'cha."

Whistling off to shoes, a harsh stench slapped my nose. I was taken aback by the foul odor. The stench burned my nostrils, and my stomach turned by the smell that reeked like spoiled milk. The unpleasant smell was trapped in my nose and seeped down to my throat, creeping in my taste buds when I followed the rancid of funk.

"Aye, what 'chu doin'?" I blasted the man sitting Indian bent-knees style in the aisle. Ash covered his peeling skin that showed through ripped jeans and jacket. He staggered on his feet with a 40 ounce in his hand.

"I-I was just tryin' on shoes."

"What's in the box?"

He opened the box, exposing shoes marred by holes and filth. "I don't know where that came from, sir," he slurred.

"Where'd you get those sneakers from?"

"I get these…I get these from my mama…for a present," the guttural voice shot an excuse. I knew our shipments like my first and last name. He still mistook me for a fool. As I thought about it, I couldn't help but wonder how the hell he'd got in the store so early.

"My man, I'm not gonna tell you twice, but you gotta leave the store."

"My mama gave me these shoes, man. My mama gave me these shoes," he repeated, with fear shivering his words.

"Did I stutter? Take off the shoes, get your shit, and leave." I gave an irascible response. He shook, took off the sneakers, and tapped dance out the store bare footed.

Shoe Fetish attacted all types of characters besides your "normal" people. I could literally sit through a whole day and laugh at the funniest things that went down inside the joint.

The air freshener in the shoe's supply cabinet swallowed the odor and opened clean air to breathe. Bored with no shipments to unpack, I scurried to the women's department where Essence worked whenever the store didn't need a lot of cashiers up front.

The room grew darker as her body sparked melodies like a harp's tune. Serving her the mo' better past through my thoughts. She bent over to pick up clothes that fell from the shopping cart in front of me. Clinging onto her backside, my eyes roamed around the back of her thighs, tracking down her aesthetics that made grown men cry.

"What's good, gal?" I finessed, and she turned around.

"You." She smirked while racking clothes on hangers.

"So I'm good, huh?"

"Yeah, everything about you."

She brought me closer to her. I held her soft waist. I eased her closer to me but she slightly leaned back.

"You know cameras are in the store, right?" She held her hips.

"Girl, I don't care."

"Well, I do." She freed herself from my hold. "I got bills to pay."

"Are you thinkin' what I'm thinkin'?"

"Uh, no."

I tilted my head and motioned toward the ceiling. She stood confused, but I broke the mystery. "Let's go to Receiving."

"Boy, are you nuts? They got cameras up there, too."

"Stop being scared. Tahleek is workin' security tonight. There's a spot where the cameras can't see us."

"I don't know, baby." She shook her head. I gently slid my hands across her fingers. My eyes spoke to hers, and she stepped to me. Seconds later she dropped back. "I don't know, Justice. I'm still pissed off about seein' you with Nanny, or whatever her name is."

"Don't trip off that. I was just showin' her how to bowl."

"Whatever, Justice. 'Stupid' ain't written across my forehead."

"I thought it was on your ass," I joaned on her, and she lightly punched me on the arm. "I'm just buggin' with you," I laughed, and the tip of my fingers slid down on her side. Her eyes traced over my hand and her eye lids fluttered. "C'mon, ma," I whispered, and she smiled, blushing through her ebony skin tone.

"I want to…but…I can't…," Her words were faint, but I persisted. I slid my hands away from her side and outlined her onion. She shivered and rubbed her thighs together. "Damn, baby…I'm not gonna lie…you're makin' me wet."

I dropped my hands from her side and softly touched her hands. "I gotta hang my jacket upstairs. You wanna come?" I held her hand.

"Yeah, I need a small break anyway."

We rode the elevator to the second floor and I hung my jacket. I leaned closer and gently kissed her ear. She looked in my eyes and stepped away.

I left the break room, unsure of what had happened; she usually kissed back but didn't for some reason. Maybe it was a woman thing.

Pressing for the elevator, the door opened as well as the door on the other side that led to Receiving. Boxes hogged the floor, and I placed them on a pallet. A breeze blew by me as two hands held on to my sides. She kissed the back of my neck, and hairs stood on my shoulder blades. I turned and grabbed Essence's hand. I walked backwards to the spot where the cameras couldn't get a good view of us.

We drifted off to an open circle surrounded by high beams of boxes that blocked the view of the camera. She lifted her black skirt and bent over in front of me. My hands ran up and down her black, thigh length fish net stockings. She turned quickly around and pulled down her skirt to blow me a kiss.

"Why are you playing games?" I griped, and she wiggled her pretty round brown that teased me to flow in between.

"Who's playing games?" she sounded like an innocent girl.

"You are. You're teasing a brotha and..."

Her kisses stopped the flow of words, and her hands went south, unbuckling my belt.

Her fingers circled around my crotch, and she kissed the tip of my nose. She stopped short in front of a wall of boxes and pulled me closer to her.

"How do you want it?" she breathed.

"Bend over and find out," I replied, and took off my button-down shirt. I threw the joint on a stack of shoe boxes and turned her around. She bent over, and I lifted her skirt and stood behind her. My fingers pulled her thong strap to the side and I instantly got a hard-on. I opened a Magnum and slid the raincoat over me. I chose to play it *safe*. I straddled behind her doggy style and kissed the back of her neck. Her thong found its way down and around her ankles once my hips kissed her backside.

The sound echoed as I stroked faster. She moaned loudly, and her legs shook with my hands massaging her waist. Spasms from the grind of my lips onto her neck made her head flip. Her body lotion tasted like red wine. I blew air over the wet spots and sent soft chills down her spine. Breaths rushed out her mouth and nose with her bush posed in front of me. She lost control as my tongue whipped over her shoulder blades. I felt her warmth rush beneath me. My hands groped her plums as I went to work and pounded out the waves of her ass.

"I want it, baby…I want it…" she whispered, and reached behind her shoulder to rub the back of my head.

Fumbling with her nipples as I slid my hands away from the rear, I massaged her breasts in circles. They were soft as dough, with the tips hardening from the warmth of my touches. That was her spot, and I played on it, fondling the twin rocks that shocked her mind around climaxing.

She tightened her walls around me and her body rocked like an earthquake. Feeling myself letting off, I rushed faster with sweat painting my face. I threw her hand off my head and grabbed both of her arms as if she was a wheel barrel. With my arms locked under hers, the intensity of holding her and the long, deep strokes pushed out the molasses she was holding in.

"Oh, daddy…yesss…yesss…I'm about to cuuum…"

She jerked her ass high with her back arched. Her knees wobbled as if she tried to break free from my hold. Juicing her with every inch of my stick, I couldn't hold on much longer. Her legs quivered, and she wormed under me as I loosened my grip. I held her close to me after feeling her come, climaxing the quickie I was looking for.

I slowed down and pulled out of her, glancing at the film of cream coating over the condom. I wiped off the beads of sweat from my brow with a napkin from my back pocket and kissed the side of her face.

"Damn, baby…" She exhaled, fixing herself back to normal. "You got me shakin' and shit."

"Uh huh, and all this time you was frontin' on the kid." I said, fixing myself together and repackaging the used condom.

"Don't gas ya'self before I take back what I said," she said while stroking my balls back and forth.

"Yeah, whatever." I picked up my pants and threw the condom wrapper in a nearby garbage can. As we got ourselves straight and fitting to jet, shoes click-clacked on the floor. I looked over to Essence; shock etched her face as she let out a light gasp.

"Hello! Is anyone there?"

I heard Joy's voice. She managed the baby/toddler's section of the department building on the second floor next to Receiving. Joy walked toward the boxes and paused.

"No one was supposed to stack these boxes this high!" She fumed, and paused again. I felt her turning toward the boxes that were stacked in front of us. "Something smells funny."

Essence and I both stared at each other wide eyed and embarrassingly smiled. Sweat beads dripped down my temple, and I couldn't let Joy see us both damn near sexed out.

Think…think…think. I thought, and looked around. An opening on the other side of the metal beams called me to flee. I pointed toward the hole in the back of the high beams. We jetted out our hiding spot, free as a bird.

"Them damn janitors need to fix those pipes so they won't stink up the place." Joy walked away, and I held in laughter as we narrowly escaped.

We sped out Receiving and separated to our departments. The bijan scented oil I smeared on my arms covered the funk, leaving no scent of lust. I grabbed a cart of shoe boxes and wheeled them toward the security booth. All I saw was white teeth sparkling from my man's grill.

"I'ma have to give you props, playboy. I've seen everything." Tahleek grinned.

"Stop lyin'," I said.

"Well, not all of it 'cuz you did a good job by goin' to the dead spot." His fat jaws crunched on a dollar bag of chips. I stood there staring at him, hinting at what he owed me. "What you're lookin' at?" Tahleek mean mugged me.

"You know what you owe me."

"You should be glad I'm not reportin' your ass to Adam." His tree trunk arms reached for his pockets. He handed me $20. "I'm not gone lie. I thought you wasn't gonna get shorty up there."

"C'mon, Tahleek. Respect my fresh." The $20 bill slipped in my pocket and Tahleek packed his bags. "Where you're goin'?" I asked.

"Home! I worked a double shift today. And it's payday."

"Damn, that's right. I'm about to get my check right now."

Tahleek and I hustled toward the cash room that was next to the manager's office. Adam stepped in front of me with a mischievous smirk on his face.

"Justice, can I speak with you for a minute?"

"Yeah." I unwillingly agreed, and walked inside the manager's office next to the time monitor.

Damn, did Adam already catch me red handed with Essence?

My heart sped to the beat of jitters. Dryness turned my mouth into a desert. I waited for the shepherd's slaughter of him firing me; walking behind him like a sheep.

Suzie sat screwfaced and grunted while tapping her feet. Adam closed the door and sat next to her. I took a seat and leaned back on the chair folding my arms while sucking my teeth.

Adam exhaled and cleared his throat. "Suzie said you stormed out the store before closing, is that true?" he asked, not really caring about what had happened.

I turned and grilled Suzie. "No, I didn't storm out the store. I had permission from Clara to leave because I had a family emergency."

"But you never came to me and told me the reason you was leaving," Suzie interjected.

"According to whom?"

"According to me. Key holders and other managers should know ahead of time when employees are leaving before recovery."

"So my supervisor granting me permission to leave wasn't enough?"

"That's not the point. The point is you left without giving a reason why you were leaving, and you were out of line."

"How was I out of line?" The tone of my voice lined between surprise and anger.

"Because you totally disregarded my authority and dared me to fire you before you walked out."

Sweat moistened the palms of my hands. Snapping at Suzie was the first thought that came to mind as she accused me of having a presumptuous behavior. I chilled after Suzie griped, but refused to stomach her reckless mouth.

"You're not catering to the needs of employees." I shot back.

"I...don't...have to cater to employees. You need permission from me before you leave. You were out of line!"

"So speak with Clara about store policy. And I don't appreciate you hollerin' at me like I'm a child."

Suzie pissed me off, but she wasn't worthy of me blowing up. I laughed at how people got their little managerial positions and acted like they ruled the world. I respected authority, but not when abused. I rather have them fire me instead of punking out because of someone's store rank. I had no problems with handling instructions from the opposite sex, but I was vexed whenever they ruled with an iron fist to make up for the fact that they were women with a higher position. Since the first time I stepped in the joint, Suzie stayed on my nerves by giving me grief. I didn't know if her beef toward me stemmed from my college degree over her GED, or that a man was better looking than her.

The room fell uncomfortably silent after the exchange of heated words. Suzie looked away and made smacking noises by chewing gum. Adam shyly glanced at her and pulled his eyes back to me. He cleared his throat and loosened his collar. He folded his hands together and sat silent before finally speaking.

"Justice is right. If Clara had given him permission, then he had the right to go. I'll make a note to all the department supervisors to let employees know that key holders make the final decisions for early dismissal."

Suzie stormed out the manager's room, and Adam exhaled with his arms folded behind his head. Everything about Suzie irked me. If it wasn't her plastic looking weave, then the suits she'd worn bothered me. I casually opened the door like nothing had happened and headed to my department. Clara didn't work until the evening, and I manned the department until then.

I've had enough. I was so sick and tired of the fascism that went on in that joint. Managers had the habit of talking to employees anyway they wanted, and the workers were taking it with smiles and giggles. Checking Adam and a few other supervisors a couple of times for speaking to me sideways, it was almost as if they got off on bossing folks around. I played my position and completed my work to the fullest, but I was no one's whipping boy. The majority of the employees didn't care if they got bossed around. They were straight, as long as they got paid every two weeks and fed their families. But to me, a closed mouth never got fed, and I turned my back on hushing up if anyone in the joint treated me like a ripped food stamp. I was a man on an island surrounded by ass kissers, working as the ying to their yang.

Sweeping away the candy off the carpet left by crumb snatchers, I looked down the aisle end and saw a lady breast feeding her child, titty out her dress shirt and all. I choked from the pink lemonade that settled in my throat and hoped my eyes were telling me lies. But nope, the child's mouth groped her breast as the lady rocked back and forth like she was high on dope.

"Check…that…out." Casper smiled, coming out of nowhere as he patted my shoulder behind me. "Ayo, fuck the strip club. Shoe Fetish is the place to be."

Casper's eyes salivated over the brown skinned lady whose breasts looked like small water balloons. She flicked her long, brownish silky hair and further opened her shirt. She was fine, with chestnut eyes and smooth skin, wearing a long skirt with a split that ran down the side of her thigh. Her rear poked out in the back of the seat, and I caught a woody from just looking at her. Shorty was probably a chick that brothers passed around the crew a few times like a 40 ounce.

"Excuse me, miss." Casper stepped closer to the lady sitting on the end-aisle seat. "Can I get some chocolate milk and some fries with that?"

He leaned closer to her, and I busted up laughing. Casper was a fool. The lady paid him no mind and rocked her newborn back and forth.

"Shorty ain't feelin' you, sun." I continued to sweep the floor with Casper flashing a half smile, like he was happy and sad at the same time.

"I'ma see if she gonna let me suck her titties right here in the store."

"Yeah, right."

"Real talk. I put that on everything I love." Casper held his square. That was when I knew he was serious.

"Suck her joints here, and you'll get locked up for indecent exposure," I warned.

"No sweat. At least I'll get locked up with a full stomach and a smile on my face." Casper looked over to the lady and whistled. "Aye, ma. Let's go to the back and do tha damn thing." Casper was raw as uncooked meat with his approaches. The lady still ignored him, but my man didn't let up. I've actually seen a few cuties answer to his boldness.

"Put a fork in it," I taunted.

"It ain't nothin'. I know what'll float her boat." He pulled out what appeared to be a roll of dollar bills. "Hey, shorty, I wanna talk to you for a minute. You treat me good, and I'll treat you better." He flashed the bankroll, and her head perked up as if she heard someone call her name.

"I don't get down like that," she claimed, talking at him while staring at the roll of green.

"I just sayin', ma. You eat when I eat. I'll hook you up if you hook *me* up."

Casper was speaking to the woman even though her eyes never left the dollar bills. Not once I saw shorty give him eye contact during the exchange. She'd *heard* him, but wasn't listening. Her eyes and ears made love to whatever amount of loot my man had in his hand. It amazed me how a piece of green paper can change anyone's views about another person in the blink of an eye. You can be the richest asshole known to man, but those dead prez would hypnotize others to overlook your shortcomings. The breast feeding broad wouldn't give Casper the time of day until he pulled out the wad of cash. She still had her eyes on the prize and refused to respect his being there. Caz just wanted a nut, and shorty eyed the dough; all was fair in sex and war.

After whispering in her ear for a few seconds, she got up and walked off with him. With the broom in one hand and pink lemonade in the other, I stopped Casper dead in his tracks.

"You ain't hittin' off shorty in this piece, g." I grilled him.

"C'mon, man. We're hittin' up my cousin's rest at St. Nick's. It's only a hop and a skip from here."

"Are you serious? You don't know what she has. She might be walkin' around with that package."

Casper rubbed his hands together. "Look, b. You only live once. And if that mean dyin' with a titty in my mouth, then I'ma go down as the happiest man who died from breast milk."

He gave me a pound and left with shorty. I was disgusted, and shook off what I saw unfold before my eyes. Casper had little to no standards. A piece of ass didn't have a face to him. He would rather eat the apple off the ground instead of climbing the tree for the golden one at the top. I just couldn't sleep with anyone on the strength of her being a female. Casper was raw in that sense. He just didn't care, as long as he got his nut off and left with a smile.

I swept up and down the aisle and felt someone behind me.

"Boo!" A voice rang loud and I jumped. "Did I scare you?"

I turned slowly, and I hadn't seen her in a few weeks. The beat from my heart kicked and a smile slicked across my face. I fixed my collar and half licked my lips to erase signs of chap.

"How you doin', gorgeous?" I hugged her as she smiled.

"I'm fine, stranger. I listened to your CD. It's tight," Sandra said, and I blushed. I still remembered her hazel eyes and well-kept micro-braids.

"Thanks, I appreciate it. So what you've been up to?" I asked.

"Keeping *my* house in order. I just came back from dropping off my kids."

"That's cool. How many seeds you have?"

"Two boys."

"That's beautiful. I hope they ain't workin' you too hard."

"No, way. My sons have manners. My husband and I taught them well."

"So where's your husband? If you don't mind me asking." I indirectly pushed her to answer what I wanted to hear.

"He's overseas."

"Overseas?" A false touch of shock salted my tone.

"Yeah, he's stationed in Iraq."

"A military man, huh? I see you like them G.I. Joe, Rambo brothas."

She laughed. "You crazy, but yeah, I can't wait for him to come home. I'm praying nothing happens to him." She turned away from me and muttered, "...because Lord knows I need a fix."

For some reason, I got the impression that she was thinking out loud.

Sandra stared at the dress shoes lining the shelves and shot toward them. Picking up the shoes to check the prices, her eyes sparkled like a chandelier. "I want these. But they don't have any my size." She looked at the shoes like a child fixing to open her gift.

"I got you, love. I'll check the back room."

As I left to check Receiving, a tornado of pleasure swept across me. Creeping with a married woman fed my ego that fled on a thin line between joy and pain. Guilt was the dead weight I brushed off my brain. The flame of desire ran wild that evening. Cheating on her mate was a possibility, but sleeping with another man's woman had never left a mark of fault. If she wasn't cheating on him for me, she would've found the next man to satisfy her longing. The way I looked at it was like how plants needed the sun and water to grow. So why shouldn't I sow my fantasy of tasting the fruit while reaping the pleasure for the both of us? The risk was great, but I had to get mine.

I came back with the shoes Sandra wanted.

"You lucky I like you like that." I handed her the box.

"I'm lucky?"

"Yeah, I normally don't do that for customers."

"Somebody's not doing their job."

"What they pay me is what they get."

"Justice, you're too much." She playfully slapped my leg and tried on the shoes. Her purple, fish net stockings turned me on as I hardened. I photographed me kissing and spreading Sandra's legs apart. The hard-on embarrassed me, but the arousal left once I stopped focusing on her feet.

"Okay, I'm done." She placed the shoes in the box and shuffled through her purse.

"Wow, that's fast. I like you as a customer."

"Why is that? Because I'm a woman who doesn't try on different shoes and make a mess in your department?"

"No, because your feet don't smell like toe cheese."

She cackled and finished packing the shoes she wanted. Her appearance flaunted the beauty that pulled me to ask for her number. My pride said "no." The flow of our conversation clicked, and I picked her brain long enough to know she dug me.

"What are you doing next weekend?" She inched toward me.

"I dunno, why?"

"I would like to know if you can come over and snap some photos of me for my husband."

"What kind of photos?"

"Um…Some sexy photos. You seem to be a cool guy. I'm not from around here, and don't know anyone to take them for me."

"I'm down," I said without second thought, and she fished through her purse to hand me a business card. It appeared from the card that she worked for a non-profit organization. So I knew she had some good-natured sense about her.

"Okay, cool. Keep in touch."

"I will." I walked away and paused for a moment. "Wait, where you're from?" I hollered.

"Texas, why?"

"Just curious."

I watched her rump jiggle like Jell-O when she walked further away from the department.

"I guess everything *is* big in Texas," I said loud enough for her to hear. She smiled, almost as if she was meaning to tease me. My eyes followed her out the store. I knew I was in for a trick with the treat being a nightmare.

Chapter 12: Five Finger Discount

It's on...

Two peanut headed looking boys dressed in brown slacks with matching button down shirts mapped down each aisle. I was waiting for how long they'd planned to stuff the gear inside their black garbage bags. My knees twitched and flagged worry as they casually checked out the construction boots resting on aisle 6. I fixed my eyes on the clock and the red tick propped on three.

Right on schedule.

My throat screamed for water, and I walked toward the fountain to fill the one liter bottle. Cool air blasted through an overhead vent and chilled the sweat flowing down my brow. I opened the Receiving room door and peeked inside with cold air brushing against my face. The emptiness soothed me, and I moved across the room after filling my water bottle. I strolled around and found the joint vacant. The morning workers had left after their shift, but I'd never forsaken the chances of them working overtime.

The clock hand marked five minutes. I went to the security booth only to find Tahleek going to work on a tall, voluptuous honey. The black panty hose that hugged her long legs sparked saliva to ease from the side of his mouth. Money was drooling like a dog that never ate in days. Her fingers twisted her short, brown curly hair with her body turned to an angle where Tahleek's eyes lusted for her apple bottom. Tahleek looked google-eyed like a child going dumb as he stared at her plums while she flirted with him.

Check!

Nervous and numb, I sauntered passed them. The lady turned to face me. Tahleek's hand greeted me. He sat relaxed while ignoring the monitors patrolling the store. The woman winked when I nodded and saluted her. I headed back to aisle 1 to check on the two boys prancing around the area in case they stole any merchandise. A guy dressed in a suit bumped into me, and I almost tripped on his leg.

"Excuse me, brotha." The guy raised his open hand like he was swearing in court as a pardon gesture. I nodded and stepped off to aisle 1. I loudly tapped on a construction boot 3 times on the top shelf.

The boys saw me and our eyes touched. The boys, wearing the tightest suits known to man, marched past me and stared straight at Receiving. My forehead moistened, and my heart pumped faster than the Daytona 500. Laughing in the dark and washing away nervousness, I couldn't wait to knock the big cheese off their feet. I thought of myself like a grim Sunday, bringing an end to the weak; wiping my ass with the scar tissue of every key holder's brain and flushing it down the toilet of oblivion.

My eyes switched from watching the boys standing in the aisles to the side wall. The clock ticked for the cue that signaled them to jet out the store. I loudly banged on the top shelf; toes tapping the floor, losing my breath, and light-headed as I dreaded each second that past. The bags bulged and flopped on their backs. They shot passed me. Balls of sweat crept down my temple and I felt like vomiting. My stomach screamed gas. The strain was pushing Felicia's home cooking upwards, and my eyes were glued onto the shelves.

Weeeiiiirrrr!!! Weeeiiiirrrr!!! Weeeiiiirrrr!!!

The alarm squealed repeatedly as the boys peeled out the back of the store. I stood up from a Buddha position on the floor and flew towards Receiving. The head start dusted my pretend chase as they got away clean.

Mission Completed.

Twice Shoe Fetish was robbed, and the heist planted a smile on my face. The grin was wiped off when Adam streaked to Receiving. He tossed his arms in the air like he was defeated. He turned anger-red with raspberry eyes that marked the tableau of a mad man.

"Where was everybody?" he fired off, but not to anyone specifically. Grunting and stomping on the floor, Adam was frightening the poor little kids witnessing him blow up from one of the aisles. He noticed their horror and caught himself from exploding. His composure cooled, and he repeatedly hand slicked his hair. "We need security. We need more got-damn security!"

Tahleek sped walked to Shoe Fetish. Adam hawked at him as Tahleek knew he was caught with his pants down. He lost track of time which cost the store hundreds of dollars of merchandise. Tahleek groaned, and I sensed his embarrassment. Adam walked past him without uttering a word and curved his anger for another time. The theft ran smoothly as I'd planned.

Golden and Makeda scurried near the Receiving room just to be nosy. I couldn't stand looking at them.

"Damn, they got us again." Golden chimed in between bites of potato chips.

"And where were you?" I grilled them.

"Mindin' our business. We ain't chasin' no hoodlums stealin'." Golden's talking while chewing annoyed me as food particles spat out her mouth.

The black rings around her sunken eyes flared. For a hot minute I thought Frankenstein was looking at me. Yep, she was that hideous looking. She pressed her hands against the Chinese wig tracked onto her head; the plastic looking hair piece was beyond unattractive. I was embarrassed for Golden, but she wasn't the one who cared about appearances.

"So ya'll wanna be nosy after they steal, right?" I griped.

"Whatever, Justice. Go over there and clean your department."

"Shut up before I choke you with your stretch marks," I said half-jokingly. "I don't say nothin' when you take long naps in Receiving."

Golden's mouth widened with red gloss caked on her lips. She was speechless. Makeda muffled her laughter, not trying to offend her "friend."

"I'm pregnant. I need my rest," Golden spewed.

"You got more excuses than a pedophile on Dateline," I joaned.

"Whatever, catchin' thieves ain't my job."

"And sleepin' is your job, right?" I shot back, and Makeda interjected.

"Okay, okay. Let's act like civilized folk, now," Makeda said, and had some nerve. She puts the "S" in savage.

Golden rolled her eyes and wobbled away. Makeda waited until Golden turned the corner and sucked her tongue in disdain.

"I can't stand that bitch." Makeda crumpled her face.

"What?" I was caught off guard.

"That heifer tried to holla at my man at my cousin's barbeque last week."

"How'd you know?"

"My cousin saw her huggin' up on him, and that bitch wasn't drunk, either."

"Oh, Lord. 'He said, she said' crap. I thought she was your homie."

Makeda devilishly laughed like she'd seen someone slip on a banana peel. "She ain't my friend. I'm using that broad for car rides to work. But don't worry. I got somethin' for that b---"

Adam strolled by the department and cut Makeda off mid-sentence, not through words, but presence. Her face untwisted to glee. She stood straight as if Adam was the store's general.

"Hey, Adam. Is everything all right?" Makeda softened her voice and erased the discharge of anger from seconds before.

"I can be better. This store is getting killed with theft. I think I need a drink."

"I got coffee in my locker. When I'm done with my project, I'll bring you a bag," Makeda kissed-up. I couldn't believe what my ears had just heard.

"Thanks, that's what I need, Makeda," said Adam.

"Okay, I'll be right here if you need anything. Just holler."

Adam raced away from the department, and I pressed my lips together to sound kissing noises. Makeda was puzzled at my gesture and took the smooches as love calls.

"Stop kissin' at me."

"I'm not kissin' at you. Your ass kissin' is disgustin'…pathetic to the 5th power, b."

"Ain't nobody kissin' no one's ass around here."

"'I got coffee in my locker. I'll be right here if you need anything,'" I mocked Makeda's brown nosing. "Sucking up to Adam for the supervisor position for the Ladies' department ain't flavor."

Her teeth clamped down on her thick lips, and she picked the rose stem from her tall, black afro to throw it at me. The stem flew above my head and missed me. She grunted and stuck her chubby middle finger at me. I laughed off the motion.

Golden wobbled back, stomach protruding her store's shirt, and rested next to Makeda. She twisted her face upon glancing at me as if she was mad at the world. If I was that ugly, I'd be mad at the world, too.

"Makeda, I'm about to take a nap in Receiving. Can you tell anyone that asks for me I'm in the bathroom?" Golden asked.

"Girl, I got you. I'll come and get you if someone comes lookin' for you," Makeda said in the fakest nicest voice.

"Thanks. Are you still rollin' with me to Shayla's party tonight?"

"Yeah, I'm down to get my drank on. I heard it's gonna be a lot of freaks at that piece."

"Amen, to that!"

High fiving and smiling, Makeda and Golden acted like sisters from another mother. The exchange between the two sickened me to my stomach. I left the Ladies' department for shoes. The negative vibe given off ripped away any respect I had for them because of their fraudulent ways.

Makeda and Golden were the store's murder mamis. Talking to them alone was cool, but the two-headed monster terrorized the joint once they mingled together. They gossiped, snitched on employees to supervisors for clocking in late, and talked behind the backs of other employees. They'd never given me any real problems, but I still showed them no love. They were the type who'll laugh in front of your face but talked shit behind your back.

I ran across Clara limping as she finally sat down on an aisle bench. She glanced at me, and her face bent from a frown to a smile.

"Justice, Justice, Justice." Clara's spirits flew as she said my name. "I got good news. I'm having surgery on my knee. I'll be out tree (three) to four months."

"That's good. Why'd you decide to go into surgery?"I asked, feeling like jumping for joy.

"Oh boy, I just couldn't' take the pain anymore. It was bothering me." Clara exhaled as if she'd finished smoking a cigarette. "Why don't you ask Adam to replace me temporarily with you for the supervisor position?" She shrugged.

Now *that* was what I'm talking about. Finally I came across a person with some sense. I got lost in excitement for a moment but brought myself back to reality.

"That's something to think about." I shrugged, not really taking her seriously.

"Yeah, go talk to him about the position. You get paid more…I think 20 dollar an hour for someone starting out. You're the right man for it."

Her words had never rung so true. Work politics licked me the wrong way and clicked the switch of doubt that lingered over me. My palms shivered from just thinking about the pay raise. I looked forward to waking up every day a few dollars richer.

Before I left Shoe Fetish, I saw a woman that looked like she'd just glided down from heaven. My eyes were frozen on her apple butter skin tone; she looked like a model straight from a magazine without photoshopped features. I followed her from kids' shoes to the front of the department store since I had to walk there to see Adam anyway.

Her swagger was like she owned the joint. I knew she was a professional woman by the way she wore the black dress suit that pressed on her figure 8-shaped body. She stood behind the counter at Bling World, the jewelry store that was housed in the building. She smiled when I walked past. I shot her a wave and kept it moving. There was no reason to act thirsty at first glance, but curiously danced on my conscience. Nosey eyes blaring from gossip folk working the registers was another reason why I didn't spark a conversation with the "mystery woman." The extra headache wasn't needed, especially since Essence tired to blow my spot in front of Nandi at the bowling alley.

I finally stepped to the manager's door and knocked. As Adam opened the door, his face was cleared from the blotches of redness that covered his flesh after the theft.

"Adam, do you have a minute?" I stepped inside the room.

"Yeah, sure. Help yourself to a seat."

I sat across from Adam and gathered words to express my interest for the supervisor position. I nervously cracked my knuckles because I was giddy; the feeling was like the first time I got my first piece of ass.

"I wanted to speak with you to say I am very interested in the supervisor position until Clara gets back from medical leave." I popped off the meeting.

Adam shifted and rocked in his seat while staring at the wall. I waited for him to open his jib and spew his Southern drawl. The vents blowing air with the ceiling lights incessantly buzzing kept the room busy from silence. His foot tapping on the floor pulled sweat from my palms.

"Okay," he muttered, and twisted his chair to shuffle through a stack of papers on his desk. "Well, we already have a candidate."

A jolt of shock hit me. "What? How is that possible? Clara just told me about her leave today."

"She told *you*, but we were aware days before. The person we hired has more experience and is the right person to supervise Shoe Fetish."

"I've been in this store for three years, and you're telling me that someone who doesn't know the store like the back of their hand knows more than me?"

Adam shrugged, and my heart dropped faster than bird shit.

Cupid's evil twin shot me in the ass and dashed my spirits. My face sank into my hands, and I slipped to a dizzy spell. Tension swelled as the automatic shotgun of politics gunned me down and dragged my cares for the store to hell. What was the point of busting my tail when a glass ceiling held me back from going up?

Heat from the florescent lights blanketed me. I felt drunk; drunk like drinking shots of liquor that chilled me after heating my stomach in knots. I glanced up and caught Adam forcing a smile. The rejection wasn't a laughing matter. I felt humiliated. I rose from the chair and left the room without responding to him. After that brief meeting, I shook off the guilt of orchestrating the thefts that plagued the store and thought of another caper to pull off.

Chapter 13: How to Beat Up a Rapper

I got off work in the evening and caught Casper buying scented oils from a vendor on 125th. He damn near bought the entire shelf because oil bottles filled his knapsack.

"Aye, black, you're preparin' for a hurricane to hit NY or somethin'?" I stood amazed as he stock piled his bag.

"It's not about jokes, sun. It's about impressin' the laaadies."

"I thought you didn't like wearing oils."

"The ladies dig it. And plus, why should I spend damn near $50 on cologne when I can cop me a month supply of oils for just $15?" He smiled mischievously. "None of them cheap joints down the block. I gets mines pure and uncut, baby boy. Pure and uncut."

I thought he was full of shit. "When did you start doin' it up for the honeys?"

"Ever since I bagged that Spanish chick on the "6" train comin' from the Bronx a few weeks ago. Shorty was open off the oils this Muslim cat gave me in Williamsburg. I copped mad numbers from females ever since then. It's a chick magnet, g."

"Yeah, I guess."

"You want some?"

"I'm good. I just copped me some in Brooklyn the other day."

Casper waved me off. "Maaan, you need to get the official joints in Mecca."

"Why?"

"Because the joints Uptown ain't watered down."

"Okay, enough with the Uptown propaganda. What you on tonight?"

"Scar-lo and his crew are throwing a barbeque at Lafayette Gardens."

"Scar-lo's crew? In L.G.?" My face crunched bitterly.

"Yeah, sun. It's gonna be official," rooted Casper, but I was still against making the trip.

L.G. can be a little wild at times. As shorties growing up in the latter part of the 80's into the 90's, my crew from Fort Greene used to rumble with dudes from that part of Bed-Stuy. The joint was a breath away from us as we lived just down the street. I got off on whipping asses even when I lost a few scraps. Running from a tussle meant your name was pussy when the rites of passage of fist fights broke us into manhood. Some cats must've loved the feel of my fists breaking their face bones since they often tested me. I was known as the "book worm"; reading books and hitting up class everyday. Knuckleheads who didn't know my hand skills found out the truth the hard way. Serving beat downs to dudes who thought I was food, I got a few passes when most heads knew how I got busy in the streets. I always thought fighting over blocks we didn't own was stupid. I fought as a *man*, and because the streets swallowed the weak, I had to knuckle up. I rolled with the punches until we grew tired of the dumbness by clicking up, friend with foe. I still felt uneasy every time I walked through that 'hood, though.

I slept on the decision to head out to L.G. for a split second. I checked my pockets and searched for a weapon in case drama popped off. Carrying a switch-blade in case Scar-lo's goons got out of line brought more comfort. Scar-lo's crew sickened me, and even though Casper grew up with them, I detested them like a sickness.

"Man, everything's gonna be cool," Casper assured.

"Uh huh, aight. I'm duffin' the first cat who says somethin' slick, word is born." I clenched my fist as if one of Scar-lo's goons was standing in front of me.

"It's not that type of party. We should head up to 145th and see if Freedom wanna roll with us."

"Aight, cool. I'm down."

The street vendors selling scented oils, books, and posters on 125th hijacked my mind away from fighting. The African brothers who sold their merchandise day and night reminded me of why I should work for self. I bet half of them, if not all, had never stepped foot in a college classroom. They rather make money without answering to somebody. Working at a job I hated sucked. I admired anyone who had the guts to take risks and slap a 9 to 5 in the mouth, or work at a job they loved. Watching other people get fat off my work was torture. Talent was in my DNA, but I lived blind to know what it was. I just knew it was *something*. Running through stages of finding myself, my life was a book with missing pages.

Casper and I caught the "A" train to 145th and walked down to Burger Town on Broadway. I spotted two girls waiting in line and we stood behind them. Freedom never noticed us. He was too busy working the registers. The girls stared at Freedom and measured him from head on down.

"Ask 'em for his number," a girl with a pony tail said to her friend. The friend sucked her teeth and removed her scarf that hid her hair that was shaped like a bun.

"He's cute and all, but he works at a fast food place."

"What's wrong with that?" The friend asked.

"I don't want that nigga comin' home smellin' like cheeseburgers and fries; stainin' my bed sheets with grease and shit."

"Girl, you somethin' else."

"That's my word. If a nigga ain't comin' home with more than a 'G', he best to not breathe near my door-step."

The girls were about to order their food when Freedom looked up at us. He ignored them and gave us pounds.

"What's good, money?" Freedom slapped hands with Casper and I.

"Ain't nothin'. We wanna to know if you down to ride out to Medina with us," I said, and he lifted his index finger.

"Hold that thought." He turned to face the girls. "Welcome to Burger Town, can I take your order?"

"Yeah, it's about time. Anyway, I wanna get a numba 2, and a numba 6 for my girlfriend," the girl with the bun angrily requested. Freedom, unfazed by the girl's tone, computed their orders in the register and walked to the workers handling the food.

"Hurry up, I gots somewhere to go!" The girl shouted with a puerile attitude.

Casper and I looked at each other with twisted faces. Impatience never allowed me to work at a fast food joint. The pay sucked, and customers who loved to talk slick added to insult. As a teenager, I avoided filling out applications at fast food joints like the plague.

I glanced over at the wall, and saw Freedom's name etched on plaques for employee of the month three times in a row. I was proud of my man. Freedom worked hard at a job he probably didn't want, but he still gave the job his life; working religiously to hush the cries of his newborn and wife. Money wasn't the root of evil since it never grew on trees. Whereas having *no* money would push anyone to the brink of cursing at the world and flipping faith the middle finger. Finding solace in work and not couch-potato his life away, he used the burger joint as a stepping stone, even if the gig wasn't the freshest. I admired my man because he saw the bigger picture. Other folks I knew scrapped blindly in the rat race for cheese and found themselves glued on the trap in the end.

Freedom paced back to the registers and handed the girls their meals.

"How can you deal with that?" Casper scowled at him after the girls left the joint.

"Man, I just ignore things like that. You get used to it after awhile."

"Sun, I would've spat on their food on general principle. But let's get off that. Scar-lo's havin' a barbeque in L.G. tonight. You should roll with us," Casper suggested, and Freedom looked down. He tapped the tip of his fingers on the counter and looked up.

"I can't, sun."

"What you mean you can't? I thought you got off around this time."

"Yeah, man, but Tamika and the baby…I gotta work overtime to make this bread."

"What are you? Part Jamaican or somethin'?" Casper joked.

"You's a funny cat. I've worked the 1st, 2nd and about to work the 3rd shift tonight. I'm runnin' on fumes right now, kid."

"Daaamn. That's wild. And I didn't know Tamika had the child. Congrats, man." Casper said.

"Yeah, sun. It's real out here…Hold on for a minute." Freedom stepped to the order window and asked his supervisor for a break. He walked back and guided us to the seating area.

"What's good with you and your shorty?" Freedom asked Casper.

"My daughter's fine. I'm hangin' in there my damn self. I'm thinkin' about goin' to the military."

"The military?" I said loudly, and the workers handling food turned their heads to face us. "Caz, you never told me you were goin' to the military."

"You never asked. There ain't nothin' out here for me to do. I'm broke with an eight-month-old daughter. I'm tired of buyin' oils and re-sellin' them on the block just to feed my fam."

"I knew your frontin' ass wasn't buyin' oils for females." I traded laughs with Freedom.

"Uh huh, but you believed me, didn't you? I'll serve my four years in the military and get out paid. It's better than sellin' drugs and landin' my black ass behind bars."

"Man, what happened with that talk about the military not being a place for a Black man?"

"Things change, g. I might as well get in how I fit in and make some bread the best way I can. I rather see different places and risk gettin' killed instead of hangin' on the block all day with the *chances* of gettin' killed, and not doin' nothin' with my life."

I exhaled and turned back to Freedom. "So when you gonna be free?"

"I can't call it. I'ma have to go hard…" He looked over his shoulder and turned down the volume of his voice. "I'ma have to go hard until they either promote me to manager, or I find a new gig."

"That's cool, man. Do ya' thing. Holla at us when you get a chance. And you better hope massa don't hear about you escapin' off the plantation," I laughed, and Freedom smiled crookedly. Casper and I traded pounds with Freedom and we bounced from Burger Town for the long ride on the "C" train to L.G.

The train screeched on the Clinton-Washington stop, and we spotted two cuties stepping out from one of the train cars. I cupped my hands close to my mouth to see if my breath was tart. I had to make sure my breeze was on point.

I stood next to a light brown-skinned shorty donning a mini skirt with black stockings that covered her thick, well-shaped legs. She worked her 5'5" frame very well, and the back of her mini-skirt bounced as she walked. Not blowing a chance to talk to her, I power walked to stand beside her.

"Excuse me, miss," I crept behind her and she turned slowly. "I'm diggin' your style, love. I would like to talk to you for a minute."

"Uh, w-well," she stuttered while walking. "I would *like* to…but I have a boyfriend."

"Aight, I respect that. So how long y'all been together?"

She thought for a second before responding. "Two years…off and on."

"Are you happy?"

"We're goin' through our problems. It's no big deal."

"That's cool. So where you headed?"

"I'm headed to a barbeque in L.G."

"Lafayette Gardens?" I was hoping she would say "yes."

"Yeah, I'm goin' that way."

"Do you mind if me and my boy walk you and your homegirl there? We're goin' that way, too."

"You must want me to get in trouble with my man, don't you?"

"Nah, I'll fall back if it's a problem. I'll just see you there so you can think about me when your man gets on your nerves." I smirked, and she smiled while walking away.

Casper and I parted ways with the girls and walked a few blocks until we hit the corner of Classon and Lafayette Ave. The smoke from the grill danced inside my nostrils and I followed my stomach toward the park. I spotted Scar-lo's crew shooting dice on the park bench with music blaring from the speakers plugged to the lamp post. I chugged down a bottle of pink lemonade I bought from the bodega, and my eyes wandered around his crew. I zoomed in on a man forking the grill while bobbing his head to the music. The sun shone on his hairless head and he turned toward us. It was Scar-lo.

I stared, and he stared back. He completely turned away from the grill and stopped forking the food. We paced at each other like two gunmen readying to draw in a Western gun fight. The sight of us walking alarmed those in the park, and the scene moved in slow motion. We stood face to face as he had an inch over me. Street rep or not, fear never colored my heart.

"Peace, lord." Scar-lo greeted me. We gave each other pounds.

"Peace, king. The food is smellin' quite lovely over there." I rubbed my stomach.

"Yeah, man. I just thought I'd give back to the 'hood by cookin' for my people's and throwin' a small carnival for the little ones. I bought mad food from the warehouse the other day." He pointed toward the long line of food on the folding tables as he read my thoughts. "Help yourself. It's enough for everybody. Eat before the rats get to it."

I fixed me a plate of spicy jerk chicken, peas and brown rice, fried bananas, and potato salad; flushed down by pink lemonade. Casper fixed his plate and sat with me. I thought about him joining the military ranks, which still killed me. I aired out the chip on my shoulder.

"Why you wanna join the service?" I asked between bites of jerk chicken.

"I need the money. I'm starvin'. My baby's mom needs diapers and we need to eat. Besides, I need discipline anyway."

"Discipline? Since when you wanted discipline?"

"I never had a pops to keep me from runnin' wild. I don't wanna do anything that'll ruin my life for me, my earth, and the baby."

I thought for a minute through bites of the rice and peas. "Become a Muslim," I half joked.

"Man, I ain't gone sell bean pies for a livin'. And I ain't givin' up swine. I hear a pork chop callin' me right now."

"You still eatin' that pig, huh?"

"I tried givin' it up. But when my old earth made some pork chops the other night, it was a wrap!"

"Aight, sun. Don't say nothin' when you get old and find tape worms growin' out your brain."

"Maaan, ain't no one ever died from eatin' pork. You righteous cats need to get off that madness. I'll hop over a cow to eat a pig's ass any day, sun."

I dropped the subject once I looked behind Casper. My eyes squinted through the curtain of smoke floating from the charcoal inside the grill. The shrill of ambulance sirens muted an argument from afar. My eyes cut through the haze of smoke and gazed at a guy pulling a girl by her strapless shirt. He jerked her back and tugged on her arm; silent yells shot out her mouth. The girl was the same light-skinned shorty I'd met at the subway with the skirt and black stockings. She was gorgeous even in her maddened state.

"Let me go, Nu-Sun! Let me the fuck go!" She pulled away from Nu-Sun, and one breast popped out her tank top. She hurriedly tucked her breast back inside and rage hurricaned her eyes. "I'm sick and tired of your shit!"

"Why you gotta do me like that, huh? Why you gotta do me like this in front of my crew, Zaire?" charged Nu-Sun, with a hair pick sticking out his afro.

"Chill the fuck out. I just asked for his autograph."

"Whatever. C'mon, girl." He lowered his voice while reaching for her. "Don't play me like a fuckin' fool."

"You buggin', man."

"Tell the truth, Zaire. I swear to God, if I *ever* find out that you slept with that..."

"It ain't even like that. Me and my girls just asked for his autograph and we went about our business." She stopped to catch her breath. "I don't say shit when you and your crew run trains on them broads from your buildin'."

"Don't try to twist shit on me. This about you jumpin' off with every rap nigga in NYC." Nu-Sun tried grappling her, but she squeezed away. Tears flew down her cheek and her bloodshot eyes hawked at him.

"Don't touch me. I don't want your nasty paws on me."

"C'mon, girl. Stop playin' and come..." He opened his mouth, but was cut off by the eyes in the park staring at them. The argument silenced everyone's conversation. The scene was like a DJ switching to a country western tune in the middle of a rap concert.

Nu-Sun backed off after failing to hug Zaire. He flung a wad of dollar bills at her that plunged to the ground. She lunged at him and swung wildly, aiming at his face. He blocked her punches and never laid a hand on her. His squad and her homegirls pulled them away from each other. Zaire aimlessly swung her legs and threw her high heels that almost hit Nu-Sun's head.

"It's over, Nu-Sun! It's over!" she shouted. Nu-Sun's face was too icy to even care.

"It's all good. You'll be back. I'm not worried 'bout it. That's what they always do."

Scar-lo's crew laughed at the exchange.

I guess I was right; her boyfriend messed around and danced on her last nerve. I wanted to approach her, but fell back on that thought. Getting caught in between drama pinned me to the bench. I fought off the need to speak with her.

Zaire's homegirls calmed her down, and one of them gave her back the shoe that she'd thrown at Nu-Sun. She fixed her outfit and slicked back her hair after looking in her pocket mirror.

"That asshole done fucked up my hair." She huffed, and tied her hair in a pony tail.

Zaire suddenly turned and caught me staring. She stopped fuming and locked her eyes on to mine. She dropped her anger and broke a smile. Even through the drama, I still dug her style. My hands trembled and I blanked out. I had to deal my cards right and not play myself in Nu-Sun's backyard, facing the chances of getting shot or my face permanently scarred.

Nu-Sun was a knuckleheaded stick-up kid rolling with Scar-lo's crew. Even though Zaire broke up with him on the spot, I suspected he still carried feelings for her, and that stopped me from making the first move. Nu-Sun's trigger finger was known to catch seizures with a short fuse, and I wasn't taking any chances of finding out if that urban legend was true.

Her feet shuffled toward me, and my hands twitched like a dope fiend begging for a fix.

Damn!

Shorty looked too fine and delicious for me to not holla at her. She walked closer with a smile that spoke of cruel intentions.

"Hey, wasn't you the guy I met at the subway earlier?" She seemed much friendly than before. I nodded, and she laughed.

"Excuse me about what happened. *That* was the boyfriend I was talking about."

"It is?" I mumbled.

"Yeah, but I'm not worried about that nigga *now*." She softly placed her hand on my thigh. "So what's your name?"

"Justice."

"Justice? Uhm, that's a pretty name."

"Thank you. It's not as pretty as you." I smiled, and redness poked out her light-skinned cheeks. Her hands shifted from my thighs to the top of my hand. I felt eyes watching us, mouths gossiping, tempers flaring; it even seemed as if the cars on the road had stopped to peep us. Her blush didn't help matters. The rush of diving head first into a conflict over nonsense sent red flags in my conscience.

"So, what you like to do?" she asked, and I sat uneasy as the wind blew over her pink-colored hair.

"I don't think now is the time. But give me your number so I can holla at you so we can go out."

She reached inside her purse, and I caught Nu-Sun and his crew staring at us. He beckoned them to walk toward our way as she pressed her digits in my cell. I looked down at her. Then I looked back at them. I looked down at her again, and my foot tapped the ground on its own. I shook away thoughts of violence, and my eyes shifted from side to side. I felt trapped with her hand resting on my lap as she dialed her number with the other. Nu-Sun cracked his knuckles with a menacing look that checked on his estranged lover. The scene dawned on me that I was nothing but a pawn for Zaire to get back at Nu-Sun. Falling off my square, I blacked out for me to even realize her chess move of using me.

A Jeep zoomed by and parked on the sidewalk with music blasting from the subwoofers. The bass vibrated my muscles that hummed with the constant boom of drums. Skid marks from the tires stained the street that cued in MC Murder Kill Kill to show off his new whip on the block. Money was a big time rapper from around the way that made it out the 'hood. He stopped and hopped out his whip with three lovely women. They were dressed in mini-skirts and tank tops that read "The Flyest Girl" across their chests.

Platinum jewelry with diamond crusted charms draped around Kill Kill's neck. The charms reflected a blue-like shine that glistened with the brown-skinned lovelies holding onto his arms. Kids from the park ran up to him and asked for autographs. Nu-Sun broke away from my direction and slid with his pack of wolves toward the vehicle.

Whew…that was close

The deafening boom from the Jeep flooded the noise level and boiled the temperatures of goons eyeing Kill Kill.

Scar-lo stopped forking the grill and split his crew apart like an open wound. He walked through the line of goons plotting for a dirty snatch. He'd finally tracked down the guy he sought for. Scar-lo stalked with the ease of a smooth panther toward the whip and wrapped his arms around Kill Kill's shoulder. They walked to the back of the park near the school with Scar-lo whispering in his ear.

Casper and I looked at each other, wondering what was up with Scar-lo and Kill Kill. Kill Kill was known to have asked Scar-lo for "favors" while on the come up. The ghetto pass allowed Kill Kill to roam freely without worrying about stick-up kids robbing him and marking his jewelry. How fitting that a so-called "gangster" rapper who graduated from Catholic school with straight A's was extorted by a real street dude. Go figure.

Scar-lo's mood switched from hot to cold. I watched Scar-lo clutch his fist in a striking pose. He stood nose to nose with Kill Kill, and his crew swarmed around him like vultures itching to feast on dead leftovers.

"Baby, it's time to go." A mother grabbed her daughter's arm and rushed out the park. Other parents followed suit.

Nu-Sun pushed away the crew and madly pointed his index finger in Kill Kill's face. Kill Kill stood helpless. They put the fear of Satan in him. His hands shuddered, and he looked frightened at the sight of fifteen dudes circling him. The three ladies who came with Kill Kill dashed across the street near the brownstones on Lafayette and left him for dead.

As Kill Kill's music blasted from the Jeep, the bass drowned out screams from blows hammered by the crew. With each body blow, his facial expressions screamed in pain. He crawled on all fours like a dog, and a short, chubby guy kicked him down to the blacktop. They showed Kill Kill mercy after ten seconds of a beat down, but the "discipline" wasn't nearly over.

A tall, muscular man who looked like he'd spent ten years in the prison gym flipped Kill Kill upside down and held his legs together. Cash and car keys flew out Kill Kill's pockets as the goons seized everything he owned. Nu-Sun patted Kill Kill down while Scar-lo directed the orchestra of ruthlessness. The bling disappeared on the neck and wrists of Kill Kill, and he was dropped helplessly on the concrete, worming away from the crew.

Scar-lo helped Kill Kill to his feet and patted the side of his face like a father consoling his son. The crew scattered off when police sirens slid in and out of the music from the Jeep. Scar-lo stood his ground and wiped away the dust off Kill Kill's leather jacket. Three police cars bolted inside the park, but no one ran, not even Casper and I.

A face I didn't want to see emerged from one of the police cars. The bastard's presence angered me far worse than witnessing Scar-lo's fake friendship with Kill Kill. As the guy walked inside the park, I had wished *he* was on the receiving end of the crew's vicious beat down.

Seeing him reminded me of the day the goons killed my old earth in front of me.

Chapter 14: When Lust Calls

"What the hell he's doin' here?" Casper pointed at the sorry excuse for a man stepping out his unmarked car.

"Beats me. He probably got constipated from eating too many donuts." I glared at Brooklyn's Chief of Police and his army of detectives. They jetted toward the elementary school to break up the crowd of goons.

Backed by a coupe of police cars crowding the sidewalks, the chief bolted toward Scar-lo and racked him against the bricks of the school. The cops trooped around Scar-lo after senselessly shoving bums around and threatening them with billy clubs.

"Didn't I tell you not to come around here parading your shit in this neighborhood?" The beefy, dark brown-skinned chief hemmed Scar-lo against the wall. Unfazed by the chief's demeanor, Scar-lo laughed it off and defiantly brushed the chief's nightstick off him.

"I'm just an outstandin' citizen givin' back to my beloved community, Mr. Officer." Scar-lo sarcastically gestured. "Don't you have real criminals to go after?"

"I got my eye on you, Rahlo Hall," the chief scolded Scar-lo.

"See, Mr. Officer. Why you gotta put my government out like that, man?"

"Because I can, Hall. Get out of my sight before I lock you and your crew of knuckleheads in Rikers for trespassing."

"Yeah, I hear you, but I ain't listenin'." Scar-lo smirked, and winked at a police officer while walking away from the chief.

The chief turned toward his army of detectives and motioned his hand for them to search the park. The DT's dashed over trash cans, benches, and flashed badges at anyone walking on Lafayette and Classon. They patted me down, but did nothing to Casper, just like when cee-ciphers never frisked him at the raid at Lucky's.

After patting me down, the chief locked his eyes on me. I hated him; hated him with every fiber of my flesh, and every fabric that stitched each cell inside my brain. I wouldn't give him a drop of water, even if we were stranded on the hot, Arabian desert.

The sunset rested behind the project buildings of L.G. and dimmed the park when the night spotted over daylight. As I saw the chief through the curtain of darkness, I wished I would've left the park with the mothers. Gritting my teeth, his face reshaped from a smile to a frown, and further fueled the fire that burned inside me to not give a fuck about him. He was nothing but a coward who died infinite deaths and a waste of hot air.

"Did you see anything?" The chief asked me. Casper shrugged, and I sat emotionless.

"Am I being arrested?" I stared angrily at him.

"No."

"Then I don't gotta tell you shit, toy cop."

The chief hand-slicked his hair backward and stood a nose-length from me. I traded stares with him without flinching.

"Is that how you talk to me?" He glared at me.

"I'm not obligated to say jack."

A cardinal drifted from a light post and flew over the chief. The red bird circled around him and dropped fouls on the shoulder of his police jacket. The greenish slop soaked on his garment, and he swiped at the cardinal to shoo it away.

"Damn, Rehtaf. Even the birds wanna shit on you." Casper laughed, and before Rehtaf raised his hand to slap him, a tall, lanky detective called for the chief for instructions.

"Chief, we're done searching the area. We found nothing of interest, sir," said the detective. Chief Rehtaf wiped off the bird droppings from his shoulder with a handkerchief before heading to his vehicle. Laughs from Casper went on, and I stuck my middle finger at Rehtaf after he skated off.

"I can't stand him, sun." My jaws locked from the mix of the evening wind and the chief's mug that sparked my resentment.

"What did Rehtaf do to you?" Casper asked.

"Nothin'...and that's why I don't like dude. He can kiss my ass from here to Mississippi."

The park cleared after awhile and cued me to head home. I gave Casper a pound and carried on to Fort Greene. I found Felicia slumped over on the stoop of the brownstone, pissy drunk with a glass of liquor wobbling in her hand. She wasn't a drinker, but always stashed a soup of "get right" whenever she drooped to depression.

"Hey, Just-isssss," she slurred, and later smiled from ear to ear. "Want...somethin'...to drink?"

"I'm cool. How long have you been out here?"

"Well, you know...I needed a drinky drink," She gulped and burped; her breath stung my nose. "Oops, sorry."

"Ayo, I'm takin' you back inside the house."

"No, no, no...leave me here."

"Why?"

"'Cuz...I wanna look up at the beautiful starsss." She slouched back and smilingly stared at the sky. "Ain't it beautiful out here, Just-issss?"

"Yeah, a real sight to see." I caught her from falling down the stoop.

She slipped in and out of consciousness, and I moved forward to pick her off the steps. My knees bent to scoop her under my arms and I almost fell backwards. I kept my balance and staggered on the stoop to the front door. She dropped her glass that shattered across the steps and the noise awakened her.

"Jussss-tissss." She rested her eyes on mine. "Do you love me?"

"Awe, Fe Fe. You're buggin'."

"You don't love me, Jussss-tissss?"

"I love you like a play cousin," I teased, and she giggled like a school girl.

"Come on, Jussss-tissss. Say you love me. Say it?"

The liquor closed her eyes and she fought to keep them open. She hummed and drunkenly flew into a tune as I hurriedly carried her to the bedroom.

"And I'm savin' all my loooooove...and I'm savin' all my loooooove...and I'm saving all my loooooove...for yoooooooou."

Oh, Jesus. She pulled the Whitney Houston on me. Repeating the chorus over and over, she later nodded off. I laid her on the bed and she rested innocently, spreading out her arms and legs. My lips touched her forehead, and she sighed as if she was conscious enough to feel my warmth. I undressed and rested next to Felicia with my arms wrapped around her waist. Her angelic face reminded me that she was one of the few closest friends I had.

I loved Felicia, but wasn't *in love* with her. Pushing her further away from intimacy had protected me from hurt. The coldness in me was the puppet master of my mind. I pushed away every woman who tried to get close ever since Mama passed. Finding the right woman for me was hard when the mirror of love reflected hate, and I had no reason to look for anything special.

***

The so-called security guards huddled around Adam and pointed toward cameras hanging on the ceiling of the store. The store opened with a meeting about theft and other things I paid no attention to. Adam called everyone to the back of the building.

"Okay, gang. I'm going over the alarm system so you'll know how the alarm will sound if someone opens the back door of Receiving." Adam clicked on the alarm that rang a noise different from the old one. "That's the sound of the alarm. Also, we've added additional cameras to the store, and extra cameras in Receiving to monitor spots that we normal didn't watch."

As Adam finished, a tall, burly man stepped beside him and flexed the boulders standing on his shoulders like a contestant for Mr. Universe.

"My name is Officer Santiago, and other guys, like myself, will dress in plain clothes and walk around the store from time to time to catch potential thieves."

Great. Just great. First the managers were watching us, and now toy cops playing Colombo were monitoring the store. I guess cameras in the bathrooms were the next move Adam had in his perverted mind.

Adam smiled like a child excited about recess. He motioned for a brunette haired, brown-eyed man to stand next to him. The man was short compared to Adam, and annoyed me as he shifted one foot back and forth. Maybe his nervousness came from him standing as the only white person in the store besides Adam. Whatever it was, dude was a nervous wreck.

The man hesitated to greet us and slowly rubbed his hands together. He cracked a smile, and felt the heat of eyes shooting at him.

"Guys, I would like to make an announcement." Adam stepped forward. I've never seen him as happy in months. "I want to introduce the new manager of Shoe Fetish until Clara comes back from surgery…Joey Santino."

The guys clapped, and I hit the roof, livid with good spirits knocked down to new lows. Hard blows hit the pit of my gut. Heat stewed from my head to my toes and washed away goodness that flooded my mind; flashing through Strawberry Fields of shooting Adam with beetles that yield measles to rip through every thread and Lennon of his clothes. I worked harder than anyone in that store, and *that's* how they repaid me?

"Hey, guys. My name is Joey. If you have any questions, don't hesitate to speak with me." Joey smiled, and Adam patted him on the back like a proud dad.

Joey, whom I called "Jo Jo", and other new employees huddled around Adam. Prince walked beside me and looked on. Adam waved for us to gather around like mindless slaves that were paid to listen to his lame Monday morning jokes. But I wasn't having it.

"So there was this girl who just bought a dog and told this guy that she dyed her hair brunette." Adam began yet another lame joke. "And the girl asks, 'what you name your dog?' The guy says, 'Dee-Oh-Gee.' The girl says, 'what does the name means?' So the guy says, 'Dee-Oh-Gee' *is* 'Dog.' You must've been a blond before you dyed your hair.'"

The new employees laughed like it was the funniest joke they've ever heard while Prince and I just looked at each other with blank glances. His jokes sucked badly. I wouldn't crack a smile even if I was hit with the most potent laughing gas known to man. Dude was just that bad. Throwing rotten tomatoes at him would've been funnier because he was *that* bad, real bad. Did I mention he was bad? Oh well, I'm sure you get the point.

We walked away from him, and I spotted Essence lurking around the shoe department, being nosey as usual.

"I see they gave you the shaft." Essence stated the obvious.

"Hell to the yeah, they did. They gave the position to someone less qualified."

"How you know he's less qualified?"

"Essence, I've been in this joint for a hot minute, and it doesn't take a genius to supervise a department." I walked away from Essence, but she followed me. I wasn't in the mood to talk to anyone, but I needed to let off some steam. So I kept going with my rant.

"Adam geeks around like he's high on coke, and Clara got an IQ of a cucumber. A retarded monkey can supervise Shoe Fetish."

Annoyed, I walked to the shoe racks and kicked over a box standing in the middle of the main aisle that almost hit Essence. I grabbed a bottle of pink lemonade mixed with hard liquor and drunk the pain away.

"Ayo, Just!" A voice rang behind me, and I saw Casper's head over the aisles. "What's really good, kid? I wanna buy some sneakers for my sister's little man."

Looking at Casper, I thought I was witnessing a nightmare. His appearance frightened me. I wondered if he was high on drugs. Essence held in laughter, but I showed no mercy. Casper waltzed inside the joint like a throwback from the 70's.

"Sun, you look like a broke Milwaukee pimp." I laughed with Essence, and she leaned on me for support. He sported black platform shoes, orange bell bottoms, and a short sleeve Hawaiian shirt with the buttons ending in the middle of his chest.

"Man...*this* is a fashion statement. Casanova ain't got nothin' on me, kid."

"All you missing is a huge ass afro and the hair pick with the black fist." I bawled against a support wall, and Essence laughed her way back to the front of the store, not wanting to look at the disaster that Casper mistaken as a fashion statement.

"Aight, aight. This is some next shit." He modeled down the aisle like the joint was a runway. He bent down to a prison pose in front of an end-aisle mirror. "There's two kinds of languages that people speak; those who got it, and those that don't. And I got *it*." He kissed at the mirror and walked to his little man after gassing himself.

"My little man needs some sneakers."

"What kind?"

"He wants those." Casper pointed to a shoe display sitting on the shelf. "He wears size 8."

I walked over to the aisle and picked the shoe that little man wanted. I handed little man the box, and he propped it against the aisle's end. He opened the box and sat down, just staring at the shoes. Looking at Casper, the boy sporting well groomed cornrows in box patterns frowned.

"What's the matter with you?" Casper looked at the boy.

"Try these shoes on for me." The boy lightly pushed the box toward Casper with his foot.

"What?"

"I want you to try 'em on to see if they fit me."

"Boy, stop playin' and try on the damn shoes."

"You try 'em on and tell me if they fit. My socks got holes in 'em."

The boy was a train wreck. The poor kid had holes in his socks and wanted Casper to try on the shoes for him. I sighed at the craziness that was happening right in front of me. Casper shoved the box between the boy's lap and snatched little man's shoes off him like a stick-up kid in '88.

"Ayo, put those shoes back on. Lil man's feet smell like he dipped them in cat litter." I grabbed a box of nylon socks that customers used for trying on shoes and handed them to little man. "Caz, I need to holla at you for a minute while lil' man tries on the kicks."

While walking to the shoe racks away from the boy, I nudged Casper and kept an eye on the boy through the shelves.

"What did I tell you about showin' up here?" I fumed at him.

"What you mean?"

"This place is too hot for you to keep comin' here, sun. It's curtains if the store catches on to us."

"Man, calm down. Cee-ciphers ain't gonna find out about nothin'. I have it all under control, baby paw."

"Aight, whatever. I'm just warnin' you. The store put new cameras in the ceilin' as well as joints in Receiving."

"Okay, and?"

"And, we gotta dead the capers and find a new hustle."

Casper rubbed his chin and looked back at his little man. His eyes scanned the ceiling and shrugged nonchalantly.

"Well, it was fun while it lasted," he said.

"Yeah, good."

I looked back at the boy and saw him walking back and forth wearing the shoes. He was admiring them in the mirror and smiled at us as we walked toward him.

"You want those?" Casper asked little man.

"Yeah, they fit nice."

"Aight, put 'em back in the box and let's roll." Casper stepped away, but later stopped and looked back toward me. "Ayo, where they got men's belts?" He asked.

"Over there." I pointed to the Men's department.

"Come with me and show me," he said, and I looked at him like he'd done lost his mind.

"You's a grown man, pimp. Go over there and get it yourself." I waved him off.

"That's foul, sun. We got a Black president, and you don't wanna help a brotha out?"

"Caz, do you need someone to help you pee and wipe ya' ass?" I asked angrily, and he looked dumbfounded. "I thought so," I answered for him, and he walked off shaking his head with little man.

Customers who expected me to walk them through every aisle in the store burned my mind's kettle. They acted like lost children in the middle of a crowded mall. Grown men and women asking me, "Where are these shoes in 'such and such' aisle" bugged me the hell out. Couldn't they see signs of shoe styles and aisle numbers that directed them to what they wanted? I wish there was a law handing out fines or jail time for shoppers' laziness. Yeah, that would teach them a lesson for sure.

My feet screamed for me to sit, and I slouched on the bench at the end of aisle 5. I buried my face between my hands and wished for the day to end. I was tired, but still worked hard like a trooper.

I picked out some hot construction boots sitting pretty on the shelf and copped me a pair. I envisioned myself rocking those joints with some navy blue slacks, a matching collared shirt with brown and cream stripes to go along with my solid navy blue newsboy.

Jemima worked the registers, and her line was the shortest. Standing in a long line was out. So I chose the lesser of two evils. She tossed me the meanest gas face when she saw me.

"What's the science, Jem?" I sat the construction boots on the counter.

"What's the what?" she was puzzled.

"Nevermind. I see science wasn't one of your strong points."

Jemima rolled her eyes and brushed my boots away from the scanner. She scanned a gift card instead, and I confusingly watched her run the register.

"Why didn't you scan the boots?" I detected her move.

"My boyfriend left his gift card. I'm spendin' his shit to get back at him."

I studied Jemima quizzically and wasn't sure if I could trust her. I smelled foul play, and I'm not talking about her breath.

I went along with her "hooking me up" anyway. Cashiers always hooked up employees in other departments, and I saw no reason to deem she was suspect even when it seemed she was lying. Jemima was a loud mouth like Makeda and Golden, but never acted shiesty toward me.

She bagged the box and handed me the receipt. Accepting the hook-up was hard. Unsure about the transaction, I pressed her about the card.

"Are you sure this *is* your boyfriend's card?"

"Yeah, man, you're good."

She signed off on the purchase and I headed back to Shoe Fetish with my mind on nothing but looking fresh.

I looked toward the shoe racks and caught a man with a gray beard staring at me. He was clean cut and looked like a wise monk who dwelled in the Himalayas. The guy walked toward me and juggled a display shoe in one hand, and guzzled a water bottle with the other. The brother was ten inches shorter than me and reminded me of a midget. Frigid air blew through the vents and I shivered with my face twisted. My front foot shifted forward and held my square.

"Hey, brotha. How are you?" he asked me.

"I'm good. Do you need any help?" I asked.

"Yeah, the price tag is nowhere to be found. Can you help me?"

I nodded, and he trailed me back to the aisle. I wormed through boxes and opened one to check the bottom of a shoe. After showing him the price, he thanked me for helping him.

"You look tired, brotha. They've been working you hard, huh?" He chuckled, noticing fatigue suffocating my face.

"Somethin' like that," I said, and for some strange reason didn't mind speaking with him. Usually I ignored customers and kept it moving, but this brother was different. Why? I couldn't tell you. Maybe it was the beard.

"If you need a new job, just call me." He pulled out his MTA business card; his name was Shan. "The city is always hiring people to join the company."

I slowly stepped back. "I'm not supposed to take your card…but I'll take it anyway." After studying his face for a few seconds, I reluctantly grabbed the card.

"I respect that," said Shan, and I cautiously placed the card inside my pocket. "Check it out when you get some free time. I've been a train conductor for 30 years."

"Thirty years! Damn, I wasn't even born yet."

"Yep, the big 3-0. I haven't missed a day nor was I ever late. I've worked my shift even on holidays, and almost missed my son's graduation."

"Wow, you must love your job."

"Yeah, that also helps. It's not work when you doing something you love for a living. It's about answering your calling, mah man." He smiled, and tapped his fist over his right chest as a goodbye.

Before I had the chance to soak in his words, a text message rang from my cell. Sandra's name popped up on the Caller ID. I forgot about the evening's photo shoot and was glad she reminded me. Shan talked about answering my calling, and Sandra's was worth picking up.

Chapter 15: Heaven's Drink

Sandra opened the door.

The outfit she wore shocked me. She possessed the sexiness that locked me onto her vibe, and the photo shoot hadn't even begun. Holding my composure, my knees almost caved in; frail, unstable, and stunned.

"Hey, baby. Come on in." She held the door wide for me to walk inside. She dressed down for the evening as I peeped the black, cat-body suit outlining her body.

"Did you have trouble finding this place?" she asked.

"Nah, I pretty much know my way around Brooklyn," I shyly mumbled.

"Okay, cool. Let's get started."

Sandra left the living room while I set up the tri-pod. Tapping my pocket to check for the pack of condoms I brought, my mind wrapped around taxing Sandra. The thought was wrong, but felt so good. It was like ditching school with the chances of mom dukes finding out and beating my ass.

I plopped the camera on the tri-pod and popped open a champagne bottle sitting next to the red leathered sofa. I glanced at the windows lining one side of the room that stared at the buildings standing in Brooklyn. My mood suddenly changed from giddy to solemn; my mouth blew long breaths. Fighting between my love for my home and lust for Sandra, I ditched morality and pitched toward selfish desires sitting on wealth. I pimp slapped the angel dancing on my right shoulder and shook hands with the little devil laughing to the left.

High heels clacked on the parquet floor and snatched my attention away from the window. Sandra pranced in front of me like a cat, and stopped in a stance that called me to come; her legs widened as she stood sideways with the ceiling lights outlining her bubble. If I was half crazy, I would've ripped off every thread that embraced her body. But like the mack I was, I sat unfazed, as if she wasn't impressive enough.

"You like?" She turned around wearing a zebra patterned body suit. I just nodded. Even my voice box was too shocked to sound off syllables.

The body suit tucked the twin pears that jiggled every time she walked. She bent over in front of me to pick up something on the floor, holding her hips that curved widely away from her waist.

"So what you're waiting for? Let's roll." She posed in front of the camera.

"Where do you wanna shoot?" I asked, swallowing spit to moisten my dry mouth.

"First, we're going to shoot here, and then the master bedroom."

"Cool."

Sandra ran through at least 10 different outfits and all of them aroused me. I fought her off…I blacked out…not able to connect thoughts and words the more her body was like a standing prose in her modeling pose. The teasing rushed blood between my legs. A brother had to think about wrinkled, old ladies to soften my wood.

Looking around the joint to swing my mind off her, the condo reminded me of a museum. Framed pictures of ancient Kemetic kings and queens like Tut, Cleopatra, Nefertiti, Candace, Selassie, and Hannibal filled each corner of the condo with statues of other Black rulers sitting on tables and counter tops. She led me from the living room to the master bedroom. All four walls of the master bedroom were colored pink with a giant mirror posted on the ceiling. Sandra was a true freak in every sense of the word.

The room reminded me of a hippie set; a water bed floating in the middle of the joint with a multi-colored light ball spotting the walls of the room. Sandra stripped in front of me and paced around her bedroom naked, as if I was a ghost. The most I've done to ease the animal desire raging inside me was the thought of me busting my ass the first time I rode a two-wheel bike.

Make a move...calm down...make a move...calm down.

Confused and horny, I just stood there like a virgin geek who only got hugs and peeks of a smut magazine. Sandra's cat crept around me, and I shooed the pesky feline away with my foot. The cat jetted off to the next room, and Sandra blew me a kiss. Her body spoke to me in bilingual patterns; one that pulled me closer to her juicy cavern while the other refused me. Loosely attracting my loins from my brain to my groin, she acted hot and cold. Mentally I was drowning in her wetness without a life saver or Morse code. Holding in screams of pain that felt so good, she fondled my wood and licked my lips, sparking my primitive desires by rubbing my sensitive spot, all the while playing games with my thoughts.

Watching her change into another outfit, my temperature flirted in the Equator numbers. The red, see-through lingerie she modeled in was tempting me. I flicked a few photos while she posed on the bed. After a few snaps, I leaned closer for my chance. She was glued to the bed and stopped posing.

Go...Go...Go...Take a chance.

I followed the voice pulling me closer to her heaven. Her nipples poked out her lingerie top. The shaved haven between her legs begged me to move faster. Her hands massaged my chest, but her head moved away from me.

Damn...

First Nandi at the Promenade, and now Sandra damn near naked in her bedroom. She blackened my already bruised ego and wormed from under me. She got up without saying a word. Disturbed and embarrassed, I helped myself to the living room and sat on the sofa. A few seconds past, and she walked back to the living room wearing the same zebra patterned body suit she'd worn before. She sat next to me and kissed me on the cheek like nothing had ever happened.

"Thanks for the photos, baby. I'm sure my husband will appreciate them." Sandra hugged me and packed the tri-pod and camera back into the case.

She kissed me goodbye. I was like a lost dog heading back to Fort Greene. I felt like a sucker.

***

Jo Jo glanced at me but quickly looked away. Keeping my distance, I wanted nothing to do with him. We never crossed paths, and he never asked me to do any task that needed finishing. I wasn't in the mood to speak with anyone after Sandra had given me the tease of the century.

He walked by me to fix the racks with his eyes hawking at the shoes. Ever since he was hired, I said not one syllable to him. Not even a letter. The less we talked, the better I felt while working underpaid and underappreciated at Shoe Fetish.

"Hey, baby." Essence tugged my shirt. "Still upset at them not hiring you?"

"Nice to rub it in."

"What? I was just sayin', dang."

"I ain't sayin' nothin' to dude." I angrily broke away the plastic that covered a pair of high heels. "He best to not breathe toward me."

"You crazy, you know that? It's not his fault."

"Bunk that. *They're* takin' over. First, they wanna take the 'hood away from us, and now they're takin' over our jobs."

Essence sucked her tongue. "Stop being paranoid."

"I'm serious. What's next? Them taking our sistas as well."

"Well…um…he *is* kinda cute for a white guy." She giggled, and my face flushed red.

"Yeah, and a fat Santa Claus can slide down a chimney, right?"

"Humph, whatever, I might want a little vanilla in my chocolate." She pressed up her breasts. "Don't be so damn mad all the time, Justice. Life's too short, ya' know?"

I ignored her, and she walked away to greet Jo Jo. I settled with stocking men's shoes on the shelves until a weird feeling alarmed me. A sixth sense told me to glance beside me. I caught a police officer hawking down the aisles, as if he was watching me trying to steal. I brushed him off and rushed the shoes onto the shelves.

Another officer hid next to a pole that stood across from me. He peeked over at my direction. Goosebumps mushroomed on me even when the room was warm. The swarm of cops crowded the department and drew stares from customers. Five officers formed a circle as one almost fell by tripping over a lawn chair. The scene reminded me of a bomb scare with K-9 dogs sniffing around the area.

What the hell is going on?

The cops made their move toward me. Shocked but calm with sweat wetting my palms, I opened another box with a hand cutter. My heart fluttered when they wheeled around the aisle in front of me, stone faced with hands on their waists.

"What's in the bag?" One cornbread-fed officer asked a guy standing across from me with his back turned. I couldn't make out the guy with him wearing a hoodie as I looked on. Other cee-ciphers inched closer to the guy and pulled out their nightsticks. The K-9s circled them, and their sniffing tightened my body like vice grips.

Desperately, the guy pushed an officer away and jetted toward the back. He didn't stand a chance, as the hardened soles under his dress shoes caused him to slip on the floor. They all tackled him and turned him over for cuffing. The dogs barked, but the officers hushed them. Wearing leather gloves, one tall, muscular officer checked the bag and found the garment loaded with stolen clothes and cologne.

"Jackpot!" The officer clapped, and they all lugged the man to his feet. Customers and employees hugged around the scene. I stepped closer for a better look at the man. His face blurred, but later cleared as I got a good look at him. What my eyes beheld forced my head to drop to the ground. I couldn't believe what I saw, but I faced reality.

How could he be so careless?

Fast Teddy, dressed in a black jogging suit, peeked at me with a teardrop following down his cheek. Cee-ciphers hauled Fast Teddy off to the streets and into the patrol car.

"We finally got one!" Adam pranced around like a boy that just lost his virginity. "We're going to use him as an example. Yes, sir."

Rich and Tahleek scrambled to see Fast Teddy arrested, but like always, they came late to the scene. Rich pulled out his pen and notebook and stepped to me. He was more like a journalist than a security guard.

"Justice, you did a good job, pal," he said.

"Wh--what? How?" I responded to the stupidity.

"You distracted the crook while the cops were watchin'. Thanks a lot." Rich was dead serious. I wondered if he was on dope or dog food because I didn't distract anything. "Adam's added security is working so far. We got police officers patrolling the store ever since we got hit for five-thousand dollars' worth of merchandise in one day."

Rich wasn't lying. Shoe Fetish and the department store as a whole was changing. The store felt like prison with Adam playing as the warden and plain clothed police as the correctional officers. Adam placed automated locks on both restrooms so security could monitor traffic, along with a buzzer to press before entering. Security also checked bags of customers and snapped photos of them upon leaving the store.

I wasn't the cause of the drastic change, but rather the whip that broke the horse's back. Cracking my knuckles with a devilish grin, I was satisfied, but pressed to do more damage. I managed to work stress-free while hooking up Casper and his crew; they all hustled well with the capers until Fast Teddy got busted. He was part of the thievery crew; the guy who raised his open hand to give me a signal after bumping into him in one of the heists.

With clean hands and no suspicion, the only worry that troubled me was someone flipping. Snitching to me was a sin, but there was no honor amongst thieves. I took a risk by skipping over the chances of me getting fired, or even worse, locked up due to someone's cowardice. The show went on with urges of me feeding my drive for getting back at Shoe Fetish for jerking me.

"Aye, big homie." Tahleek swooped over to me after Rich left to speak with the police. "Watch 'cha back, man. They watchin' you."

"Who?" My eyebrows slanted by surprise.

"The managers and cee-ciphers. Be careful, mah dude," he whispered with a serious look etched across his face. "You didn't hear that from me, man."

"Good lookin' out, sun." We gave each other pounds, and I watched Tahleek follow Rich.

I wondered if they *were* on to me. They watched me before, but never had Tahleek walked up to me with a confirmation. The walls were caving in on me. The quick sand in the hour glass of me jetting out of Shoe Fetish was running out. Exhausted by work, I pushed every inch of strength I had to move forward as my heart yelled for me to leave. The crack in my heart was packed with muted prayers, screams and broken wings that flavored bitterness in the crevices of my existence. My veins were the streets, with my spirits riding on fumes before the wall of fear blocked me. Blank thoughts, pockets of lint, and a broken watch clothed the walking dead, but not me. I trudged forward and pulled up my bootstraps to reach my goals. The fight only made me stronger and I refused to give up.

The night lit with the sun's reflection darkening the Harlem streets. I clocked out, but not before cee-ciphers with their K-9s checking my book-bag. The search was annoying, but that was the price to pay after rebelling.

My celly buzzed and flashed Nandi's name on the text message.

Hey u. I'm n Harlem rite now @ the Lenox Lounge. Are u @ work? She asked.

Yeah...I work down the street from the L Lounge. I responded.

Do u wanna meet up?

Sure :)

I had something to look forward to after an evening's work of processing shoes. I skipped down 2-5th and flipped on excitement. I hadn't seen Nandi in a good minute. I wanted a glimpse of the queen who looked as if God had dipped her in the purest brown sugar, and the night gave me that chance.

Half empty on a slow Wednesday, the Lenox Lounge was still jumping, even on a work night. Blues tunes finessed the room when I saw Nandi from afar. Not wanting Nandi to think I was sweating her, I played it cool as she waved at me from the back room.

Candles flaring inside tiny glasses on tables fanned away dimness that almost shadowed the lounge. I squinted to get a clear view of her, and after a few seconds of dimness she clearly appeared as if the moon was shining on her through the roof.

"Hey, stranger." She hugged and kissed me on the cheek.

"Long time, no see."

"Yeah, yeah, yeah. A sista been busy with music. I stopped by just to get a few drinks."

"By yourself?"

"Uh, yeah…why not?"

"I'm just sayin'. A beautiful woman with no man around is a shock."

"You're such a charmer, Justice. You talk to every woman like this?"

"Not every woman is Nandi." I winked, and sat next to her. She pulled out her wallet and called for the bartender.

"Two Long Island Iced Teas…on me." She offered to buy drinks. Her gesture stunned me.

"Wow, you ain't from around here after all."

"I'm not the average woman." She smiled, and lifted her drink next to mine for a toast.

We chatted for a good hour about what we did during the week. I was comfortable enough to drink beyond my limit. I was pissy from five glasses of Long Island Iced Teas and fought to keep my eyes open. My nickname for the drink was "silent killer"; the effect hits you after gulping it like it was Kool-Aid because of its sweetness.

"You're such a light-weight." Nandi playfully pushed me over on the sofa. She wasn't affected by the fifth drink.

"I'm cool. I'm cool." I played off drunkenness, but the liquor soaked me.

I gave up fighting off the intoxicated fruits that held my body hostage. I leaned on Nandi's shoulder for support. Relaxing with her on the sofa was like the liquor was teasing my emotions and fucking my mind at the same time. The mirage of that good feeling was birth by liquor, but I knew to stay away from a façade to the mind. I hadn't felt so brand new in months while hunched over on her lap floating on cloud nine.

"Ooh, snap. That's my song!" Nandi grabbed my hand and damn near yanked me from the sofa. "Come on and sweat out the liquor." She led me to the open area next to the bar.

"Cause I Love You" drifted from the jukebox, and the soulful rift of Lenny Williams made me forget I was drunk. Holding Nandi sobered me as her chocolate-coated skin was the smoothest I'd ever touched. Dancing between the "Oh's" of Lenny, we grooved as if we'd known each other for years. The lounge turned dark, and no one mattered to me even though I aimlessly glanced around while slowly grinding up on her.

"I'm glad I've met you." I spilled, and felt her smiling.

"I'm glad I've met you, too. Not a lot of good brothas are around, ya' know?"

"Yeah, I feel you. But it's not about them. It's about me and you."

"Is that so? What makes you different from the rest?"

"Action speaks louder. Let's just say I put in what I get back."

Nandi tightened her grip with her arms strapped around my shoulders. I wrapped my hands around her slim waist and kept pace with the rhythm.

"Yeah, I dig that." Nandi sighed. "So when's the last time you cried?"

The question threw me off guard. I flipped through my memory Rolodex, fishing for the moment that left me vexed at some point in my life.

"Um, let's see." I thought for a few seconds. "When my mom passed away."

"Oh wow, sorry to hear that."

"Yeah, but shit happens." Not caring about my old earth passing away at that point emaciated the pain in my voice. I emotionally pushed Nandi away from me but held her closer. "That's the past, and this is *now*."

I lifted my head from her shoulders, and we stared face to face. The white dot in her eyes reminded me of stars, and I slowly pecked on her eye lids. I felt the warmth from her lips as we danced a hair apart. Sparks flew and darts of heat poked my heart to kiss her.

While leaning forward, a picture of her dismissing me at the Promenade held me back from kissing her. I pushed away that memory and manned up. She eased closer to me with her eyes closed. She hugged her lips onto mine. The quick move stunned me as I rubbed her hips; her lipstick smudged my soup coolers. Nandi leaned back but I took a kiss. We tongued in the middle of lounge with all the cares in the world thrown out the window. The flow of the rhythm danced with the lock of our lips as the floor clamped my feet to the carpet.

The song faded, and I slumped back on the sofa feeling like I was walking on water. My eyes pushed to stay open, but tiredness KO'd me. Glancing at the reflection of me through Nandi's eyes, she was the last memory I had for the night; the best memory I had since the last time I saw Mama alive.

Chapter 16: The Queen Bee

She mounted on top of me and whispered in my ear, "I want you, my king...I want all of you inside me."

The room was dark, and her eyes shined like the heavens that lined with the windows to her soul. She bent over and kissed me, but I took control and turned over on top of her. Her legs opened with nectar moistening her kat, calling me to slide between and ease all of me inside her. Breathless and weak, she peeled off the black stockings that hugged her warm thighs. Her eyes begged me to dip inside and fill every corner of her slippery walls. Stroking back and forth like the ball of a clock, my fullness gently stretched her wetness. She shrieked, unable to handle my girth. Intense euphoria colored her eyes and her love muscles gripped me, throbbing with each thrust and soaking me down. I felt the warmth of her wetness as it forced me to stroke faster, wanting to take all of what she gave me. She pressed her lips together to hush whispers of curses. Verses of my thrusts circled steadily as she shot moans that walked on a thin line between breathing and weeping. Tensed with my muscles weakening, my hands clinched the bed sheets, fighting off the urge to come. She clawed her nails deeper into my back and pulled me to waterfall inside of her.

"You want me?" I whispered, filling myself about to collapse. Her lungs slipped to catch her breath.

"Y-y-yeah...yeah. Give it to me...give it to me." She gasped for air, and I heard the song of her heartbeat with my mouth cupped around her breast.

She moonwalked inside the folds of my brain, eclipsing my mind's light to black and white as I soaked inside her purple rain. Moving to the rhythm of her breathing, I eased deeper inside; cussing, thrusting, and sucking on her titties before busting off. She erupted and creamed over me as I let go, releasing every bit of tension that built up. Panting with sweat touching our bodies, we rested on the dampened sheets and I closed my eyes, only to open them again.

***

I woke up with cold sweats flowing down my forehead. The day's brightness blinded me, and I used my forearm as a shield. Frantically looking around to familiarize myself with the room, I knew I wasn't home. My eyes roamed around and saw posters of Prince cluttering the purple walls of the room. Nandi, staring out the window wearing nothing but a purple robe, looked over to me and smiled.

My breathing calmed from the sight of Nandi as I remembered the first half of the night. I thought of urban myths like drunken folk finding themselves in a tub of ice with some of their organs removed. And with that in mind, I felt my ribs, and was glad I was together in one piece. Nandi's smile ceased that horror.

"Feeling better, baby?" She sat on a pad next to the window. I sat silent, still surfing around the room. "This my aunt's house."

"Where are we?" I asked, half calmly.

"New Jersey."

"Jersey? How did we get to Jersey?" I looked around for my clothes like a prisoner of war.

"The bouncer from the lounge carried you to the cab, and a neighbor helped me bring you up here," she said, and later read my mind. "I folded your clothes and put them over there."

She pointed to the ironing board with my clothes neatly folded. "Good lookin' out, love."

"My pleasure. I also made *us* breakfast; turkey sausages and pancakes. I mean, that's if you're interested."

Yes! She doesn't eat swine.

I was left speechless, and clutched the bed sheets like a homeless child witnessing an angel. No woman besides Felicia had ever cooked for the king without me asking. She walked out the bedroom while I dressed, still shaking off the mild hangover from the night before. I got my gear in check, and worked on the plate of that "feel good" before breaking out.

After eating breakfast, I thanked her for the love and we kissed for a good minute before I broke out to Brooklyn. I rode the first PATH train smoking to Manhattan and then hopped on the "A" back to Bed-Stuy to hop the bus to Fort Greene.

I walked to the brownstone itching for a shower. I caught Caprice crying, sniffing, and shaking on the stoop of Felicia's brownstone. Puzzled, I tapped Caprice on the shoulder, and her head lifted from her folded arms. Tears smeared her eyeliner and redness swelled her eyes. I nearly flipped before she had a chance to speak. Her cries lit the match and sparked the cocktail bomb of fury.

"What happened?" I repeatedly tapped her shoulder for eye contact.

"He…he…"

"What?"

"This guy…he touched…" She sniffled; the crying dampened her speech. "This guy at school…he won't leave me alone."

"What happened, Cappie?"

She wiped away the wetness from her eyes and cheeks, and sighed before continuing. "This guy at school won't leave me alone. He keeps botherin' me. The nigga lifted my skirt up and felt between my legs today after gym."

I grabbed her arm without second thought and lifted her off the stoop. "Come on."

"Where we goin'?" She was resistant.

"To see the punk who felt up on you. Where he rest at?"

"Gates Ave."

I held Caprice's hand, but she tugged on my jacket and pulled away. "Hold on. Why we're goin' to Gates?

I looked at her like she was stupid. "What the blue cheese you mean 'why we're goin' to Gates'? You said he touched you, right? So I'ma touch *him*." I yanked her arm again, almost dragging her.

"No, Justice. I don't wanna go," she cried.

"Fuck that. We're goin'." I dragged her even more and walked down the block until she stopped completely. She looked at me and sobbed more harshly than before.

"It's not that serious, Justice. I don't know why you're stressin' it."

"You can't let any dude touch your body, Cappie. Your body is a temple, and if you let one pass with a cop and feel, then every last one of them will be itchin' to do it. That's why we're hittin' up Gates so I can set the precedent and lay down the law." I fought off hostility toward her, but she was tapping on my patience.

"How we're gonna get there? I got no loot for bus fare. He stays on the other side of Gates," she said, and I looked around for a bodega to break a five for change. I spotted one down the block, and told Caprice to stay put. I busted the five and met with her on the corner. Handing her eight quarters, I saw the look of "I don't wanna go" heating her face.

"Look, I don't want any trouble, okay?" She didn't budge. I laughed before kissing her forehead.

"You ain't gettin' into trouble. But there will be trouble…for them."

I grabbed her arm and we hopped the B52 bus. Caprice annoyed me with her pleads on the ride there. I drowned her out, and focused on what I planned on doing to money who violated. Once the joint stopped, we walked a few blocks to Gates, also known as "God Avenue" to a lot of older dudes who ran Brooklyn back in the day.

She pointed him out to me when we got there. The tall, lanky, light-brown skinned boy was shooting dice amongst his friends on a stoop. They never saw me coming. I blacked out with my flesh hopping mad and my consciousness tipping on a tight rope; smoke damn near blowing out my ears and nose. I was outnumbered 6 to 1, but odds didn't matter to me.

"You don't gotta do this. You should talk to him. They touch on girls all the time at school." Caprice tried changing my mind, but only fueled the fire with gasoline.

I paused and folded my arms with my eyes brooding down at her. "So did you like to be felt on by him?"

"Aaah…no." She shrugged.

"Do you think money should've felt you up without your permission?"

"No."

"Case closed. Sometimes you can't talk to people. Sometimes you gotta knock a muthafucka in the mouth to get your point across."

No more was said after that. I bit the gun by picking up a bottle and busting it on the concrete, signaling my war cry. They all turned in unison, and the culprit's eyes widened in fear.

"That's him," she confirmed, and it was a wrap.

POP!

I dropped him clean on the pavement with no questions asked.

The Tyson special between his jaw bone and neck floored him. He twitched on the ground like a goldfish begging for water outside its fish tank; he gasped and choked with his soul ripped apart, hoping that life would hurriedly spew from his lungs. My cold stare dared any of his teenage goons to step to me, and they stood there motionless.

I stood over him while he rolled on the ground. His crew not helping him only fueled my thinking that this cat was worthless and pathetic. Grabbing him by the collar, I dragged him to Caprice. He put up a weak fight of breaking away from my grip. I tightened my hold to the point of almost choking him. He desperately swung his arms and hit the air with feral cries. I clamped down on his back with one knee and pulled his long hair to face Caprice.

"Say you're sorry!" I commanded, and he held his jaw that was most likely broken.

"My jaw…" He squealed, sounding like a pig in pain. I violently shook him like he was a baby rattle as he babbled words I couldn't understand.

"Fuck yo' jaw, nigga. I said say sorry!"

He looked at Caprice, and mustered all the energy to apologize. "I'm…sorry."

"He called me a bitch, too." Caprice fired me up even more.

"Oh, you called her a bitch, huh?" I played with him by tugging on his collar. "I want you to say, 'I'm sorry beautiful Black queen, original woman, mother of civilization, queen of the universe.'"

"What?" The boy seemed confused. I tapped him on the head.

"Repeat it!"

After two failed tries, the boy got it on the lucky third. I dropped him on the floor and dug inside his pants pockets, raiding his wallet of twenty dollars that now belonged to Caprice.

"Broke ass punk don't even have enough money for a weekly metro pass," I spat at him, and walked away with Caprice, brushing off remorse. The joy of knocking him almost out cold thrilled me and sent a rush that urged me to do it again.

Why'd he violate Caprice? Why?

I asked myself, but the boy had it coming. Yeah, I could've talked to the young brother first, but the burst of misplaced hate targeted him as my prey. One half of me wanted to rewind the scene to talk it out with the little man, while the other loved the way I held someone's life in the palm of my hand.

The more I walked with Caprice back to the brownstone, the more I erased away the guilt and shook hands with the street instincts of "hit first, ask questions last." Not taking any chances of getting jumped, I used the boy as an example in front of his crew by humiliating him to teach a cruel lesson; not to violate women and anyone of my fam.

"How was the Spring dance?" I asked Caprice, shaking off the incident.

"It was cool. Me and my homegirls were the flyest bitch---um, girls there." She corrected herself. "And I won the spelling bee."

"Yeah, I heard." A light bulb clicked in my mind. I reached inside my pocket. "I bought you somethin' from the department store."

I handed Caprice a gold bracelet with her name etched on it. Her eyes lit up with tears glossing her pupils. Drops eased down her cheek. She reached over and hugged me.

"Thanks, Justice. I thought you forgot," she said.

"I've just been mad busy workin'. I had to make it up to you."

She wrapped the bracelet around her wrist.

"You're the future, Cappie," I said. "Don't waste a bright young mind like yours, because without you, there's no future."

Caprice smiled, and I gave her the metro card I got from the punk I floored so she can head home. I hugged her and walked her to the subway. Sleepless and hungry, I jetted back to the brownstone and stacked a mountain of leftover salmon on a plate. Reheating the fish in the oven, I looked outside and saw Scar-lo whisk down the block in his car. Felicia entered the kitchen to pour a glass of water. Suddenly, I remembered the conversation Scar-lo and I had in the park several weeks earlier.

"How did Scar-lo know about you losin' your job?" I surprised Felicia as she paused.

"What?" She frowned.

"Scar-lo told me you lost your job. And when I asked him how he knew, he acted like he was the four corners of the universe. I hope you're not fuckin' him."

Felicia slammed the pot on the counter. "You got some nerve worrying about whom I'm laying with. For your information, Justice, no, I'm not fuckin' Scars. He knows because he's seeing one of my homegirls."

"Uh huh."

"Uh huh, nothing." Felicia slammed the fridge, almost spilling the water in her glass.

"I'm just sayin'. I know you want a baller and all. Since you claimed I was makin' chump change." I smirked, and she froze, glaring at me like an eagle stalking its prey.

"Fuck you, Justice. Fuck...you." Felicia stormed out the kitchen with her red robe almost falling open, exposing her nakedness. I laughed to myself and fell out on the sofa to soak up the energy to head to work that evening.

***

"As-Salāmu `alaykum, mah brotha." Casper held a bean pie in hand while sporting a bow tie with a black suit.

"You Muslim now? I thought you couldn't live without pork?"

"Nah, sun, I got a new hustle. I'm sellin' bean pies up and down Fulton Ave."

"Funny dude." I wasn't the least amazed at his latest hustle.

"Man, it puts food on the table. Frontin' like I'm a Muslim ain't nothin'. But I can't give up swine. That's for sure." Casper set aside his stack of bean pies on an end-aisle seat. "Who's the white boy?" He pointed at Jo Jo.

"Some sucka ass clown the store hired over me for the supervisor position."

"Wow, that's crazy. They jerked you over *him*?"

"Yeah, sun. I wanted to smack the freckles off Adam for playin' me. I've been workin' hard at this store for a minute, and this is what I get in return?" I asked, but to no one specifically. "That's aight, though. I won't be here for long."

"I feel you. But on that note, I'ma bounce like a bad check. I got bean pies to sell. I'll holla at you later."

"Peace, king."

Casper strutted out the store and pitched bean pies to anyone who walked past him. Dude was a character.

I thought about the bonus checks that were coming, but doubt we'd receive a red cent knowing the amount of theft that went on in the store. I left the department and trucked to Adam's office. Just my luck, he was finishing interviewing for the Men's department. Stuck between the long lines that flooded the front and seeing Jo Jo's mug, I waited around the office, and pretended I was fixing the shelves of hats near the manager's door.

Five minutes had past and a woman with a juicy bottom and bodacious body walked out the door. She looked like a dancer straight from a Luke video. My eyes couldn't escape her caboose that was the size of two giant cantaloupes.

"She's a real dynamite, isn't she?" Adam smiled so wide that I thought his face was about to stretch.

"Yeah, a real atomic bomb," I answered sarcastically.

"Well, is there anything I can do for you?"

"I was wondering about the bonuses we're supposed to be receiving around this time..."

"No, no, no," Adam rudely cut me off. "There are no bonuses this year. We got hit hard by theft and Corporate isn't issuing bonuses until we improve on security."

Just like I thought, the company had short arms with deep pockets. It wasn't my fault the store didn't have skin tight security. Jewelry, cologne, designer boots and jackets were popular items for sticky fingers.

"Justice, can you step in my office for a minute? I would like to speak with you." Adam stepped inside his office and I followed. He rested on the edge of a table and exhaled. Thinking of why he wanted me in the office, I expected the worst, but refused to drum up bad luck.

"There's been suspicious activity going on in the front counter with gift cards. Do you know anything about it?" His eyes squinted and studied me. His question threw me off the bridge.

"No," I answered, giving him full eye contact.

"Are *you* sure?"

"Adam, I don't know the problem to even give you a good answer."

"Management found gifts cards that weren't audited and kept on record. I looked on the camera and found you use a gift card for the boots you're wearing now."

Ah, damn. What did I get myself into now?

"Okay, so what you're saying?"

"I'm saying employees are illegally activating gift cards by pretending to use them to scan items in the store."

"I know nothing about what you're taking about. All I got was a pair of boots from shoes. Whatever happened after that, I know nothing."

I knew I shouldn't have let Jemima use her "boyfriend's" gift card to buy those boots!

"We're investigating more about the situation. So I hope you're telling the truth," Adam said as if he was looking down on me. I damn near exploded.

"I have nothin' to lie about. I don't know anything about gift cards. You're sniffing up the wrong tree if you're lookin' for someone to place the blame on." I purposely said "sniffing" as a pun.

I stood calmly and left Adam in the dust. The fuss over gift cards left a bitter taste in my mouth with a sweet lesson. Mama always told me anything that came too easily or free wasn't worth having. Thinking I was the only bandit in the store, Jemima was the last person I would've thought of conning the joint. She talked a great game but never backed up her claim. I couldn't put it past anyone to act normal in the store anymore.

Prince walked beside me and tapped my shoulder with a wide grin. "Guess what, sun."

"What's good?" I gave him a pound.

"I'm movin' to Now Cee." Prince showed me his transfer papers to a Charlotte branch of the store. "I'm jettin' out of here next month."

"Congrats. Why you're bouncin' out to North Carolina?"

"The rent, sun. It's crazy up here in NY. I get the same amount of money down in Charlotte and pay less rent. A three bedroom townhouse down there only cost nine hundred dollars a month. A studio in New York will cost you more than that, sun." He tapped the papers on the palm of his hand like it was a lottery ticket worth thirty million. "Man, you should roll, too. It's real chill down there, and they got some fine ass sistas down south, sun. Thick as hell, and will cook for a brotha."

"Nah, man, I'm good in Brooklyn."

"Why you so concerned about BK? Brooklyn ain't goin' nowhere."

"And I ain't goin' no where, either," I protested. "I'ma make it somehow. Just 'cuz the city wanna hike up property and rent doesn't mean they gonna force me outta here. Check what I'm sayin'?"

"Yeah, but check what I'm sayin'. Why sweat to make ends meet when you can meet ends with the same pay in an open market like the south?" I thought while Prince continued. "They don't got what New York got, sun. I can take the NY hustle down there, set up shop with businesses by investing in property with the money I'm makin' at work, and get paid! It's time to enterprise and stop fuckin' around with just livin' on borrowed land. A man ain't free until he owns land."

"I feel you, but my heart rests in Brooklyn. I can't see myself down south."

"I understand, man. Well…I see you on the other side."

We gave each other pounds and went our separate ways. Prince had a point, but living somewhere other than the Rotten Apple was a vision I couldn't grasp. Letting high rent and taxes get the last laugh and shackle my desire of staying in New York was out. Fighting my way to success was the only option.

The hands of the clock nailed my life on the cross with my strength ringing around the drain, leaking out my feet as time past by. I wasn't finished with stocking shoes on the racks before closing. Jo Jo left for the day but pinned a note near our schedules stating I was to only recover shoes.

While I worked the aisles like a mad man, Golden snooped around and cleared her throat, trying to scoop my attention.

"Are you done with your department?" She shot me a nasty attitude.

"Nah, why?"

"'Cuz you gotta help with the Ladies' department."

"What?" I look at her crookedly.

"Ladies was hit the worst out of all the departments and we need help." She was pissing me off.

I ignored her and tilted the display shoes in a 45-degree angle like Clara had had instructed before her surgery. That didn't stop Golden from carrying on when I was doing *my* job by fixing shoes.

"Justice, Ladies' is lookin' bad and you gotta help us so we can leave early."

"Don't tell me how to do my job. It's three of y'all over there and I'm the only one closin' in Shoe Fetish. Your department would've been done a minute ago if you weren't playin' Sleeping Ugly in Receiving."

The verbal dart pierced her ego. She stomped back to her department. The tongue of man was sharper than a slap of hand as she was defeated without me physically confronting her. Golden was the shit stain I hoped would get fired in a heart beat.

I finally finished recovering and checked back to the brownstone. I almost busted my ass when I stumbled over suitcases after unlocking the door. I looked at the tags on a handbag and saw that someone was flying out the country. Felicia waltzed in the kitchen with another suitcase, feeding my curiously as to why so many packed bags crowded the joint.

"What's good with the suitcases?" I asked, being nosey.

"I'm visiting fam on the island." She left for a second and rolled another set of suitcases in the kitchen.

"You didn't tell me you were bouncin'."

"Yeah, I know. It's a last minute thing. I need to get my head straight before the rally in downtown Brooklyn. My grandparents own a ranch, and I'm gonna chill with them for a while."

Felicia and her mother finished packing, and I helped them to the cab on their way to JFK airport. I kissed Felicia "peace" on the cheek, but her mother and I dropped eye contact.

Without Felicia and her old earth pestering me, the king had the throne to himself. That only meant one thing: I could invite Nandi over and finished what I've started.

Chapter 17: Swipe Bandits

"Close your eyes. I got a surprise for you."

"You better not cut my neck or somethin'."

"C'mon, baby, close them. I got something for you when I was out on tour."

I closed my eyes, nervous about want she had in store for me. I didn't like surprises, but I did it for her. She placed the envelope package in my hand, and my fingers surfed over the joint, trying to figure out what it was. I opened my eyes and saw two tickets for a go-go concert in DC.

I jumped up and hugged her, almost suffocating the sister. Elated with joy, I backed off and snapped to my senses. My eyes squinted with my vibes distant from her, as if she'd done something wrong. I wasn't sure if I could trust her. I thought of her buying me go-go tickets as suspect.

"How did you know I liked go-go music?" I asked, and she smiled.

"I checked out your personal page on the internet. I saw that you liked go-go, and I copped me two tickets for us while I was on the road," she chided affably, and I blew a short sigh of relief. "You better be careful what kinda info you leave on the 'net."

"Yeah, I know that's right. Thanks, love." I shrugged off my paranoia and felt kinda foolish. Nandi going out her way to find out what I liked hit a soft spot in my heart. It wasn't what she gave me, but how she went about doing it.

We took the Chinatown bus from NY to DC a week later to hit up a go-go spot. Chuck Brown was playing in front of a packed crowd, and he did the damn thing. He sung his classics with call and response yells as congas, kettledrums and cowbells got us amped. His set was live, and we broke a sweat from dancing from his tunes that lasted for 2 hours; one of the best two hours I've ever experienced.

I got hooked on go-go ever since I heard the E.U. band's "Da Butt" jam on *School Daze*. I was addicted ever since. Nandi was worried about the violence that sometimes plagued go-go clubs in DC. The city had shut down mad spots over what Nandi had called, "some nigga shit." The joint we hit up was peaceful, and everybody had a ball.

Ba doom...pop pop...boom boom...pop, pop Ba doom...pop pop...boom boom...pop, pop

The cabbie drove us to a hotel in Northwest DC, and I got to see the sights. It amazed me how a ghetto was a neighbor to the White House, but then again, I wasn't; Harlem was next to plush apartments on the Upper East and West sides of Manhattan. Gentrification was also hitting DC hard, but I playfully pinched Nandi's cheeks to dwell away from what was hurting me back home.

We checked in and collapsed on our bed after showering and changing clothes. Dead beat tired from dancing, I wasn't thinking about sexing Nandi until she strutted from the bathroom wearing boy-shorts and a tank top. Hot under the skin as heat mopped across my crouch, I dropped my thoughts and slouched away from her, aiming my focus on the phallic shape of the Washington Monument. As I looked out the window, she rested beside me and tapped my shoulder.

"Hey, baby. Don't tell me all that dancin' got a young man like you tired," she laughed, and I flipped over to face her.

"I've just been thinkin'; thinkin' about not living to be an unfulfilled adult," I said.

"Then don't be."

"Easy for you to say. You don't know what I go through each day."

"It's hard for me as it is for you. You think me going on tour with my band was an overnight thing? I worked my tail off to get where I'm at, and I'd never let anyone hold me back, even when there was times when I wanted to give everything up."

"Yeah, I feel you." I exhaled, and got some shit off that bogged me down.

"Turn around so I can massage your back," said Nandi, and I refused to pass up a free massage.

"You must be in a good mood," I said.

"I'm in a good mood because I wanna massage your back?" She chuckled.

"Yeah, I wasn't expecting that."

"That's just how I am. I know things ain't easy for you. I bought those tickets so you can get out of New York and breathe; see places. If I'm happy, then you should be, too."

"I didn't know you liked me like that. You kept frontin' on me," I said, and she laughed.

"I wasn't frontin' on you. I move when the time is *right*. I won't lie to you. If I like you, I'll tell you. If you think I need to change when you see something that's wrong with me, I'll change, to make our relationship better. I'll change to make you happy, as long as I'm happy with you."

I was floored, but in a good way. I almost broke down and told Nandi how bad I wanted her, but past hurt silenced me. I saw her in a different light as her hands pressed over my back muscles. Every female I fooled around with were just fuck buddies for a quick nut. I ran through females like red lights, and didn't mind cutting them loose if they did or said something stupid. Nandi went out her way to please me and I liked her even more. Yeah, Felicia was there, but she was just a friend. Nandi was a potential lover, and so far she was hitting every spot. She wasn't a bitch, hoe, slut, or any other madness. She carried herself as royalty, and I had the utmost respect for her. I respected her mind because she never used flesh to attract me; I glanced at her face without thinking about how nice her ass was.

I turned over to kiss her. She wrapped her arms around my shoulders and tongued me. My hand navigated below her navel, and hers blocked mine.

"What's wrong?" I asked.

"Mother nature's calling."

"Yeah, right,"

"Real talk. See for yourself."

I tapped my hand between her legs and found out she was on her period. Pissed because I finally had her alone, I gasped after feeling the maxi pad.

"It's all good, ma. We can just kiss the night away." I kissed her nose and chin, and she lamped on top of me for the rest of the night. I never thought being sensual was just as blissful as off the wall sex. Hey, you live and you learn.

***

Jo Jo was closing with me for the night and we worked separately during the evening. He wasn't wearing a casual shirt, but rather one with a painting of the Wu-Tang Clan emblem. I laughed to myself and approached him. I didn't like looking at him, but at least dude had some style when it came to music. He fumbled with stamping price stickers on boots while clamping security bars on them. I helped him out and sparked the conversation.

"What's good?" I greeted Jo Jo. He was surprised that I uttered a sound to him.

"Hey, what's up?"

"Nothin'. I'm diggin' your Wu-Tang shirt."

Jo Jo raised his eyebrows at my unusual friendliness. "Oh, thank you."

"Aight. I thought you only listened to the Osmonds or somethin'."

He laughed and gave me eye contact. "Yeah, I like the Osmonds. And I like The Jacksons as well."

"The Jacksons? What you know about The Jacksons?"

"I know a lot about The Jacksons. But they aren't better than the Osmonds."

"What?" My shriek alarmed folks in the shoe department. "Tito's afro got more talent than the Osmonds."

"Whatever, dude." He smirked.

"Whatever, nothin'. Hell, even the Partridge Family got more talent than the Osmonds." I grabbed a few shoeboxes from Jo Jo's stack of new products and stamped stickers on them. "The Osmonds are better than The Jacksons my ass." I laughed to myself, and got a kick out of the small talk.

The crowd simmered down and I worked on a mountain of shoeboxes with Jo Jo. He worked quietly and never ran his mouth like Clara had. Jo Jo never bothered me, and *asked* whenever he needed help. I did my job, and I guess he recognized that. Just let me loose and I'm fine. I didn't need a babysitter for a supervisor, especially the ones who whined every five seconds when customers destroyed the department.

Picking his brain was the only way I felt comfortable mixing with him. A gumbo of questions shifted while I stacked construction boots on the shelves. Dodging children running wild in the department, I stayed with the agenda of digging up info about Jo Jo. Time almost robbed me of knowing anything about him as the clock moved on wheels. I stayed close to kids' shoes to make sure parents weren't using their crumb snatchers as a tool to steal. After the kids' section cleared, I moved like a fox with thoughts of a sniper.

"So where you're from?" I asked Jo Jo while helping him stock the last box of stilettos.

"Queens...Flushing. But I stay on 110th Street."

"That's peace. So how'd you find out about the opening here?"

"I just walked in. I got laid off my computer programming job and I was looking for a new gig."

"Damn, that's crazy."

"Yeah, it is. But luckily my wife and I saved enough money to hold us over until the market gets back rolling. The company I worked for had laid off five-thousand workers nationwide. There were people who've been working there for 30 years but still got the ax. It's sad, but hey, what are you gonna do?"

I nodded, but wasn't finished with him. I had a grind to axe with plans of chopping down the whole tree. "So did you have any background with supervising retail?" I slipped in the question, hoping he'd take the bait. He thought for a minute before answering. I should've worded my question another way. I sensed he was on to my motives.

"No…not really. I worked at a grocery store when I was a kid. But that's about it."

Adam's a lying bastard!

Ice ran through my veins, and the indifference toward Jo Jo was snuffed out when I realized he had nothing to do with the bogus hiring. Stung about something I already had guessed, I needed a walk to clear my mind. I stepped outside for fresh air to get away from the smell of bullshit.

A barrage of police sirens shrieked from afar. Red and blue emergency lights swirled across buildings and flipped in front of me without cars sitting there. The hairs on my flesh erected from the fury of sound and colors that lighted warnings. I felt funny as something wasn't right. I left the light and meddled in the dark by ignoring my gut feeling. Casper's face flashed amidst the splash of sight and noises, but I didn't think too much of it. Bored with nowhere to go and nothing to do, I lamped outside for a hot minute and walked back to the department store.

I headed to the cash room to grab my check. Suzie's evil grin was standing in the way. She grabbed the check envelope sitting inside a file folder. Clearing her throat with exaggeration, she handed me my pay. She basically held the check for hostage as I reached for the envelope.

"Aren't you forgetting to say something?" she asked, and I wasn't in the mood for games.

"Say what?" My voice cracked.

"Say 'thank you' when I hand you your check."

I was taken aback, but kept cool. Arguing with her for playing with my money would've been too easy, but her bullying me wasn't happening. I half snatched the envelope away from Suzie and gave her the meanest grill known to man.

"Suzie, you give me a hard time every time I see you. I haven't done anything to you, but you still come at me with static."

"I'm paid to keep the store in order, Justice."

"Aight, bet. Then I deserve two checks: one for working, and the other for putting up with your bullshit."

I smiled crookedly and slicked out the cash room, quietly shutting the door before giving her a chance to talk back to me. Was I afraid of getting fired because of me cursing at her? Not really, as I've heard her say much worse to other employees. She was a real bitch to people. I think she had a strange fetish of me verbally abusing her through our squabbles. All I needed was a whip, chains, and a dominatrix outfit to make our encounters fit so well.

I walked down the aisle leading to Shoe Fetish and saw Golden speeding toward the exit. With tears flowing down her face, Golden stormed out the store in a flying rage. Dying to know what had happened I tapped Makeda on the shoulder and asked her about Golden.

"What happened to Scary Krueger?" I was joaning.

"Adam caught her sleeping in Receiving. He fired that bitch on the spot." Makeda showed no remorse.

"How did he find out?" I asked, and Makeda smiled devilishly. "You grimy for what you did, Makki."

"Whatever. The bitch got what was comin' to her," she laughed all the way back to the Ladies' department.

I thought she was foul for ratting on Golden. Adam had rarely gone up to Receiving unless departments needed help with bringing down shipments from the docks to stock on the floor. I guess Makeda tipped her off to freckle face as Golden had it coming. I never liked Golden anyway. I wouldn't eat at the same table with her even if Jesus was the host.

A black briefcase was sitting on an end-aisle bench in Shoe Fetish. I was tempted to open the joint, but that would've been ignorant. Maybe a million dollars was in the briefcase as a sign of good luck since I found it. I grabbed the briefcase and rested it on the supply shelves. I wouldn't want anyone sneaking through my belongings, so I killed the idea of rummaging through the joint.

I spent the next few minutes sweeping the aisles. A short, cleaned shaved white man wearing a black suit frantically searched around the department. I stepped to him and saw that his face was drenched with sweat.

"How can I help you?" I asked.

"Yes, did you just so happen to come across a suitcase?" he looked nervous, but I wanted to test him.

"What color was it and how did it look?"

"The briefcase is black with a gold combination on each fastener. I'm afraid because I didn't lock it."

"What initials are on the top of the briefcase?" I shot at him.

"C.D.," he answered, and I walked him to the briefcase sitting on the shelf.

He hugged the joint like he'd just met his long lost son and shook my hand like a mad man. "Thank you, thank you, thank you. I have my whole life in this briefcase."

"What's in the briefcase?"

He looked surprised by raising his eyebrows. "What? You didn't go in it?"

"Why would I? It's not mine."

"Where are you from?"

"Brooklyn. But what difference does it make? Your briefcase is safe and sound, and no one went through it."

"Oh, all right. I own a jewelry store in the Diamond District. I have nothing but diamonds and platinum chains and watches in here. You know, the bling bling, like those rappers say." The way he said "bling bling" was rather corny. I pitied him for trying. He tapped the briefcase and dug inside his pockets to hand me a business card. "My name is Ron. Ron Stern. Call me if you need anything. And thanks again."

Yeah, I need a new job.

He scurried out the department and almost knocked over an old lady on a walker. She cursed at him, but he jetted like a cheetah.

As he bolted out the joint, police sirens circled outside the store like a disco ball. A crowd ringed around the sidewalk and I followed the colors flashing. Cops waved off onlookers away from the scene as they curiously looked on. I thought cee-ciphers were out to arrest the guy with the briefcase full of ice, but he walked past authorities as they ignored him.

A cardinal flew above the crowd and almost hit me before landing on a light pole. My nerves went dead, and my heart was light while I stalked outside the automatic doors. I had the same gut feeling from the first time I walked outside and I knew something wasn't right.

The scented oils on 2-5th hit me once I fully stepped outside to glide to where cops were brushing folks away from the scene. People crammed the streets as if Michael Jackson was moonwalking nearby, and I thought a riot was about to pop off. Cops cleared the area with nightsticks and picked apart the crowded street.

I got a full view of police cars and saw Casper slouching in the backseat a few feet away from me. My jaws dropped, and my lungs pushed out breaths of despair. I saw a pair of cops sit between him in the car. Redness covered Casper's face as the chase was over; no more clothes to boost with loot from hustling them around the way. He shook his head "no" without tears running down from his eyes. He showed no malice toward me. I sensed his callous glare was more of an "I fucked up" look.

I knew he shouldn't have pranced around the store as if we weren't the ones robbing the joint blind. Some of the thousand of dollars' worth of merchandise the crew had stolen was plotted by me. The store lost a large sum of money ever since I dropped the bombshell on the train with Casper. First, the cops arrested Fast Teddy in the store for running with a duffle bag filled with shoes, and now Casper got knocked.

Fast Teddy, an older brother who was part of the crew, had jacked the store for its cologne, but got greedy and then handcuffed. The boys dressed in church clothes in the first series of robberies were stick-up kids from my block. They did well, but Fast Teddy's cockiness got the best of him. While he worried about how much jail time the judge was itching to throw at him, my concern dragged on the possibilities of someone in the crew ratting us out. My hands weren't completely dirty because the cameras never caught me, and it was my word against anyone who decided to snitch. Fast Teddy would've been the first to flip and sing to detectives and switch his story by claiming I'd forced him into the plan. I didn't care about him as much as I did about Casper. Caz heading to Rikers was blood on my hands as I peeped the cop car hauling him off into the sunset. I was pissed at him for showing his face at the store, but I took the blame for pulling him into my mess.

Intermission #2: Nowhere to Run…Nowhere t o Go

A man once said, "If you could have one wish, what would it be?"

I said, "To grow wings and touch the sky."

He said, "You have wings. I'm surprised you can't see."

I said, "What do you mean? I got no wings to fly."

He said, "Break off the chains and you shall flee."

I said, "What chains do you speak of, and why?"

He said, "Around your mind, break 'em apart and you're free."

I said, "I'm not ready, and if I do, I'll die…"

Monday, August 18th, 2008 6:24pm

I HATE MY JOB BOOK 3: (The Burn)

King Dhakir

Chapter 18: Running Out of Time

"Do you know an Azeem Combs?"

"Yes, I do," I responded to the beefy-looking detective. He had been grilling me for the past fifteen minutes about recent store thefts.

His breath reeked of beef jerky, and his green-colored teeth added to his "take no prisoners" attitude. He rubbed spit away from the cleft between his chin and left saliva stains on the back of his hand. The questions were nothing to me, as I dodged every bullet that was shot.

"Did you have anything to do with the recent thefts that happened in this store?" The detective turned beet red.

"No, I didn't."

"Is that so?"

"Yeah, I didn't have anything to do with thefts."

"Well, not according to Azeem Combs, street name Casper."

A film of sweat trimmed the front of my hairline, and the detective who looked like a corn-fed country redneck skimmed over his notes.

"I don't know what you talkin' about, mah dude," I said.

The detective mockingly responded, "Well, *mah dude*. I think you do know what I'm talkin' 'bout. I'm talkin' 'bout you being behind a series of thefts that cost the store several thousand of dollars."

His country accent irked me. I jerked back in my seat to find comfort while he lurked around the room with coldness in his eyes. With each chew of tobacco that foamed inside his mouth, I wondered if he wanted to call me "boy."

"You got me twisted. I don't know why I'm here. You have no proof or evidence of me taking part in anything. You can take it to my lawyer if you wanna ask me anymore questions." I called their bluff.

"Okay, fine. Suit yourself."

He looked at Adam and nodded. After the detective dismissed himself from the room, Adam sat directly across from me, seemingly gathering his thoughts.

"You're breaking my heart, Justice." Adam shook his head, but I was unnerved. "I see your boy got caught with his hand in the cookie jar."

"What you talkin' about?" I played dumb, ostensibly ambiguous about his claim.

"Your boy, Fast Teddy, tipped off the police about Azeem Combs, whom we saw talking to you on various occasions on camera."

"And? What does that gotta do with me?"

"We think you got something to do with it. It was too much of an inside job for the thefts to run so smoothly."

Adam shot the dagger in my heart. With his last comment, I knew I shouldn't have put too much trust in crack headed ass Teddy. Casper had begged me to put Fast Teddy on the gig, but Teddy was too chicken hearted to go through what I had in mind. I never respected a man who stole from his family just to support a 10 dollar an hour crack habit. He did every drug, from shooting heroin to smoking on a glass dick to get high. Fast Teddy used to look out for Casper when he was a superfly hustler back in the day. I guess Casper putting him down was pay-back.

"I don't know why I'm in here." My rebuttal struck a cord when Adam rubbed his face.

"If you wanna play it that way, be my guest." Adam shuffled some police documents with a half smirk on his face.

They were closing in on me, and I needed to plan ahead. Quick! I didn't have a lawyer, so I had to play chess. I wasn't a rat ass bastard. Confessing meant giving up Casper, but telling Adam and the detective I had nothing to do with the thefts was great, kinda like sexing the mayor's daughter in his bedroom.

I knew the detective was pushing me over the edge by claiming Casper had ratted me out from stories Mama used to tell me. She'd used scare tactics to force local hoodlums into giving confessions by either claiming that a member of the crew was snitching, or threatening to lock up their families on a conspiracy charge. I knew the game all too well.

Leaving the manager's office and walking past the register, I spotted a temporary agency down the street from the department store. I never paid any attention to the joint, but I trooped over there during my lunch break. As I strolled past the lobby into the reception area, a lady who reminded me of a Kemetic queen greeted me when I stopped by her desk.

"Good evening, sir. How may I assist you?" she asked, with a smile that stood out from her apple butter complexion.

"Yes, my name is Justice King, and I'm looking for a temp to perm assignment."

"Oh, aight, please have a seat. I'll be with you in five minutes."

After waiting for the five minutes that past by faster than road runner, she came back with the paperwork, cheesing as if she was hit with laughing gas.

"Once you fill in the application, I would like for you to use the computer over there to test your typin' speed. That's if you wanna work in an office, you know what I'm sayin'?." She pointed toward a corner computer stand.

"Sure, I have no problem with that," I said, trying not to stare at the nipples poking through her blouse like bullets. "And what's your name, Miss?"

"Oh, I'm sorry. My name is Lanette Davis."

"Nice to meet you, Lanette." We shook hands, and I took a seat at the computer to fill out the applications for registration at the agency.

Working at a warehouse wasn't what I had in mind. I chose to apply for the clerical/administrator positions. The typing and office program tests were easy. I scored well on both alphabetical and numerical advanced typing tests and printed my results.

I overheard Lanette speaking on the phone to clients looking for employees. She tickled me when she changed her voice, from when she greeted me at the door to her talking on the phone. She went from sounding like she was a straight up 'hood chick when talking to me to a "Valley Girl" when speaking with clients.

I finished the test and application, and handed the paperwork to Lanette.

"I'll contact you as soon as we find any positions available." She smiled, and I pieced together her face in my memory.

"Thanks. By the way, you look mad familiar." I measured her face as she twirled her long, brunette hair. "No, really. I'm not tryin' to holla at you or nothin', but you do look crazy familiar. Do you shop at Shoe Fetish down the street?"

"No, but I work at Bling World," she whispered and carried on. "I work two jobs because I need the extra moolah."

"Aight, cool. I knew I saw you from somewhere."

I sipped on the last of the pink lemonade and remembered when I spotted her swaying away from the shoe department. She was the "mystery woman" whom I always saw working near the front registers where Bling World was located. She handed me her business card and crossed her thick thigh over the other. I thought I saw sparks fly when she said "Call me if you have any questions."

"I'll call you all right," I murmured to myself before walking out the door.

I texted Casper's cousin, Wakeetah, after work and told him the news. Wakeetah and Casper were night and day; Casper was 10 years younger than Wakeetah, Casper was light and Wakeetah was black as charcoal, Casper was loud and crazy, and Wakeetah was soft spoken and calm, Casper hustled and Wakeetah taught at an elementary school in South Jamaica, Queens. Well, you get the point.

Wakeetah texted me from the Haile Selassie Housing Projects further Uptown for a news event. He was there to support a friend facing eviction at a small news conference in the wild 100's. I didn't know why they faced eviction, but I figured the reason was the same as folks getting put out from their homes in Brooklyn.

The "A" train dropped me off deep in the hundreds. News vans crowded the streets in front of the brown brick project buildings. I peeped a brown-skinned woman speaking madly on stage that stood high on the street. Her fist pumped the air with authority as her words hit me harder than moonshine.

"...we've been living in this neighborhood through the crack-era and gang wars, and now they wanna kick us out when they finally fix things up." She blasted on the podium with conviction. "The new Harlem is not for Black people. They wanna get rid of us and remodel the projects and brownstones and we won't benefit from any of it!"

Chants of "power to the people", "Amen", and "save our homes" erupted from the crowd of hundreds that flooded the block. I caught the tail end of the press conference but got a chance to check out the cameramen interviewing folks on the street.

"Stop throwin' up them signs and respect the event," An older head scolded some young boys standing next to him for throwing up hand signs for the cameras. I knew they weren't flashing signs for the deaf. They left with their tight-pants sagging damn near to their knees. I felt bad for them. Kids nowadays have no sense of style whatsoever.

As the day went on, I felt like I was at a Black Panther's rally or something. The majority of folk dressed in black pumped fists in the air; donning red, black and green sweat bands across their wrists. I shivered from witnessing the movement as I'd never seen a crowded street full of Black folk unless a mob fight was going on. But that night was different, with a fist punching injustice in the face instead of fingers standing by themselves.

Shouting through frustrated tongues with hearts pumping out despair, the soul of Harlem shifted through its last footprints in the sand. A community synonymous with a Renaissance that later transformed into crack sells and hustlers flirting with death and packed jails, residents juggled with the changes of struggles that was once left in vain; the past was swept through the storm with their tracks washed away by rain. No light was gleaming down on them anytime soon, unless they did something about it. Hope was tapering off when the walls of sleep silted over the fire of their minds. Scrambling with nowhere to go, most felt hopeless and stuck in the dark, as a nation without a future is like the sun without its shine.

Cops stood on the sidewalks with horses, itching for violence to pop off by tapping batons in their hands. I brushed off their paranoia and doubted a riot was going to spark unless the horses went crazy and stomped over people.

Wakeetah texted me to see if I've made it Uptown. I wormed through the crowd to meet him on the other side of the stage with my hands waving in the air to catch his attention.

"What's good, baby boy?" He hugged me as I towered over his five-foot-seven frame.

"Ain't nothin'. I just got off the plantation on 2-5th."

"I hear that. I'm ready to bounce anyway. I've been here politickin' with fam since Noon. I want you to meet a lady friend of mine." Wakeetah led me to the other side of the stage. His friend was the lady I heard fuming as I got there. "Qu'Asia, this is Justice, a friend of my cousin, Casper."

"Nice to meet you, Justice." Her tiny hands shook mine as I gazed at her chestnut eyes.

"Likewise, queen. I'm diggin' your afro."

"Thank you. I appreciate the compliment, love."

Wakeetah cleared his throat to snap Qu'Asia out of her daydream and butted in our brief exchange. 'Keetah was a trip sometimes.

"Are you ready to go?" He asked Qu'Asia.

"I'm going to stay here with fam and the reverend. I think I need to be with them for awhile before I go crazy."

"What's goin' on?" I was lost.

"It's a long story, but the landlord gave us a two-month deadline to move out. The whole projects is going to be turned into luxury apartments. I have nowhere to go. There's not a lot of places for me to live in New York with a $200 a week salary workin' at the supermarket."

"Wow, that's crazy." I grimaced.

"Crazy ain't even the word, honey. I've been livin' in Uptown for 30 years, and worse comes to worst, I'll have to stay in the shelter with my three children because of this mess."

I was lost for words, and my mood hardened. Helping out the sista rang over me, but there was nothing I could do about it. Hell, I was struggling to help my damn self. My eyes held in cries from flowing down my face as everything around us was changing. I still saw the same people: blue collared workers living honestly and underworld dwellers who were fiends or crack sellers. Rotten milk and unsweetened honey left folks hungry when sheriffs knocked down their doors for eviction. False promises of hush money and jobs from politicians robbed my peers of their options. Thinking about those who lived better than themselves, many of them wished to move their skeletons to bodies that passed for white and high-class while blaming their brown melanin. The less fortunate became junkies with gelatin brains after shooting heroin to ease the pain of losing their rest. I wondered if things couldn't get any worse. I've watched folks in that same 'hood try to live beyond their means with the checks they'd spent. The clothes and shoes they worn had cost more than their rent, pushing me to the point where I'd almost lost sympathy for them.

I looked over to Wakeetah and saw him reaching for Qu'Asia. "It isn't over yet. We're going to do something about it." Wakeetah bear hugged her.

I poked my back pocket for my metro card and found the flyer about the rally in downtown Brooklyn that Felicia helped organize.

"There's a rally in BK soon. I think you should check it out." I handed Qu'Asia the flyer.

"Thank you, Justice."

We hugged like we'd known each other for years, and the swarm of cheers from the background silenced her sobbing. I gave her a handkerchief and departed with a "peace" before Wakeetah and I headed for the subway. We took the "A" train to 4th Avenue with thoughts of Qu'Asia haunting my mind; her family bouncing from shelters, scrambling for food, tussling with others trying to steal what was theirs, and her brown eyes dimming from a shine to bleakness.

The train ride to downtown was quick to my delight. Wakeetah and I transferred to the "B" train to Flatbush. He annoyed the hell out of me with his complaints about riding to Brooklyn, worrying about getting robbed or something. My man was funny like that. I wanted some new kicks at Dapper Don's on Flatbush Ave., and muted Wakeetah's paranoia. The pair of navy blue suede loafers sitting pretty on the display shelf had my name written all over it. I was copping those joints at any cost.

Dapper Don's had the freshest shoes not only in Brooklyn but all of New York City. If you wanted any color combination shoes, Dapper Don's had those joints. All the ballers, players, and fly girls shopped at Dapper Don's for his shoes and gear because he carried the exclusive joints. Working there instead of Shoe Fetish would've made a world of difference. Oh well, I could only dream.

Weaving and bumping through the crowded avenue was annoying until we finally reached Dapper Don's. We weren't there for a minute until Scar-lo and his crew of thugs bulldozed their way inside the joint.

"I want all of those, sun!" Scar-lo happily looked at the brand name clothes hanging on the wall. Scar-lo handed the manager a stack of money that looked like bricks as he walked over to the customers shopping.

"Everybody gots tah leave." He shooed away everybody in the joint as they left without refusal.

"It's time for us to leave now," Wakeetah whispered, but I wasn't moving a muscle.

"I came here to shop. I ain't leavin' until I get what I want," I talked loud enough for Scar-lo and his goons to hear. I wasn't scared not one bit. Scar-lo was a wolf who smelled fear. A hint of fright turned sheep into lions, and I stood on my square.

Scar-lo pulled out another stack of dead politicians like it was nothing to him.

"Let 'em live. I want them to see how we ball since he keeps frontin' on the squad." He laughed, and damn near bought out the whole store in front of my eyes.

I heard about cats buying out the bar, making it rain in strip clubs and shutting down malls, but never in life I've witnessed it up close. Scar-lo even pulled out a bottle of champagne to toast Nu-Sun (his lieutenant) while his other little goons shopped until they got tired.

His show-off style spoiled my joy for shopping. It was like the room turned from cool to warm when I thought of shoving the $500 leather jacket he held in front of a mirror down his throat. Damn near broke with a bullshit job, I envied Scar-lo. His freedom to buy anything he wanted was choking my patience of living on a straight path. Teaming up with him to sell drugs was a lot easier than going to college. The ice glistening on his neck and wrist was calling me to join his team of goons to stack cream, but my own vice with setting up thefts at Shoe Fetish was enough drama. Drug dealing was a one way ticket to the grave, and I wasn't a slave to fast money.

Scar-lo stopped shopping like he'd run out of breath, and half the store was empty. He stuck his thumb up like "okay" to his crew and jetted off into his luxury car.

After I copped the loafers, Wakeetah and I were on our way back to Church Avenue to catch the "B" train. I gave Wakeetah the whole scoop about what had happened, and how Casper got knocked by the police. I even told Wakeetah I had set up the thefts since I trusted him.

"How much time you think the system gonna give him?" I asked.

"Who knows…hopefully not much since it's his first offense." Wakeetah kicked rocks as he walked on. "Justice, how can you be so intelligent and dumb at the same time?"

The answer fumbled between my mind and mouth. I quietly stared at the traffic passing us by.

"Why didn't you just quit your job?" he asked with hurt in his voice.

"I don't know, man. I was comfortable…I guess." The words from my mouth trailed off, as *actually* quitting my gig had never leaked out my dome even during the days I hated working there.

"Comfortable of what? You have a college degree. I know you can do better than working retail. That job's for high schoolers, sun." Wakeetah scowled at me like a big brother. "It's bad enough we have too many brothers in jail for doing dumb shit. I'm *really* surprised at you because you're a lot smarter than cats wasting their time away on corners."

"Yeah, I know."

The truth burned, but I faced the fire standing. Wakeetah was right. I just didn't know how to leave, or knew what the future had in store for me if I did fire my boss. Shoe Fetish was like an abusive relationship where the victim stayed with the lover, and I walked around with whip marks on my brain.

"What was your graduating GPA in college?" Wakeetah asked.

"3.6."

"3.6! Man, you could've easily bagged a few scholarships for law school, sun. I have connections with several scholarship programs offering money for Blacks and..."

"I don't want a scholarship because I'm Black." I cut him off; my pride spoke.

"It's a lot better than working retail, that's for sure. Hell, they owe us free education anyway." Wakeetah dug in his wallet and handed me a business card. "Call this number. He's a good brother, and should be able to help you out. Opportunity knocks only once. So answer it."

"Cool. Thanks."

I stuffed the business card in my back pocket as we crossed the turnstiles to hop on the iron horse. Wakeetah went his way, and I went mine, hoping that the dark cloud covering my tomorrows would stop following me so I can breathe sunshine.

***

Dressed in black army fatigues, combat boots, and hair tied in a pony tail, Felicia looked like she was called to war.

"What's good, GI Jane? You's a soldier now?" I studied her angle.

"Nope, just trying out some gear for the rally."

"Aight, just make sure you don't scare the neighbors." I dropped my book-bag on the ground and lamped on the sofa. "How was the trip to the island?"

"It was mad cool. My abuelos gave me some money for the mortgage that'll last me for a few months. But other than that, it was a nice getaway from the city."

I stood and stamped $500 in her hands. She looked at the stack of 10's and 20's, but brushed off the money.

"No, no, Justice. I don't want your money." She grimaced.

"What you mean, you don't wanna take my money?"

"Baby, you don't have to do that. I can handle this on my own."

"Stop talkin' crazy, Fe Fe. I've been livin' here rent free and now it's time for me to help out."

She still wouldn't take the money. So I stuffed the loot inside the bra she was wearing and bounced to my love nest down in the basement. Felicia chased me downstairs and slammed the loot on the nightstand next to my bed.

"Justice, I don't need your money." She stood firm on her square.

"What's gonna happen if you get kicked out? Huh? What then?"

"I can take care of myself. Come to the rally with me if you really wanna help."

I sucked my teeth and stared at the ceiling while resting. "I ain't goin' to some damn rally to watch a buncha negroes run around singin' that 'We Shall Overcome' shit."

"You being selfish. The least you can do is help me fight to save the brownstone and spread the word."

"Shit, you don't want me to give you money! I'm not wastin' my time downtown. That's all I gotta say."

Felicia went haywire and slammed the door, damn near shaking the room.

She'll get over it.

I turned toward the window and stared at the stars. Billions of lights glittered the more I watched the night. I fantasized about touching them. Stars rolling in expensive cars with gorgeous groupies had never moved me like the ones up above. The moment was when my memory switched to episodes earlier in the evening.

Witnessing Scar-lo damn near buy out the store clicked. It was eating me alive, and I knew selling dope was the easy way out. Running the crime route only led to a dead end. I was broke, but not poor. I just needed to do something to make money and myself happy. The marriage between patience and I was stressful, but I knew living through the worst made a better heaven. Dope dealing and knowingly killing my 'hood would've eaten my conscience alive. I wanted to make a difference in the 'hood, not destroy it. But before I could reach for the stars, my past would ultimately come back to haunt me.

Chapter 19: Sinking Ship

The door bell rang. I sat and waited for three more rings to follow.

ding...dong...ding...dong...ding...dong

I sprang from my king-sized bed, and my head swelled with nothing but her image. I opened the door and put on the cool face as she stood in front of me.

"Peace, beautiful. You look stunnin'." I marveled at her from head the toe. Nandi was rocking some navy blue open-toe dress shoes and a long, purple jersey dress with navy blue lining. The sleeveless top that cropped from the middle of her breasts to neck brought heat between my thighs, and my eyes almost couldn't bear glancing at her.

"Thank you, my king." She walked inside and turned around, expecting me to hang her navy blue leather jacket. Any other girl would've got the gas face, but Nandi was galaxies away from the average pigeon.

"So what you got cookin'?" Her eyes lit up.

"I got a lil sumthin' sumthin'."

I threw down in the kitchen by cooking yams, cornbread, kale, Cajun breaded fish fillets, and a side bowl of black-eyed peas. After Mama passed, Grandma taught me how to cook almost every Southern meal known to man. But I'd *never* touched the swine like pig feet, ham, pork hot links, and chitlins. I didn't see how folks could eat something that smelled like shit before cooking. Eating pork was close to AIDS as far as I was concerned.

The fire from the Kwanzaa candle holder lit the darkened dining room, and I watched Nandi enjoy the meal. Surprise carved her facial expression with each bite. I laughed to myself since she didn't expect me to cook so well. Just call me the new-age "Renaissance Man."

"Who taught you how to cook?" she asked.

"Uncle Benson."

"Stop playin'. How'd you learned to cook food so deliciously?" she mumbled between bites while feeding my ego. "Let me find out you had someone cook this for you."

"I learned from the best." I patted myself on the back. "It's all in the wrist, baby. All in the wrist."

After we ate, I held her hand and led her to the basement with a trail of purple roses stretching from the dining room to my bed. The champagne popped, and we drank the night away. Her feet shuffled against my shins with her fingers circling around my chest. Her titties perked out from her dress and teased my hands to massage them. Breathing hard with each twirl of her nipples, she bit her bottom lip and unzipped my slacks. I firmly gripped her hips and nibbled on her neck. She fell back onto the mattress with her eyes closed. I slipped the dress off to the ground and dipped my face between her thighs. Kissing around the hairs above her pearl, my mouth tasted every drip of her honeywell. She shivered and madly massaged my head as she groaned from each twist of the tongue.

I slipped away and ran across the strap of her lace panties. I pulled them down with my teeth, and they rung around her ankles and fell to the floor. Sucking on the toes of each foot, a burst of air rushed from her mouth with heat circling her feet. I licked the arch of her foot and eased my tongue back up to suck both of her inner thighs.

She shrieked when I nibbled up and down both thighs, seriously teasing her as I dribbled close to her wet spot. I turned her over and massaged her shoulders. Tasting the scent of peaches smoothing inside my nostrils, my tongue ran down the crease of her spine. She quivered from licks from the tip of my tongue as her muscles relaxed. Reaching for the blindfold on the nightstand, I flipped her over and she yelped.

"What you doin' with that?" Nandi rubbed my chest in half suspense.

"Shhh, relax…Baby, I got this." I wrapped a Zorro mask around my eyes and placed a black cloth over hers. I licked across her lips. She shuddered under me. Wetting her cleavage with a bottle of gold Alizé, I kissed the liquor off her flesh from the nipples down to the puddle over her navel.

The kisses freed her and locked away stress that tensed her body. Her hands fondled my crouch and called me to overwhelm the wetness glazing over her pussycat. But I pulled away…teasing for her to go the extra mile to please me. She tried to get hold of my man but instead felt air. The mystery blinded her until she felt me in the rawest form, laying up and slowly taking me inside her mouth.

Twisting the pleasure spot of my brain, she worked me like a candy cane. I was frozen on the outside with electricity running through my veins. Her thick, soft lips hugged, pressed, and sucked me to a point where I wanted to scream "I love you," and give half of what I owned.

She lied back on the pillow and split her other lips with two fingers. The vagina monologue filled the banks of my desires by talking cents and daring me to draw money shots inside her sugar walls. I eased back and straddled on top, feeling her titties pressing against my chest. The tip of my erection tapped her cervix, and she squirmed from each stroke. Clawing my neck and back with her nails, she pushed me to ride faster and whispered for more. Her finger tips pressed against the balls of my shoulders with her tongue licking my Adam's apple. The tickling pushed me deeper. Tears of pleasure leaked out her eyes through the blindfold. The moon shone inside the darkened room and I stopped…I held her hand and lifted her off the bed.

"Let's go by the window," I whispered, and she followed me as she held my hand. I stood behind her and licked the outs of her ears. "Bend over and put it in for me."

Facing the moonlight with me behind her, I held her waist as she bent over. I poured scented oil on her ass and rubbed it all over her, flowing down from the base of her back to her hamstring and legs. I filled her up deep inside her pink. Her walls massaged around my stick as if she was forcing me to cum while I slid in and out, fucking her with my fatness swallowing deep inside her cherry.

"Damn, you good," I breathed, popping my hips onto her rear. She whispered for me to thrust deeper. Her thighs shook with intense jolts of shock.

"Ooh, shit…hit it harder." She threw her ass back onto me, slapping against my hips. I felt liquid warming out its shell. I slowed down from the sensitivity that pushed me to nut inside her. "Don't stop, baby…don't stop. Keep goin'." She egged me on, but I was done; not holding anything back.

Thoughts of pulling out were rubbed out. I madly picked up speed, hitting it until she bathed me with warm cum that slid down my shaft and around my nuts. I uncontrollably released the last of my might inside her triangular prism and took deep breaths to keep up with her. Panting with her back coated with sweat, she turned around and dropped to her knees. She kissed the tip of my erection and gently squeezed for the nut to spring out like getting the last of the toothpaste. Toes curling and eyes rolling, I was light footed; my senses tingling as she played me like a flute, stroking each vein beneath her tongue and massaging the last of my hardness. I felt like squeezing myself inside out as her warm mouth worked on my knob. Weak from the shivers of tongue tricks and the up and down licks, I crouched down from fatigue and collapsed on floor. I kissed her nose and forehead, and rested my sweat-drenched body on top of hers.

***

I woke up next to Nandi as if she was a new woman. Remembering that she cooked for a brother in Jersey, I hooked up some French toast and scrambled eggs. I spilled the last batch of pancake mix in the drain, so I fixed us some brown sugar oatmeal from scratch.

A hand fingered my back, and an arm wrapped around my shoulders. Hairs stood on my skin when she kissed my shoulder blades and glazed her lips on the back of my neck. I turned around and caught her smiling. Her chocolate-coated skin turned me on instantly as she stood there naked.

I lifted her onto the countertop. We lip locked with the breakfast cooking. It seemed like the eggs were set off by us doing the mo' better when the heat arose from the stove. The skillet sizzled and popped loudly as we went on. The food wasn't the only thing cooking that morning. The quick appetizer jump started our day, and we ate breakfast after trading climaxes.

Speechless and rested, we lamped in the basement and laughed while watching the second season DVD of *The Boondocks*. I didn't have to go to work until the evening. So we napped until the time clocked for me to trek to Harlem. Thinking about calling in for the day, I realized a brother's pockets were looking guilty. Nandi was important, but love didn't pay the bills.

She caught the NJ Transit while I damn near skipped to Shoe Fetish from the subway, happy as I'd ever been since working there. Suzie grilled me, but I didn't mind her. Usually I would've mentally cussed her out. I was too chill to let her get to me. Prince was hanging up clothes on a rack in his department when I saw a guy with a hunchback limp his way.

"Hey, brotha!" He held up pair of pants in front of Prince. "I wanna buy this."

Confused and hesitant to leave the rack, Prince nodded his head, unsure of the question. "Yeah, you can buy the pants."

"Nah, brotha. I wanna buy just one leg. Not the pair."

"Mah dude, you need a pair of pants in order to wear them."

"The sign says 'on sale: men's pants'." The guy went on, pestering Prince.

"Yes, I *can* read, and the pants are on sale."

"So I wanna buy a leg."

"You can't buy a leg."

"So why call it a pair of pants when I can't buy a leg?"

I was rolling, and damn near choked on pink lemonade from laughter. The guy's mismatch pants legs (one was orange and the other was navy blue) confirmed his seriousness as he strutted away, shaking his head.

"Dude's a character, sun." Prince smirked while placing shirts on hangers.

"I needed that laugh. I can't believe money asked you that stupid ass question. I ain't laugh that hard since Jemima fell on her ass walkin' off the bus." I held on the clothes rank for support, crying myself to tears.

Prince left the rack and we walked to my department. He saw Jo Jo and tapped me on the shoulder. "What's good with the white boy?" he asked, sounding a lot like Casper.

"Jo Jo's cool. I got no problem with dude. He doesn't step on my toes and I don't step on his."

"That's peace. Oh yeah, I've been meaning to ask you about the shorty you met in Medina a few months back."

My forehead creased from pretend cluelessness. "Who? Nandi?"

"Yeah, her. I know you hit that, Just. I know how you gets down." Prince cheesed.

"She wouldn't let me." I looked away.

"Shorty fronted on you?"

"Well…um…she was on her period." I told a "light" lie; referring to the time when Nandi and I lamped in DC.

"Doesn't matter. You should've put on the rain coat and hit the power u."

"Chill, I'm good with that." I grimaced, and was disgusted by Prince's suggestion.

"I don't know about you, but when it's time for me to hit the snappy nappy dug out, ya' boy goes hard, sun. Nah-mean? Ayo, I'm out!" Prince gave me a pound and skipped off to lunch. I stood there, not knowing why I just told Prince a story. Sleeping with Nandi was something I could never tell anyone, not even Casper. Any other girl would've found her name hollered in male gossip, but not Nandi. Not telling Prince about my intimacy with her was like lifting the world off my shoulders and walking away free.

I helped Jo Jo with stocking shelves with new women's construction boots. We didn't talk until ten minutes into working on the project.

"What's good?" I asked.

"Nothing, just the same story; working and taking care of my family."

"That's cool. I hope your family takes what's given to them," I said, subliminally referring to Felicia turning down my offer to give her money.

"Yeah, I'm just taking my time until the job market builds up again. You know, there's a meeting later today."

"Meeting?" I was surprised.

"Yeah, well, I guess you wouldn't know since Adam told the supervisors first. But he called for a storewide meeting earlier this week. He has some important news."

"Good or bad?"

"Beats me. I'm just as clueless as you are. The meeting starts at five."

Time ticked with both hands sitting on five without signs of Adam. I anxiously waited while stocking shoes and fixing shelves destroyed by savage customers. I wondered if their apartments looked like junkyards after rummaging through boxes like alley rats. The aisles looked a mess.

Six o'clock past…then 7…later 8. I still saw no signs of Adam. Maybe he was busy powdering his face with nose candy since he always moved 40 going north. The clock flew past 9, and Adam called over the intercom for the entire store to meet him near the entrance after customers made their final purchases.

Adam stood with some of the big cheese of the company. I was scared shitless. Flanked by the head of Human Resources (HR) and the Regional President of Sales (RPS), Adam sinister grin was nothing but trouble.

"I apologize for the lateness. The meeting was supposed to start at five, and it's now 9:30." Adam opened the meeting near the registers. I loved the irony of the head honchos' lateness. "I thought it would be important to address major changes in the building and give everyone a heads up about the problem the company is facing. I'll let Mr. Lynch take over the meeting and relay the news of these major changes."

Tall, lanky, and pale-skinned, Yugo Lynch's appearance begged for a sun tan. He stood there looking homeless. He was Head of HR and spent most of his time surfing the net for exotic "dating services"; an older women whom I used to fool around with was one of his "dates" and had put me on to his debauchery. The desk receptionist had literally caught Yugo with his pants down; downloaded porn popped up on his laptop screen. The average person would've got fired, but not Yugo. His pops held major stock in the company and he was let off the hook with only a warning; nepotism at its finest.

Yugo stepped forward wearing an all white suit. I wanted to curse him for sporting white *after* Labor Day. What a cornball.

"Again, sorry for the lateness. As you all know, the economy is bad, and the company is taking a huge hit."

Yugo's candor was that of carelessness. "The company is projected to lose money, and is in the process of closing down 13 stores nationwide with 500 lay offs."

Employees in the store gasped in unison, and chatter filled the room. I swallowed the red pill of knowing how many people were laid off and waited for Yugo to bust water.

"So without further ado, anyone holding the yellow slip that we gave you earlier should come with me. And the rest with the green slips goes with Julie." Yugo walked away and expected folks to follow him without saying a word as if he was Moses.

Prince had the yellow slip while I held the green. We looked at each other without speaking, but our eyes spoke of worry. He followed the ant line of employees awaiting their fate. The weight of facing the axe sat heavily on my shoulders. Reality slapped me like a freight train. I was sick of Shoe Fetish, but I wasn't ready to leave.

Julie, a short, light-brown skinned woman, was left standing with us while the rest nestled upstairs. She was the RPS, and I'd spoken with her a few times during store visits. Hesitant to speak, she forcefully smiled. Her eyes scanned at what was left of the store.

"Okay, guys. Those of you who have green slips means you're *staying* with the company," she began, and emphasized *staying*. "The others you saw walking upstairs with yellow slips are getting laid off."

My mouth dropped. Not because I wasn't laid off, but because Prince was part of the group that got the axe. I relaxed for a moment and back tracked when Adam had mentioned about the company losing thousands of dollars. I didn't know he'd planned on firing damn near the entire store.

"Please show support when your fellow employees come downstairs," said Julie, and the rest of the day was solemn.

Folks cleaned out their lockers while some smoked away the pain outside. Some were angry, happy, or stunned about the news. Security even had to stop an employee from throwing clothes on the floor in the Ladies' department. She took her anger out on the store by whistling through each aisle and flooding the floor with jeans, shirts, and other garments. Security got hold of the contentious girl and dragged her outside when she refused to stop. The scene reminded me of a trashy talk show topic gone wrong.

Tears soaked the cheeks of employees, mostly women, who got the yellow slip. They smoked outside, still shaking from the sudden announcement of the lay offs.

"This is what I get for bustin' my ass for these muthafuckas for twenty years of my life!" A lady fumed between puffs. "The hell with them!"

"I don't know how I'm gonna support my family." An older man worried. "I got four kids to feed, and this job was my bread and butter."

Most of those who got laid off were older, between the ages of 35 and 55. I guess the company thought they'd save money by keeping the younger employees since they were new to the job scene.

I stepped back inside, and saw Essence standing next to her register. A short, heavy set woman angrily strolled near Essence with fire in her eyes. Evita approached Essence with eyes blazing rage and clenched fists.

"You bitch." Evita winced, and spoke words of hell. "You took my job, hija de puta."

Evita stormed out the store even before Essence could respond. I watched the scene unfold and laughed. "What's good with, 'Vita?"

"That heifer is just mad I took her job." Essence laughed it off.

"What you mean?"

"The company demoted Evita because she had to go to El Salvador to fix a problem with her green card. She was gone for mad long, and Adam promoted me to replace her as front supervisor."

Evita had worked for the company for five years and managed the front cashiers. Adam wasn't too fond of her. He used her green card problems as an excuse to give her the boot as front supervisor. Adam was as slimy as a pot of okra. He gets the "laughs in your face but reports you to Corporate behind your back" award for store manager.

I saw Prince handing Adam the keys to his locker. Those laid off had two weeks until the store terminated their status. Some folks grabbed their things regardless of the grace period. Still shook from the meeting, Prince walked toward me while reading the notification of his release.

"Damn, sun." Prince crumpled the notification and slid the sheet in his back pocket. "Now I most definitely gotta move down to Charlotte. It's a good thing I saved 10g's."

"I didn't know they were layin' off folks. I'm surprised they didn't get me." I shrugged.

"I knew they wouldn't. It's only you, Jo Jo, and some other chick in the morning. Your department is under budget."

"True dat," I said, but thought, *if only he knew half the story.*

Although Prince had a point, I knew Adam had wished I was laid off. Some chick worked in the morning, but I rarely saw her since I usually worked in the evening. So that usually left me by myself, or with Jo Jo working the night shift.

Seething because the company released him, Prince handed me a New York Globe and was disgusted at the headline.

CRASHING THE PARTY: Foreclosure Rocks the Hamptons

"You know the economy's bad when rich folks in the Hamptons are struggling." I opened the newspaper and skimmed through the article.

> *10 homes in the Hamptons have been foreclosed in the past 6 months due to the falling economy. Residents living in the area known for its celebrity and beach parties are struggling to pay bills for their high priced homes. Banks have seized the homes of delinquent borrowers while others are trying to sell their homes to avoid foreclosure.*

"That's crazy, b. It's lookin' like we're headed back to the 80's." I folded the newspaper, not believing I had little to no other options besides school and the military.

The 80's was a gritty and crazy time for inner cities across America. Crack, gangs, and unemployment swallowed neighborhoods and took homes by storm. The Reagan era was a lightning rod of vices that burned bridges between the Civil Rights-era and a generation where money was God.

The lay offs awakened me, and I saw life differently. I've always thought owning a business was risky until I faced living jobless in a blink of an eye. Life was nothing but a giant risk, from walking outside not knowing what the day had in store for me to constantly following orders from people who literally held my livelihood in the palms of their hands. The company laying me off would've defeated my purpose for setting up the thefts. I wasn't finished carrying out my plan. My heart was burning to see the store crumble in front of me. And while thievery was only the tip of the iceberg, I found out I wasn't the only disgruntled employee robbing the store blind.

Chapter 20: Dumb Criminals

Adam stormed in front of me, face beet red and sweat sliding down his temples.

"Justice, can I speak with you inside my office?"

Oh, Lord.

"Aight." I lazily followed Adam, looking forward to more grilling from him and the detective who looked like an extra from the *Dukes of Hazard*.

An amalgam of pain and giddiness gripped my stomach like a lion hugging a cactus; I worried about someone bitching up and flipping on me. The trip to the office was like walking the long mile to death row. The slow walk gave me time to sow a chain of comebacks as a defense.

Adam pushed the door and opened the flood gates of drama. My livelihood was at stake. I saw the same detective with the annoying country accent, and Gloria, a lady working the registers, sobbing insanely with her head buried between her legs. Seeing her sitting inside Adam's office surprised me more than anything.

"Gloria, did Justice have anything to do with employees illegally activating gift cards?" Adam frantically cut to the chase with Gloria bawling in the chair. I was taken aback because I knew nothing about illegally activating gift cards.

"Gloria, tell the truth. There's no one here but me, you, and Detective Keeley." Adam pressed her.

Detective Keeley handed Gloria a tissue. She wiped the eyeliner that smeared across her cheeks, making her look like a raccoon. The silence brought tension in the room as the lights in the ceiling buzzed noise. Gloria exhaled, and I was afraid that Adam and the columbo had forced her to blame me for a crime I didn't commit.

"No..." Gloria cried, muffling between sobs. "No, Justice didn't have anything to do with it." She jerked back into her seat and brushed the tissue under her eyes. I saw disappointment in Adam's and Keeley's faces.

"So who was in it?" Keeley pushed himself into the conversation to make him feel important. Gloria didn't budge, and rocked back and forth in the office chair. The cold stare from Keeley to Gloria sung anger; she was too timid to give up names. Adam and Keeley wasted my time. They could've struck the fear of God in Gloria without me sitting there.

"If I'm going down, then everybody is going down with me." Gloria blurted out, almost regretting what she'd just said. "All the cashiers except for Essence, Timothy, and Ben were illegally using gift cards to make purchases."

Adam and the detective damn near gasped in unison. Even I was shocked at the revelation. "The Receiving crew were in on it, too. You can even check the cameras and the purchases on them."

Adam turned steamy red and slammed his fist on the table. "I can't fucking believe this shit happened in my store!"

"How did you find out about me swiping cards?" Gloria asked.

Adam faced cleared, and he let out a brief laugh, as if she should've known the answer.

"You used the gift card in Florida, and Corporate picked up on it. You signed your name on the receipt after using the gift card at a Florida store, but another receipt from a customer in this store had the same gift card number." Adam sarcastically shook his head with a 'you dumb ass' smirk toward her. "We tracked down the customer, and the customer said he'd never used the gift card. Not mention that we caught you and other employees not scanning merchandise, and using the gift cards instead to activate them."

"Am I going to jail?" Gloria was frightened, and Adam and Keeley both glanced at each other.

"We don't know yet, but we want the money that was stolen back to the store."

Tired of the nonsense, I wanted to leave. "Since my name is cleared, can I leave now?"

"Yeah, but we're watching you, too, pal." Keeley chimed in while chewing tobacco. His teeth were green, and looked like he brushed those joints with seaweed.

I left work after the so-called interrogation, relieved about Gloria not falsely accusing me. Gloria made the fatal mistake by signing off on the receipts, and unknowingly leaked evidence to Corporate. All parties involved were basically caught with their pants down. At least I wasn't the only one rebelling in the department store. Lucky me.

Leaving from work was like a caterpillar turning into a butterfly as I headed back to Brooklyn. The sun shone for a few minutes until clouds covered its shine. Rain trickled down and drizzled before flooding the streets. I sped walked to the brownstone before I got drenched. Running through the stench of bums and a flock of young boys hugging the sidewalks on corners, I finally reached the brownstone.

No one was home, and boredom crossed me until Nandi hit me on the hip. She was back from the brief trip on the Northeast tour with her band and wanted to kick it with me. I remembered the show at Club Libra that the new neighbors across the street had mentioned. I invited her to roll with me.

We met at the spot around 10, and the joint was dark and dingy. The joint reminded me of a haunted house without the fake spider webs and Halloween characters dangling from the ceiling. Nandi and I were the only brown faces in the joint, but I didn't care. I looked forward to a good time.

A tall, lanky guy bumped into me and spilled some of his drink on my dark gray slacks. I was heated, and the guy held on to a chair to straighten himself from stumbling.

"My bad, dude." He stood on his feet, and his eyes looked like they were drowning in liquor. "Let me buy you a drink."

"I'm good," I said, standing next to Nandi.

"No, man. It was my fault. I wanna buy you a drink. I'm sorry for spilling my drink on you." He slurred, but I protested.

"Nah, money, I'm okay."

The guy dug in his pockets and handed me a twenty dollar bill. "Have fun, bro." He patted me on the back and went on his drunken way.

I reluctantly took the Jackson, but what the hell, it was a free drink. I ordered two Long Island Iced Teas, and the drink hit me like a Mack truck. Fighting to hold my liquor, I consequently held on to Nandi for support.

"Oh, brother, not this again." She rolled her eyes, and I tried to save face.

"I'm good. I'm good." I came back, but she laughed at my effort.

The show started with the MC introducing my neighbors' band as The Jokers. They donned red and green court jester outfits, sported the twin bell hat, and rocked on stage. I gave them an "E" for effort and "T" for nice try. They were type corny.

The wailing guitars played by Rob echoed throughout the small stage room. Jess sung on the mic as lead singer. She was a pretty dope singer; her voice carried each note without cracking. Pete banged on the drums, and the crowd jumped around like they were in a mosh pit. My body shook from the vibes let off by the bass guitar while the keyboardist jammed with the melodies. I loved it, because the show was a lot better than some of these half assed rappers today who shouldn't dream of touching the mic.

The Jokers ended their 20-minute session, and I greeted them as they packed up on stage. I congratulated the band on the dope show, and Nandi traded business cards with them. I wasn't into rock music, but their set knocked hard. We stayed in Club Libra for a couple of hours and bounced after we got tired of the guitars that vociferously smothered the club. I wasn't sure when Felicia was coming back to the country. So taking Nandi home with me was too risky. Not having my own bachelor pad killed me because I had to calculate *when* and *how* I was planning on bringing some cuties back to the brownstone without Felicia catching me in the act. Most girls I've dated had their own spot, and I never had to worry about motel money. I asked Nandi if she wanted to chill at one of the rock hills at Central Park North. She was down with the idea, and we lamped there for awhile.

The condos stalking alongside Central Park motivated me to succeed. Working at Shoe Fetish lessened me as a person with a college degree, and I needed to push myself to the limit. I thought about what Wakeetah had told me earlier about scholarships as well as Scar-lo spending money like it was water. Hustling books inside a classroom was better than rotting inside a cell and letting the system molest the greatest part of my life.

I glanced over at Nandi, and she sat there looking at the cars breeze by. Her aura emptied the garbage that spammed my mind, but my mouth never moved an inch. I refused to pour my heart in liters and express how I really felt. Her darkened features were like a masterpiece in the arts and leisure section of the Times. Ruckus rang out when police dogs barked at streeters trying to break into parking meters for change. The noise shifted my eyes away from the sugars of her grace that raked my taste buds, to cee-cipher chasing fake thugs down the block. Suddenly, the rally in Brooklyn set in. I flashbacked to my and Felicia's past conversations.

"There's a rally goin' on in BK about gentrification," I mustered out, and she held on to my arms. "Do you think I should go?"

"Sure, why not?"

"Well…the brownstone I'm livin' in is owned by a lady friend of mine. I've been livin' there for a minute now, and she'd lost her job. She doesn't have that much money to pay for the mortgage and that whole block is gonna be remodeled into luxury condos. I wanna give moral support, but I think protesting is a waste of time." I paused for a few seconds and ran my thoughts. "But it's crazy to me that the brownstones in Brooklyn were originally dirt cheap, but now the prices are gonna be bananas if developers get their way. I wanna help, but a movement is more than makin' noises."

"Yeah, but what can we do?" Nandi shrugged.

"I don't know. I have a better chance at seein' Tupac at the mall than seeing unity amongst Black folk. Everybody's doin' their own thing and don't wanna help each other."

"I know how you feel, but don't give up too soon. I think you should go. Your friend was gracious enough to let you stay, so you should at least help her out."

I shook my head, half listening to Nandi; not out of disrespect, but my mind was overwhelmed with so much emotion. "What did we get after those *I Have a Dream* speeches? Yeah, we made some progress, but we're still so far behind. The days of marching are over and…and…"

"We need to rethink how to go about getting what we want." Nandi finished my sentence.

"Exactly! Marching and rallying are symbolic victories. We need something that's physical. Hootin' and hollerin' and askin' for apologies will not get us anywhere. That shit died in the 60's."

"But, baby, I still think you should go. Nothing happens overnight. There's an old saying, 'patience is a bitter plant but its fruits are sweet.' And there's no use in throwing in the towel so fast." The words that left Nandi's mouth was like honey to my ears, and she went on. "We still have house niggas who only want a buck, and niggas saying they keep it real when they're really destroying the 'hood. But we need to keep pushing. It's a beautiful struggle being down, and the only way to go is up." She caught her breath from dropping a long-winded jewel. I was amazed by her awareness.

Nandi impressed me with her thinking, and I was moved by her level of intelligence. Most females gossiped or talked about the next chick's fashion, but Nandi's knowledge eclipsed them. Talking to her was refreshing, kind of like a storm after a drought, a glass of water in a desert, or your favorite song the first time you heard it. The more I spent time with her, the closer we were married through the mind.

We tongue kissed for the next ten minutes and left the park because she had to troop back to Jersey. I didn't want her to go. I wanted her to stay...she captured my brain without locks and chains and rocked my boat without childish games.

"I wanna roll to Jerz with you," I said.

"Come with me? You must be out of your mind, Justice."

"That's funny, because my grandma said I bumped my head when she put me in the washing machine."

"Ha, ha, cute. A sista needs time to herself. I know my aunt ain't gonna let you spend the night," she was quite frank about it, and sensed disappointment on my face. "Aaaah, I'm sure you got a few hoochie mamas you can call."

"What if we become man and woman, and I cheat on you with one of those hoochie mamas?" I played on her "hard to get" angle.

"Hmm…I'll probably swallow a bottle of pills and kill myself." She looked at me very grim. I wasn't sure if she was playing along or was serious.

"Whatever, ma. I wanna kick it with you for the rest of the night," I protested, but Nandi refused to budge.

"Next time, baby." She kissed me on the lips. "Peace."

Nandi hitched a cab to Penn Station, once again leaving me in the dust. After she left, I got a text from a number I didn't recognize. I texted the number back and the caller was Sandra. Erasing her number after she'd fronted on me at the photo shoot, I pushed her out my mind. I didn't expect her to call again. I called the number, and she picked up after the third ring, sounding like a phone sex operator.

"Hey, handsome." She finessed her words. I was unsure how to draw her out. So I put my cool on.

"What's good?" I asked like I didn't care about her calling me.

"Nothing. Just thinking about you."

"What you were thinkin' about?"

"Thinking about you coming over here to finish that photo shoot we had," she said, and a set-up came to mind, but there was no reason for Sandra to double cross me. I tossed around the idea of doing right, but my thoughts went left and got lost in temptation.

"I don't know, ma. It's kinda late." I baited her.

"Eleven is not late unless you're a little boy." She teased, and I tried not to give in.

But as we went on, my mind played tricks on me; shadows of Sandra prancing around wearing zebra panties with the matching bra lit up inside my mental camera. Horny from hanging out with Nandi, I was like a dog wagging its tail. I failed the test of not thinking so frail because I was such an emotional wreck. I checked my watch, and it clocked a little bit past 11. Sandra was only a couple of train stops away; her condo was in downtown Brooklyn near the train yards.

"I'm on my way."

I clicked off and crashed into the palm of her hand.

Chapter 21: Fire Your Boss

Sandra opened her bath robe and stripped naked. She smeared the chocolate syrup covering her breasts all over herself as if it was body paint. She licked the rest on her finger tips and winked at me. She dipped to the floor and jiggled her round brown while I sipped on a glass of hard liquor. The drink cooled the heat that brought a river of sweat to flow down my temples.

The show Sandra put on turned me into a boy who'd never seen a woman dance naked before. She performed a split and bounced up and down like a tennis ball. The teasing fixed my eyes on her and pulled me to realize she could've seduced a drowning man into drinking a gallon of water. She wormed on the floor, and squirmed toward the sofa. Ice flooded my veins as I sat unnerved; pretending her moves was amateur.

I glanced around and saw no trace of wedding photos that once graced the top of the end stand near the sofa. I paid the missing photos no mind and kept snapping pictures of her. The camera was her personal mirror, and she made no bones about showing her lust in front of me. She strutted over to the sofa and rested on my lap. Twisting in front of me, she blew air on my neck and licked in circles. My thighs numbed, and my heart beat sped its rhythm. She grinded her love on me and wrapped her arms around my shoulders. Wiggling her milk shake tempted me to buy a side order of kisses with a body that would make a seasoned reverend scream "Hallelujah!"

I palmed her bubble and felt the warmth pulsating from the rear. Moans whispered in my ear as the chocolate from her nipples smeared on my button-down shirt. I was tight about it, but she unbuttoned the shirt and pressed wet kisses on my chest.

Paralyzed by shock, I was physically there, but my mind drifted off in space. I slipped in and out of consciousness from the liquor hitting me. Sandra unzipped my slacks and tipped over my bottle of leftover pink lemonade. The drink spilled on the burgundy Persian rug, but Sandra was too deep in freak mode to even care by fingering the top of my underwear and caressing my chest.

She unbuttoned my pants and pulled down my boxers. I couldn't hold back the expression of pleasure. The hard liquor freed feelings that overwhelmed me. The 80-proof liquor was the truth serum that grabbed the root of my emotions. My mind drove from ecstasy to guilt in a split second, flashing to kissing Nandi earlier that evening as Sandra slurped me up and down like a Popsicle.

Shifting between my legs, she traced her tongue down my shaft, inking a string-along with my wits passing outside its margin. Liking without loving, bliss without feeling, and a soul without thoughts, she clothed me with each bob of her head. It felt wrong, but I couldn't put my finger on it, as she played my hunger for her like the seasons; setting my fall by pushing me to spring inside of her.

Suddenly I snapped out of the trance in an instant. "I can't do this." I brushed Sandra off me. She crunched her face as if she'd smelled something funky. "I gotta bounce…I gotta bounce," I crazily repeated.

"What!?" She was vexed, got up, and held her hips.

"I gotta go." I zipped my gray slacks and damn near tripped over a stiletto. "I'm sorry, Sandra. But this ain't the time. I'm goin' through some things right now…"

I jetted out the condo faster than Flash Gordon, not knowing if my feet had touched the ground. Not even an Audi 5000 could've caught up with me. I staggered outside the joint like I was working out my legs for two hours straight. Tensed with no sense of direction, I spotted a park across the street and trekked for refuge until I got myself together. My sense recessed in an orgy with every nerve in my body. I swerved off to the park and sat on the bench, crying uncontrollably. But even in tears I never felt an ounce of pain. My body was crying for me. Tears released frustration of a man who grasped all the tools needed to survive in society but wasn't going anywhere. Every inch of me cried for change, but I didn't know how to go about making the right moves.

Swinging on bra and thong straps, my mind was drenched in debauchery that later wrenched through the pores of my skin, sweating out apologies to my mama that her son wasn't living right by making a mockery of a man. Feasting my eyes with nakedness wasn't the cause of my breakdown. No, I was too strong for that. I was looking for something that was already there, and that's when I realized *that* something was with me all a long.

I clicked back to Sandra after the tears dried. If I was with her any other time and night, she would've got the business. Sexing her in front of the wall window facing the projects that crowded Brooklyn was a fantasy. I just wasn't in the right mind to turn daydreams to reality. I never thought I'd turn down sex from an attractive woman like Sandra. Maybe it was fate, or me coming to age. Whatever it was, I felt like a new man.

***

I was dead beat tired when an elderly woman crept near me as I stood by a wall of bottled water. She stepped in front of me and looked around like a lost child trying to find her way home.

"Excuse me, ma'am. Do you need assistance?" I asked, and she ignored me. Her eyes panned the main aisle that separated the departments in the store. She scratched her gray-colored hair and stared at my chest before acknowledging me.

"I need a pack of bottled water," she said, slowly.

"Do you need help takin' the water to your car?" I asked, and the lady sighed as if she was annoyed by me for helping.

"No, I just come from surgery..." She stopped, and continued to stare at my chest.

"Uh...okay."

"And I don't wanna get any sicker. Blacks and Hispanics have diseases, and I don't want you to carry the water to my car."

The comment was so ignorant that I wanted to laugh. So I played around instead of getting mad.

"Who you think packaged the bottles in the warehouses and shipped them over here?" I was being a smart ass.

The old fart didn't answer, and looked around the store until she found a white face, the *only* white face in the store at the time, which was Jo Jo.

"Him...him...I want him to carry the bottles to my car." She frantically pointed to Jo Jo. Absorbed with laughter, I walked over to Jo Jo and told him what the lady had said.

"Are you serious?" he asked with the same laughter I had.

"Real talk. You should help her. I don't want her to catch the bad case of niggaritis."

Jo Jo helped the lady, and I trekked to Receiving. I took a break by reading beside metal beams that held a mountain of boxes. I heard footsteps walk out the elevator and heard a cacophony of hooting from a male and female.

Ben was macking (or at least trying) on Essence; she wasn't listening to his riff raff. I laughed to myself while reading a book on Entertainment Law. I paid them no mind for a second, but decided to look around the other side of the beams.

"What's good, baby? Let's play army so I can blow you up." Ben grabbed Essence's arm, but she pulled away.

"What? You lame, Ben. Get a life and stop buggin' me because I'm not feelin' you like that."

"Not feelin' me? Baby, you should get with a nigga like me and stop talkin' to Justice. Swing my way, ma."

I laughed to myself. Only lames would use another man's name as leverage to pull a female.

"First of all, I'm not your 'ma,' and second, you just mad 'cuz I won't give you none." Essence snapped.

"You just poli-talkin'. You missin' a lot 'cuz you missin this." Ben grabbed Essence. She angrily jerked away.

I watched as Ben clutched Essence from the back and dry humped her. I got pissed when he bumped into a wall of boxes that spilled on the floor. I just stacked those boxes earlier during the evening. What he did was the straw that broke the goat's back.

"Dead that shit, money." I stepped from the shadows and confronted Ben. "Leave her alone."

"Stop hatin', Justice. Keep readin' your encyclopedias and let me get mines."

He let go of Essence and took a step toward me. Essence stood next to Ben. I thought she was going to smack him for violating, but she didn't.

Ben was no match for me, and fighting a high school kid on the job was a waste of energy. No kudos for not only serving a young poo-put like Ben, but also showing off in front of a female. I got the impression that they were playing around from the laughter in the elevator, but I guess Essence had enough.

While Essence backed away from Ben, I sensed drama and didn't want any static to go down. I opted to extinguish the fire before I did something I would later regret.

"Aight, go ahead and get yours. I got no problem with you, money." I fell back from wanting to hit him because of cameras capturing the scene.

"Whatever, duke. I don't want her anyway. You can have her." He came back, and I ended the tension, at least in my mind.

I turned away from Ben and he pushed me into a stack of boxes. Shaking from the blast of shock, I turned to face him and ducked a flying punch when he swung. I grabbed and rung his neck and yoked him up against the wall. He choked and turned blue, gasping for air. I felt a hand pulling me back, but I was too hot headed to back off him. In my mind, all I heard was "Keep choking," even when Essence was really yelling, "Stop, Justice."

I finally let go and he dropped to the hard concrete. My hands shook like a crack addict suffering from withdrawal as Ben's erratic behavior was his downfall. First I thought they were joking, but then things got drastic. So I got relentless and gave the young kid the business.

Ben folded in a fetal position, wheezing and holding his chest like he'd been shot. Essence held her chest in disbelief but still didn't feel sorry for him, nonetheless.

"Now what you gotta say?" She shot at Ben. Breathing was labor, and he was too weak to draw a response.

I took the elevator to the main floor and forgot about him. I worked on a few boxes with Jo Jo and saw Ben staggering across the department minutes later. He glanced over but quickly looked away from me as if my eyes were the sun that blinded his courage.

The store was closing and I finished recovering Shoe Fetish. Jo Jo let me out early and I clocked out. I saw Ben sitting in the manager's office with tears flowing down his reddened eyes. I couldn't believe what my eyes were seeing; a wannabe thug begging the higher-ups for attention to punish me.

"Oh, so now you snitchin' on me, huh?" I taunted, and he sat quiet like a mute. "You ain't so bad now, punk. Never play games with grown folks."

I got the impression that he'd snitched to Adam about me yoking him. How could he rat after picking a fight with me? The baby paw found out about never stepping to a grown bull; he folded after I crushed his fake thuggery in less than five seconds.

While the low-life was singing to the quasi-managers, I had to figure out whether I was fired, or worse yet, facing charges.

***

I never went home after yoking Ben at the store. I lamped at one of my lady friend's spot in Canarsie for a few nights as a getaway until I got my mind right. The best medicine was out hustling the old timers at Lucky's. Shooting a couple games of pool took my mind off the drama. Ben got what was coming to him. He started the fight, and I finished it.

Shooting pool usually lifted my spirits. I won a few dollars and lost some. The feeling of winning was like the good old days. I played a few games and maintained my evening away from worry.

I drove on the fast lane of cash flow and cruised on a winning streak of close to a thousand dollars. Greenbacks peeled off my fingers while I lounged on the sofa across from the pool tables. 10's and 20's flipped from my finger tips and it felt like I'd won the lottery. I saw cee-ciphers stroll inside and dwarf my spirits to midget size. My heart pounded and my mind raced around confusion. I saw nothing but a brick wall in front of me with invisible chains holding me onto the sofa.

They looked around and walked toward me. One officer pointed his finger toward me and the other led the way. I dipped the loot inside my pocket and waited for them to approach. I wasn't sure if they were after me or other dudes at the spot since a lot of shady characters lamped at Lucky's.

"Is your name Justice King?" A tall, burly cee-cipher asked me.

"Yeah, what's good?"

"Can you come with us to the station for questioning?"

"What for?"

"About a fight that happened a week ago at your place of work, if I'm correct?" He asked, and I nodded. "A complaint was filed against you. The victim pressed charges."

"Victim? Homeboy rushed me!" I was exasperated.

"I wouldn't know, but come with us so we can get this situation straightened out."

I held out my arms because I knew the drill. Cee-ciphers slapped the cuffs around my wrists and walked me outside to the police car. The cuffs damn near cut off the circulation in my wrists as I sat uncomfortably in the back of the joint.

They held me in central booking on a $100 bond. The bond hurt me because that meant a brother had to crack open my savings account over a small scuffle. I stripped down to my boxers, socks, and wife beater, and they locked me in a one-man cell before they took my mug shot. One officer locked the door and asked me to slide my hand through the opening to take off the cuffs. My wrist felt freer than Harriet Tubman as I made the best of relaxing on the steel bed.

I quivered inside the frigid cell and counted money in my head just to keep my mind off the cold. Cracks filled the four walls of the 8x12 foot cell, and blotches of moisture stained the concrete floor. A light hanging from the ceiling dangled back and forth with flies tangled around the bulb.

Then my life flared back to an album of images from the past.

Shower sex with Felicia…Old Man Willie's laying lifeless on the stretcher...arguing with Suzie…the "New" Brooklyn…Scar-lo extorting Kill Kill…the arrest of Casper and Fast Teddy…knocking out money who harassed Caprice…fighting with Ben...Sandra's strip tease...Kissing Nandi.

My mind swirled in a hurricane of pictures until I heard a clash…

BOOM!!! BOOM!!! BOOM!!!

The officer thumped on the door. I jumped up as if fire was lit under my ass. I slid my hands inside the opening so the cee-cipher could slap the cuffs on me again. The cuffs were lighter than before, and he walked me around the lobby for my mug shot.

"Let me guess. It was over a girl, wasn't it?" A short, stocky guy with fuzzy hair asked me while looking behind the photo camera.

"Somethin' like that."

He smiled, and took shots of my front and side.

"Are you in school?" he asked.

"Nah, I graduated college."

"Where?"

"A school that remains unknown." I've never told anyone the name of the university I attended since I felt molested after graduating.

"What was your major?"

"Political Science."

"Wow, so what you doing working at Shoe Fetish?"

"What is this? Twenty Questions or somethin'?" I was annoyed and cut the conversation short. I wasn't in the mood for small talk, especially with an officer who was imprisoning me for an offense I didn't start.

The "questionnaire cop" walked me back to the cell, and I rested on the bench in a daze. A group of officers strolled by and rolled a television set near the cell. One held the videotape while another had a silly facial expression, smiling like a clown.

"What you doing picking on innocent young boys?" one of the officers joked.

"I'm the victim. He picked on me." I countered.

"Well, we're about to see right now."

I was confident about the cameras in Receiving clearing my name. A guy with long, black dread locs plopped the cassette inside the TV, and the black and white footage of Receiving appeared.

The footage caught Ben harassing Essence, and the cops giggled like little school girls.

"Is this how you whipper snappers talk to girls nowadays?" laughed a tall, olive skinned officer.

I brushed off his smart comment and was anxious to clear my name. The camera rolled when Ben followed me as I turned my back. I smelled freedom in the air. I stared at the TV and nervousness flooded my stomach. The concreted chill breezed through my socks as I watched the last seconds of Ben pushing me.

Standing on my feet awaiting for a release, my eyes were glued to the box. My mouth dropped when static turned the screen into a puzzle of black and white spots. The static lines cleared, but a sharp pain flew through my stomach, almost as if someone had shot me. The screen cleared only to find that someone had recorded an episode of *Martin* over the time when Ben started the fight.

What the fuck?!?!

The original theme song of the show blared from the speakers and I collapsed on the floor; dazed, weak, and distraught.

A shadowy figure hovered over me and lifted me from the ground. My blurred vision couldn't make out the person sitting me down on the cold cell bench. I later regained sight. Rats fighting over crumbs in between cracks of the concrete took me back to when I job shadowed Mama on the day she was murdered. But instead of Mama walking down the corridor, all I heard was a masculine voice from my side.

I looked over to my right, and *he* sat next to me. I'd rather have Ben sitting in the same cell with me than him. The Sarge of the precinct brought me a warm cup of cocoa and I declined.

"You've never drank cocoa before?"Chief Rehtaf asked.

"You wasn't around to see it if I have," I spewed at him, and his face reddened. He stood from the bench and summoned other police officers inside the cell. I wasn't sure what was going on, so I rested while facing the white paint rotting away on the ceiling.

"Mr. King, you're out. You can go home now." Rehtaf motioned for me to leave the cell with his hand.

"What?" A surprised look stormed across my face.

"Yes, you can go. The girl who got harassed by the guy you choked stepped forward and gave us all the information we needed."

"And you believed her?"

"Why, yes. How else would we have known about you hanging out at Lucky's?" He winked his eye, and walked off with his men.

I slapped my clothes back on and strutted outside the precinct. Rehtaf sat in his car in front of the joint. He was throwing hints, but I ignored them. I ditched him, and he damn near drove on the sidewalk to park beside me.

"Hey, Justice. Why don't you let me take you home?" Rehtaf insisted.

"It's against the law to ride on the sidewalk, ya' know?" I threw another smart aleck remark.

"It's kind of a long walk from here to Fort Greene."

"I'm good. Besides, I don't want the wolves findin' out I'm bummin' rides from five 0." I stared straight, but he persisted.

"Is that how you treat someone who posted your bail? C'mon, man. At least let me talk with you for a minute."

"I don't know if I can do that. Mama told me never take rides from strangers." I turned the corner, and he followed suit.

I trooped up the block and stopped at a bodega to cop a bottle of pink lemonade. When I stepped outside, Rehtaf was standing outside his car and later walked in front of me. We stood face to face, three feet apart, and I gulped from the bottle, waiting for him to yap about whatever.

"Listen, I know you're mad at me, and you have a reason to be, but let me talk to you for a minute. Please." He begged, and I showed him mercy.

I answered him by walking toward his car and helped myself by opening the door. "You shouldn't unlock your whip in these parts. Cats love to steal and joyride beat up cop cars around here." The sarcastic remarked forced Rehtaf to smile, and we went our way to Fort Greene.

I saw heads nod as Rehtaf crept by certain 'hoods. Hustlers shooting dice on the block scrambled when Rehtaf grilled them. He'd gained a lot of respect over the years as police chief, but I still hated him. He wasn't there when I needed him the most, and my eyes wandered off to the Brooklyn scenery of brownstones and tall project buildings until he strong armed my attention.

"Why are you so quiet?" He tapped on the steering wheel and popped in a *Stylistics Greatest Hits* CD.

"I ain't got nothin' to say," I responded, and grooved to the tune of 'People Make the World Go 'Round.'"

"There's a lot to say. I haven't seen you in awhile."

"Good. I wanna keep it that way."

He looked over to me and sighed. "Why you keep pushing me away, Justice?"

"Why should I let you in my life? You wasn't there when I rode my first bike, when I got into my first fight, when I had my first date…my graduations…hell, you never even taught me how to shoot a gun. My mama taught me how to bust an oo-wop for my 10th born day at the firing range. If it wasn't for her teaching me that, I would've been gone years ago when I shot that guy who murdered her."

Rehtaf exhaled. "I understand why you're angry, but let me make it up to you. I want to be a part of your life, Justice. I missed out, and I just want to be your friend."

I didn't answer while we neared the brownstone. I looked around for a spot for him to park. I didn't want anyone seeing me with him.

"I'll think about it. You can park right there." I pointed to a corner three blocks away from the brownstone. He screeched near the sidewalk, and I hopped out the car in a happier mood. "I'll catch you on the rebound, Chief."

I gave him a salute and carried on.

***

Adam looked surprised when I stepped inside the manager's office. He knew why I was there. He sensed it, but didn't believe it. The moment was what I'd been waiting for since I got tired of slaving there. He sat firm like he'd seen a ghost. His eyes were the only part of his face that moved. I cleared my throat and handed him my name badge and letter of resignation. He unfolded the letter and read.

"Usually they give two weeks' notice, but I wanna leave today." After handing him the letter, Adam's mood soured.

"What you mean you're leaving today? We got a big project for you to do, and you're the only employee we have for Shoe Fetish besides the other girl in the morning." Adam's temper hit the roof.

"No, I'm cleaning out my locker. It's time for me to move on."

"So you just gonna dick me over, huh? Just leave the store all of the sudden after all the things I've done for you?" he vented.

"Things you've done for me? Adam, I had to negotiate for vacation time, go through unnecessary questioning for the swipe cards, your constant bullying of employees, and you playing favorites by giving employees more hours than others." I ran down a list of screw-up jobs. I intentionally left Jo Jo out the conversation.

"I could have you locked up for theft, Justice. Remember? Your boy, Casper, and what's his face? The Fast Teddy guy," he threatened. I slid closer to the door and let out a light laugh.

"I knew your true colors would come out. You never cared about me, or any other employee in this store. And now you wonder why I'm leaving." I smirked with my hands on the door knob. "If you can arrest me, then go ahead arrest me, because I'm out."

I left the office and felt emancipated. Leaving the office was like getting rid of dead weight with a clean slate to start over again. Adam slammed the door as I walked past the registers like a lion strutting high and mighty in the jungle. I pretty much ignored the wall of eyes staring from the registers. I didn't know any of them because Adam had fired damn near all the cashiers from the swipe card scandal. I inherited my stress of working there to them because I was gone. Goodbye and good riddance.

I took the elevator to the lunch room and bagged a few items like my work boots and box cutters. Essence walked in before starting her morning shift. Her mouth stuttered, and she stood stiff when we caught eyes.

"What's good?" I greeted her even though I knew she'd tipped cee-ciphers off about me hustling at Lucky's the day I was handcuffed.

"Nothin'. I'm fine." She glanced at my bag. "Did you quit?"

"Yeah, I had to break out."

"Why you leavin'?"

"It was either me bouncin' or them firin' me anyway. They got my head on the platter because of the thefts that happened over the last few months."

I finished packing and hugged Essence for a final "peace." We locked lips like the good ol' days and I promised her I'll call.

Before jetting outside the store, I saw Jo Jo step inside to start his shift. We had grown closer over the few months since he was first hired. I got the job done since he never pestered me; that was the way I liked to work. The supervising styles between Clara and Jo Jo made me realize that the actual job wasn't bad; it was the people who made life shitty at the job.

"I'm outta here," I said.

Jo Jo was puzzled. "Why? You just got here."

"No, man. I'm done. Finished. Finito. I cleaned out my locker and am no longer employed with the company."

Jo Jo stared at me quizzically, like he was daydreaming.

"Any firing involved?" he asked.

"Yeah, I fired my boss." I gave Jo Jo a pound, only this time he gave me the correct fist stamp like I'd taught him.

"So, where do you go from here?" he asked, and I shrugged.

"Law school. Doing somethin' I *want* to do."

"Cool, dude. Hey, keep in touch." He fished through his wallet to hand me his business card. "I might need your help to get me outta a jam someday."

I nodded, and walked out the joint. After I left the department store, I walked down 2-5th a freer man. I cracked the ball and chain holding me back and mustered the courage to break away from Shoe Fetish. Earning less than the worth of my degree was highway robbery. I still needed some change before heading off to law school. I scheduled an interview with a law firm to get my feet wet until the LSAT came around.

As I carried on, fond memories bubbled over, as well as some I wanted to forget. Leaving the department store was a nasty divorce, and I left with everything, including my sanity.

Chapter 22: The Interview from Hell

Interviews were the worst, but making pocket change before heading to law school beats eating ramen noodles everyday as a broke student.

Lanette, the lady from the temp agency, hooked me up with an interview at a law firm. The temp assignment was the perfect opportunity to gain some knowledge before I was scheduled to take the LSAT…so at least I thought.

I waited in the lobby for five minutes donned in a brown suit and matching suede loafers until two men approached me with wide smiles. They looked like clowns, but I took my mind off from joaning on them and maintained focus.

"Are you Justice King?" a guy with blue eyes and blond hair asked me.

"Yes, I'm Justice King. Nice to meet you." I extended my right arm and shook hands with them.

"My name is Jack Meoff," the guy with blue eyes said. "And this is my business associate, Stu Piddass."

Piddass was taller than his partner and I, and looked rather nervous, as if he'd never seen a brother before. I disregarded his giddiness, and Jack Meoff directed us to an empty conference room to start the interview.

Heat from the vents pulled sweat from my neck and I wiped my brow with a napkin. I grabbed a seat and sat across from Meoff and Piddass. I loosened my collar and dropped my leather carry bag on the floor.

"Do you mind if I take off my jacket?" I asked.

"Sure, go ahead," Meoff responded, and Piddass looked at me like I was speaking alien. He was already rubbing me the wrong way.

I took off my suit jacket and placed it on the back of the chair. They both hawked at me while I handed them my resume. Their foreheads creased while studying the one-paged sheet of my history.

"I see you attended State University," Piddass said in a stuck up way. "Hmm, a very good school."

Dude was beyond condescending. I stayed cool with my hands folded on the table. Working with Adam and Suzie was a blessing in disguise because I knew how to handle characters with snooty attitudes. Stu Piddass's breath smelled as if he'd swallowed a skunk. I held my breathing every time he spoke.

Meoff leaned forward with his hands also folded together.

"Tell me a little bit about your background." Meoff's high pitched voice brought fright to my ears. He sounded like a man butchering a song by singing off key on Karaoke night.

"I attended State University with a bachelor's in Political Science, and graduated with a 3.6 GPA," I said, in interview talk, and my history raised eyebrows. "I made the dean's list three times as an undergrad, and was once president of the Me Phi Me National Honors Society."

Meoff intensely studied my resume. "Okay, it looks like you have good qualifications for the job." He shuffled through his notes, and Piddass glanced at his watch every ten seconds. "Well, Mr. King. What the company is offering is a *copier* position."

"A copier position?" my voice turned high-pitched.

"Yes, a copier position."

"Correct me if I'm wrong, but I got the impression that the position involved assisting lawyers with court cases based on the job description that was posted."

"Well, yes and no," Piddass butted in. "You *will* assist lawyers, but only with copying their court documents for eight hours along with a 30-minute lunch break."

These folks are insane! I thought to myself, and I pushed for more questions out of them to see if I could lobby for an office position.

"Are there any other positions available for clerical work?" I asked.

"Well, um…um, no." Meoff stuttered, and looked over to Stu Piddass. "Only the copier position. Let me remind you, if you take this job you can only take one day off during the year."

"What happens if someone in my family becomes sick, or if I need sick days?" I glared at them.

"Well, we would have to let you go. This job is very intense, and we have to make sure you're here every day of the week."

"So if I broke a knee cap, you'll still expect me to come to work with one leg?" I played with them.

"Not to that extreme, but when, excuse me, *if* the time comes, we shall see."

These cats were insane. Standing on my feet copying papers all day was degrading to my degree. I was baffled at how they pushed for me to copy papers without making the smallest effort to recommend me to a desk position. At least working clerical could've held me down until law school. Working without days off was like juggling fire without gloves. Even though the position was temporary, I still wasn't settling for less.

"Are you're interested in a slower paced or faster paced environment?" Piddass asked while staring at my resume.

"Which one do you think is more productive?" I responded half-heartedly with nothing to lose or gain.

"I think the slower pace is good for you."

"Are you saying I'm slow?" I chuckled, and Piddass whispered off a sinister laugh.

"No, no, no." Meoff grabbed the conversation away from his partner. "We think it'll be a good fit for you."

After Meoff finished, it was time for *me* to lawyer them.

"Do you think the copying position reflects my degree?" I asked, but to no one specifically.

"No, it doesn't. You're actually overqualified for the position," answered Jack Meoff.

"So if I'm overqualified, then why wouldn't you refer me to a position that remotely reflects my degree instead of having me stand for eight hours copying papers?" I asked, and "stuck on stupid" and "parked on dumb" were too lost for words.

I nodded and sucked my teeth with a crooked smile. "It was nice meeting you, sirs, but there's no way I can take this job." I politely shook their hands and went on my merry way. I bought me a bottle of pink lemonade from the vendor in the lobby and waited outside after calling a taxi. The trip to Long Island was a waste of time and money, but regret was a learning experience.

Shoe Fetish was a severe let down after graduating and I wasn't continuing that trend. My old earth had once told me, "Nobody will ever give you what you're worth. You only get what you negotiate." And I took heed to that jewel.

As I waited for the taxi, my cell phone rang, and I answered.

"Hey, Justice," the female voice greeted me. "What's good?"

I didn't recognize the person on the other end, but I went along anyway. "Nothin'. Just got outta this wack ass interview. I'm headed back to Brooklyn now. What's good with you?" I asked, still unsure of whom I was speaking with.

"Nothin'…nothin'." The woman hesitated and lightly hummed to her next words. "I have somethin' to tell you."

"Uh…okay, whassup?" I expected the worst and hoped for the best.

"I'm pregnant."

Chapter 23: FEAR (F.alse E.vidence A.ppearing R.eal)

I couldn't recognize the voice, and Caller ID didn't help; *unavailable* popped up on my cell's screen. I flipped through my mental rolodex and was vexed about the unfamiliarity of the feminine voice on the other end. The habit of talking to scores of women over the years had left my ears too numbed to recognize a voice without a name.

My tongue dried, and the news fried my brain into suspense. The pit of my stomach twisted in knots as the "p" word hit me like the kick of a shotgun to the knee caps. I hoped the call was a joke, but it wasn't April's Fools Day. Either way, I had to face the music.

Please, don't let this woman be some hoochie mama.

"Excuse me?" I calmly asked, after hearing the "p" word.

"Justice...I'm pregnant." The voice on the other end cracked.

"Where are you calling me from?" I asked, as a slick way to squeeze the hint of which woman I was speaking with. "The number shows *unavailable*."

"I'm at my aunt's apartment in Jersey."

Nandi!

I was relieved, but worried at the same time. I've never had a long conversation with Nandi regardless of knowing her for over a year. We'd text each other to make plans and meet, and rarely conversed on the phone. I wasn't a phone person anyway. I'm a product of a generation spoiled by technology.

"Why are you calling me from a private number?" I asked.

"Um...I don't know. This is my aunt's house phone. My phone died."

"Do you want me to meet you in Jerz?"

"Yeah, my aunt's on vacation. That'll give us time to be alone."

The train ride to Jersey was the worst. Mild dizzy spells and lightheadedness tipped me over my seat. I rocked back and forth to an imaginary beat like a schizo, and outside the window looked like colors were messily splashed together. Luckily, the train car was empty enough for me to not make a fool of myself. I was chained and held down; castrated with my sperm sedated and shackled by locks of fear that battled my well-being. Seeing a brighter part of me was love, but hate spilled and overflowed my mind with venom that chilled my heart. Not thrilled about an extra mouth I couldn't feed, I felt broken like a man limping beside the woman bearing his seed. Thinking about fatherhood was smothering me during the longest 10-minute train ride of my life. I came back to my senses after meditating like a Buddhist, and looked to face the music and not betray my heart like a Judas.

Nandi picked me up at the station in a SUV and drove us back to her aunt's rest. Tiredness drained her eyes as she slouched on the sofa. I sat opposite her on a love seat as words escaped me. I didn't know what to say or do.

She sat upright, and the sight of her beauty amazed me even when she looked fatigued.

"Are you okay?" Those were my first words to Nandi since talking to her before the train ride.

"I'm good, just thinking."

"Aight, cool." I thought for a second to string the conversation along, still driving myself back to reality. "So how and when did you find out you were pregnant?"

"Yesterday night when I took the test, and another at the doctor's office just to be sure." Nandi stared at the pregnancy test lying on a towel next to a bottle of pills on a wooden table. "I was tired and started vomiting. I thought it was because of jet lag and constant touring. But I took the test, and it came out positive."

"Funny." I chuckled, and her eyes lit up.

"What's so funny?" She asked.

"I thought you were pregnant on the wrong side when I was walkin' behind you."

"Oh, boy. Get off my butt." She playfully threw a sofa pillow at me. "My head is killing me. I'm gonna take some of these aspirins and call it a night."

Nandi swallowed and chased the aspirin with a glass of water. Silence reheated the room after laughter cooled the mood. The silence was awkward, as if we'd never met before. I stared down at the floor with my head resting inside my hands. My heart was happy for us having a newborn, but my mind called that feeling a liar. The quietness was my chance to cool the fire and speak what I was thinking throughout the train ride.

"Are you getting an abortion?" I asked, and she was taken aback; a smile had lived on her face until a frown killed it. The room remained quiet…dark…and bleak. I felt the eyes of every appliance and piece of furniture inside the apartment scowling at me.

"What? No. Hell no! I'm not getting an abortion. Are you nuts?" She flared, and her eyes heatedly blasted at me.

"How are we gonna take care of the baby?" I snapped back.

"I can't believe you'd asked me that, Justice. There's more to raising a child than money," she underscored her point with a dash of contempt.

I was mentally shot with no room to think. My head spun and lost control. I had to leave and go somewhere and breathe. Short breaths left me paralyzed with my heart banging my chest. The love seat felt hot and consequently pushed me out the door.

"I'm not hearin' this right now. I'm out." I sped off and Nandi chased after me.

"Justice, where you're going?"

"Somewhere." I opened the door knob, but she Kung Fu gripped my arm.

"You're not leaving without telling me where the hell you're going." She protested. I forcefully knocked her hand away and ran off. "Justice…Justice!"

I never looked back or even thought of stopping after hearing her pleading yell. I ran until fatigue overwhelmed me. A park was down the street from the pad and I sat on a bench to catch my breath. I sipped on the last of the pink lemonade I stashed in my pocket and slumped on the bench. I relaxed while staring at the clear, blue sky bleeding across the horizon.

The war between my mind and heart ripped my spirits apart. I needed a moment of peace to desperately clear my head. Staring at the Manhattan skyline from the Jersey side of the Hudson River, I swerved around the curves of my past; thinking of my childhood that was caged in the big city. The sun never shone on grass and only bled over buildings that suffered from heat; swallowing the attitudes of most urbanites like myself. I wandered around with sweltering thoughts of anger on stacks of metal with nowhere to breathe as holes burned my pockets. Softening the pain with games of superstition like never repeating "Bloody Mary" thirteen times in the mirror to avoid bad luck, I'd thought clearer, and realized the bitch had cursed me before I was born. Torn between life and fantasy, I searched for faith from within and fought to the top. My wrongs helped me understand what was right and I sought to correct them. Some say I was heartless, but nah, I wasn't. I just didn't have time to grow as a man and elude decay. How can I listen to the beat of my heart when everyday I followed the pattern of train and work schedules, alarm clocks, and two weeks of received pay?

Switching back to the scenery, the park finally bored me. I scanned around to find anything funny to snap me out my funk. I saw an older guy teaching a little boy how to ride a bike. He held on to the bike and let go after a running start.

"Come on, son." The man cheered his child on. "I'ma buy you that video game today if you ride without falling."

The boy finally rode the bike without his father's help after falling a few times. He rode around the park and stopped at his dad.

"You my main man. Let's go get that game." The dad passionately hugged his son, and the boy jumped up and down; even his eyes were smiling. His pops kissed him on the forehead and carried his bike to the car after throwing away the training wheels. They hauled off and left me alone in the park.

My eyes watered uncontrollably, but I wasn't crying. The sheet of water blinded me and I wiped them off with a handkerchief. My pops wasn't around to teach me how to ride a bike, let alone call for the 20 plus birthdays he'd missed. I envied and hated the boy with the bike at the same time. He was my innocence and guilt wrapped in one body. Glad to see the boy and his dad leave the park, I had time to think alone without focusing on my crippled past.

I closed my eyes until a spark from the barrel of a gun lit the dark and reopened them.

POP!!! POP!!! POP!!!

Clashes of gun shots piercing through Mama's body slapped the wires of my brain. The memory turned into a crystal ball when haunting pictures of the future took over: Nandi in labor without me by her side, her pushing a stroller alone, teaching our child how to ride a bike, taking our child to school and helping with homework, child running wild in the streets with boy jailed before 18 or girl pregnant before graduating high school, child hating me for not being there.

Wait. Hating me for not being there?

I was kicking myself in the ass. I've been doing wrong for so long that I didn't know the feeling of doing right. My will to walk a straight path was the life boat that saved me from floating off shore and drowning in shame.

As I jumped from the bench with a burst of energy, a cardinal swooped alongside the railing. The red bird stared at me crookedly and flapped its wings. I didn't know whether to strike or look, as the red bird danced on the edge before flying off into the sunset. I thought I was going crazy because the red birds have been following me ever since my old earth passed away. I guess weird things like that happened to some folks.

The skies blushed indigo with frost skating over me. I stood from the bench and jetted back to Nandi's place. She was either hurt or hated me for bailing out on her. I wanted to patch things together. Sealing up open wounds was my only ticket to getting back close with her. Instead of running away from fear, I pulled up my boot straps and faced my masked blessings head on.

I knocked on the door…No answer. I called her phone, but she wasn't picking up.

"Nandi, it's me, Justice!" I hollered at the living room window but fell short on my luck. Repeatedly calling with no answer, I grew worried and anxious. I trooped around the building and checked out the apartment windows. The lights were out, and the joint was dark as night. The white blinds, opened half way, were the only reason how I peeped inside.

I saw a giant rock on the ground and thought about busting the 2nd floor window, but that would've been a crack-head move. So I chilled for a minute, and wasn't sure if she was knocked out or had changed her mind to go out. Her SUV was still outside, but she disliked driving and didn't mind catching cabs.

While dialing her number, I was cold as hell and damn near panicked. Remembering the bottle lying on the wooden table, I ran to the rear of the apartment and banged on the back door. I still got no answer. Maybe she was dead or lying unconscious on the floor. She was probably ignoring my calls, thinking I was a low-down dirty creep, or maybe she played sleep just to irk me.

Rushing back down the steep stairway, I flagged down a cee-cipher cruising in a police Jeep. I peeped the officer looking at me dead on and he drove off, as if he never saw me. Pissed with a grain of patience, I charged back inside the building like a raging bull drunk on desperation.

Beating on the door like a mentally-ill patient, all I remembered was the conversation Nandi and I had after the show at Club Libra.

"I'll probably swallow a bottle of pills and kill myself."

The second those thought-to-be prophetic words manifested in my mind, I heard police sirens wail from afar. I stopped beating on the door and saw the same officer from the Jeep that past me by.

"Is there a problem, sir?" The officer asked with fury surrounding his blue eyes.

"I'm tryin' to get inside my lady's apartment. I think she'd swallowed a bottle of aspirin," I explained, still heated about him passing me by, like that Pharcyde song.

"Okay, but I got a call about a disturbance on this floor."

"Yeah, that was me! I've been beatin' on the door tryin' to get my lady. I'm not sure if she's alive."

As I paused to calm down, Nandi opened the door seconds later wearing a purple bathrobe with her locs wrapped in a towel. The officer caught himself from gawking at Nandi, and turned away from looking at the cleavage of her breasts.

"What's all the commotion?" Nandi confusingly glared at me and then the officer. Sensing the officer was sort of a peeping Tom, she closed the small gap that exposed the split of her breasts.

"Miss, I received a disturbance from a neighbor about the banging of a door on this floor…" The officer said, but I cut him off.

"Baby, I was beatin' on your door because I thought you overdosed on aspirins after our fuss." I exhausted my reasoning in one breath. Nandi was amused, and covered her mouth to keep from busting out laughing.

"Boy, you…are…a…mess." She cracked a smile and giggled. "I was in the shower. I didn't hear anything until I got out and heard you with the officer out here."

Nandi turned to the officer. "Sorry for the misunderstanding. I guess one of the older ladies in the building made the complaint."

Dumbfounded and peeved, the officer left without the action he was looking for. I embarrassingly walked inside the apartment.

"What made you think I OD'ed on the bottle of aspirin?" she asked.

"You were mad because I walked out. I just thought of the worst."

"I don't go loony because some guy leaves me. No offense, baby, but it takes more than a man to drive me insane."

I was relieved, and hugged Nandi like I hadn't seen her in years. "My bad for walking out earlier. I apologize. Will you forgive me?"

"You crazy, you know that, right?" She said, and passionately kissed me soft on the lips. I guess that was her answer for forgiveness.

Carrying Nandi to the bedroom, I gently laid her down for "make-up sex." We laughed later about me almost hurling the rock to break the window and the cop speeding off when I flagged him down. We also opened the floodgates to our past; trading spills about skeletons in our closet that brought us closer. I told her about the relationship between me and my father, and the murder of my old earth. She told me about a past miscarriage and how she'd used to perform in Chicago subways to pay the rent. I trusted her, and she trusted me. We gave each other our trust. I lost confidence in the word after life took Mama away from me. If I couldn't trust life with the most precious jewel that made me happy, then who could I confide in? Who could I run to? Because trust is more than a word; it's a lifestyle. The oath that creates a bond is meant to go to with you to the grave and not easily given away. I fought and picked myself apart until I found someone closer to share my hell to raise heaven. I thought trusting someone was the hardest thing in life, almost like catching a lightening bug with chop sticks. Once I caught the bug of trusting my other half, I saw the light, and stood out the dark of living in a cave of misery.

We eventually fell out during old episodes of *Good Times.* I haven't rested well in months, and with a good woman by my side, I had another reason to over look my tomorrows.

Chapter 24: No Justice, No Lease

The barrel of the rifle was aimed at me, and the shooter on the roof stood frozen like an assassin. I was a goner if I made the wrong move.

The scene was like I was the only person in the crowd that the shooters marked for death. The barrel was pointed at anyone standing in its crosshairs. No one had noticed the men covered in all black aiming at us except me. I stood close to a lamp post just in case bullets flew my way. The men surrounded each corner of Brooklyn's Capital Hall's roof and seemed prepared for a riot to break out from protesters.

Lines of picket signs swamped the front steps of the joint. The flood of protesters swept the streets in full force with feelings of unrest. Screams from protesters donning red, black, and green were shouted from the mouths and bullhorns of angry Brooklynites. They swarmed the streets like ants surrounding bread crumbs as the police with riot gear stood in the entrance area.

The matching gear of marchers spoke unity amongst the youth and old, mostly Black and brown; fighting for property they considered a family legacy. Flashbacks of marches in the Civil Rights era dawned on me when I saw hundreds of people pumping their fists, hell bent on saving their land.

Click...Clack

Aiming, focusing, and clutching their guns, I thought I heard the shooters' fingers easing on the trigger. I was standing too far to know for sure. Cardinals floated down from the sky and landed on the steps of Capital Hall. My body shivered on its own when the red birds swooped down. I fixed my eyes on the men posted on the roof, possibly plotting to gun us down. I looked around with Caprice and checked out various signs plastered on pickets of marchers.

Death Over Taxes...Burn Brooklyn Burn...No More Condos!!!...Click Clack, Gimme My Shit Back!

Protesters shouted the slogans and alarmed authorities. The blue coats scrambled in three points of the area: the entrance, sidewalks, and streets. A short, slender, brown skinned man dressed in green army fatigues lamped in front of a news camera crew with his team soldiered behind them. He drank from a water bottle before spewing ether to the mic.

"If you ain't fightin' for a cause, for the love of your 'hood, and you're killin', robbin', and stealin' from your own people just to make a buck, then you ain't doin' thangs!"

"Right on! Build! Build!" shouted protesters behind him, waving black bandanas.

The man caught his breath and carried on. "We need to get together, stop hatin' on each other, break bread, and put our money together to build a better neighborhood for our family…"

"…because if you die over a 'hood that don't belong to you, and kill a man who looks like you for that 'hood, then you ain't a real nigga…you just a dead nigga!" finished another guy from his crew.

Mouthing off gun shot noises while pointing to the sky with fingers shaped as guns, they all shouted together, *"R.B.G! R.B.G! R.B.G!"*

The camera crew looked spooked. They scurried to the next group of protesters near the steps, wishing to escape from the rowdiness of the brothers they'd interviewed. Felicia and the women of her organization were dressed in black fatigues and talked to reporters on the mic. Caprice and I walked over to Felicia and caught the tail end of her talking on camera.

"We need a change in the community. Our families lived here for too long to lie down. They can take our land, but never our freedom," Felicia blasted on the mic, but cut off her statement when the crowd fired a clash of vociferous cheers that scratched my ear drums.

Shaking off the noise, Felicia looked over and seemed surprise to see me at the march with Caprice. She hugged me, and her eyes glossed with tears.

"Thanks for showing support. What's up with the change of heart?" She asked.

"Just wanna check out the scenes. That's all." I smirked, looking around paranoid.

"Uh huh, sure," she joked, and we both turned our heads toward the podium standing in front of the entrance. The councilwoman pranced out the glass doors of Capital Hall and stepped to the podium to address the audience. She appeared nervous by struggling to hold a cold glare to fight off fear sparked by the crowd.

"Please, please. Quiet. I need your attention, please," her soft voice chimed into the microphone. The crowd hushed a few seconds later and drove their attention to the top of the steps.

"The local councilmen, and women, and I are working vigorously to resolve the problems of gentrification. We are working around the clock to make sure the situation is handled properly and correctly. We appreciate the support, as we're trying our best to serve the people of Brooklyn."

Not satisfied with the breaking news, the crowd erupted with anger, and the blue coats moved in closer to protect the councilwoman.

Councilmen and women from various districts of Brooklyn had set-up a meeting with city officials to discuss living arrangements for displaced residents who couldn't afford the increase of rent and land taxes. I thought the meeting was just a show of saving face, and the protesters reflected those same feelings.

The blue coats frighteningly waved their night sticks in the air and almost sicked their dogs on the crowd. Loud barks echoed from chained patrol dogs. They wrestled with leashes to run and attack marchers nestled between barricades that blocked off each lane. Bricks and bottles were thrown at the blue coats, and authorities sprayed rounds of mace. Taken aback by the sudden outbreak of drama, I slid away from the commotion while tugging on Caprice's jacket.

POW!!! POW!!! POW!!! POW!!!

Rifle shots sang louder than the opera and I ducked for cover. Panic smothered the streets as people ran aimlessly like a stampede of bulls in Spain. I covered Caprice for safety. My eyes chased after Felicia, but she vanished. I managed to find her through the wave of feet dashing wild on the street. I held Caprice's arm and ran past a man wrestling with a blue coat. We dashed for safety inside the subway, not taking any chances by staying there.

"Cappie, stay here. I'ma go find Felicia." I left Cappie by the turnstiles. She refused to let go of my arm.

"No, I wanna go with you," she cried.

"It's too dangerous for you to go out there, Cappie. It's more safe for you to chill here than upstairs."

I kissed Caprice's forehead and ran back to grab Felicia. I didn't see any signs of her, and I blacked out. An alarm sounded off and my patience hit the roof when scrambling to find her. Pushing through screams and ducking wild fists, I spotted Felicia in a shoving match with a blue coat. I stumbled over bodies lying on the street to help her but wasn't quick enough. The blue coat fired mace and blinded Felicia. I went nutty by making a left on fury and parking on crazy.

Felicia stumbled to the ground and held her face. I shoved the blue coat off her. I swung my fist and the blue coat flopped to the ground in a twist from my hit. And that was when I heard a shot....

POP!!!

Hot air whizzed past my face like a hot curling iron. My skin turned warm, but I wasn't in pain; it felt like a mosquito bite. Instincts told me to grab Felicia despite the traffic and peel off to the subway before snipers let off more rounds. Protesters trampled over the blue coat I'd fought off as adrenaline rushed my body to lift Felicia off the ground. Locked up behind bars over another scuffle wasn't my ideal way of supporting a cause. So I scurried to get Felicia out of there in a hurry.

Broken bottles, feet stamping and police sirens rolled as background music. The wind hitting my back pushed me to the subway as I carried Felicia to safety.

We hopped on the iron horse to Bed-Stuy to jet back home. As we rode the train, the side of my pants became damp. I saw Felicia bleeding. Blood leaked through Felicia's thigh and she waved her hands in horror, as if she'd seen a giant rat run by her. The blood soaked her black army fatigue pants and drew a puddle on the seat next to us. I looked around the train like a mad man for help. The bastards around us just stared like nothing was wrong.

"I need help! My friend's been shot." I cried out, but no one budged. "Are you muthafuckas deaf? My shorty's bleedin' and she needs help."

An elderly woman reluctantly stood and wrapped her hair scarf around the bullet wound to stop the flow of blood. Dry blood spotted the area and onlookers sat like statues during the hysteria. *Only in New York, folks. Only in New York.*

The train halted to the next stop, and I rested Felicia on the bench, still pissed from the lack of help from folks sitting in their seats like mannequins. I wanted to slap each and every last one of them for living.

As Felicia rested, I looked over to Caprice. "Cappie, go upstairs and use my cell to call the paramedics," I directed, and Caprice dashed to the street level for better service. "Great, now I gotta wait for the ambulance that's slower than the pizza man," I mumbled. Felicia's eyes fought from closing.

"I'm...tired...Justice," she hissed. I clapped my hands to keep her from falling in the kin of sleep.

"Stay awake, baby." I kissed her, and sketch-like pictures of my old earth passing away in my arms was drawn over Felicia. I shook it off and focused on Fe Fe.

"I promise to give you a foot massage once we get back home," I joked, and she laughed, only to shriek in pain.

"Stop, you play too much. It hurts when I laugh."

"You're not passin' on me, mami."

"Stop fretting...I'm good."

"Shhhh, stop talkin'."

The subway's temperature went from humid to cool when I was alone with Felicia. The tunnel's dimness drew an air of nothingness with not a person in sight. Breathing heavily like an asthmatic needing his inhaler, my muscles tightened and crammed with the ache that pounded my head. The roof of my mouth dried like cracked sand, and licking it did no good. Felicia's eyes continued to open and close like she was fighting sleep. Her breathing took long pauses as she fought to stay awake. The breaks between breaths tore my nerves apart. I didn't know what to do, except talk to keep her alive.

"Fight, Fe Fe, fight!" I egged her on, and she smiled crookedly.

"I'm...good," She whispered off. "I'll...be...okay."

She mustered all her strength to clutch onto my hand. She squeezed with the courage that held on. Sweat soaked my forehead and blinded me by trickling down my brow like a drizzle. The hairs on my flesh bristled from shock. Grizzled from the ambulance wait, anger sizzled over my nerves from flashbacks of Mama chasing robbers without back-up. Everything was moving in circles, and my breathing sped as if I was smoking crack with the bad case of the shakes.

Don't close your eyes…keep 'em open…Gotdammit, don't die on me, now!

Before I mentally broke down, footsteps click-clacked from the middle of the platform. Four paramedics rushed down the platform and aided Felicia. Seeing the meds rush towards us calmed the truculent attitude I had had towards them; a crew of them let a few of my dudes die like animals in the middle of the street when I was younger.

They carefully lifted Felicia and power walked to the ambulance. Caprice and I joined Felicia on the trip to the hospital. I held Felicia's hand tightly while she rested on the padded stretcher. The paramedics cleaned the bullet wound and stuck IV's in her arms. A short, stubby paramedic lady studied my face, and I was annoyed. I glanced at her with the "what the hell you're looking at" stare, and she reached inside her first aid kit.

"Sir, your face…you're bleeding," She pointed to the cheek where I felt the hot air whiz past when I heard the shot. "It looks like a scrape. Can I check it out for you?"

I gave her the go ahead.

The sharp pain felt like a bee sting. I looked in the small mirror lying next to the first aid kit. The scrape stretched from the top of my jaw bone to the side of my chin. Blood covered my fingers, and the paramedic dabbed peroxide on the graze. I sat on the ambulance bench, still in shock as gun shots and black dots around Mama's face haunted me on the drive to the hospital. I blew a sigh of relief, even when the beast laughed in my face with its ghosts clouding over me.

***

Felicia slowly opened her eyes once I walked inside the hospital room with purple roses. Doctors wrapped bandages around her left thigh and stuck an IV in her arm to ease the pain.

"What's good, ma?" I handed Felicia the roses, and she rolled her eyes. "What? You don't like 'em or somethin'?"

"Nah, I wanna get outta here. I've been here two days too long. The food sucks. It tastes like glue."

"God bless hospital food."

"Tell me about it. They tried feeding me bacon and ham for breakfast, but I told them to kill that. Ain't no swine going in my body." She clutched the roses and smelled them. She nodded and placed them on the counter next to the hospital bed.

I flipped the channel and popped in the *Chappelle Show Season* 2 DVD in the player. The comedy took my mind off almost losing Felicia as I relaxed on an incliner chair lying next to the hospital bed.

"Why did you come to the rally?" she asked after an episode went off.

"I told you, to support."

"Don't give me that shit. I know you, Justice. I know there was a girl you wanted to check out downtown."

"Seriously, I thought about it, and I knew I had to show some love."

Felicia glared at the ceiling and thought. I knew Felicia was sensing someone had pulled me to the rally. She flipped through the channels and wasn't really paying attention to what was on. I felt her mind skipping through reasons why I'd *really* shown my face. I'd known Felicia for years to know that she understood me. She knew I didn't budge unless lured.

"You think the rally was a success?" she broke her eyes away from the television to mine.

"After what went down? I can't call it. That probably made them wanna kick us out the 'hood even more."

"Yeah, it's whatever now. I got a couple of interviews…well, at least I had, but now I gotta pass them up because of this."

Felicia slumped in the bed. Her eyes glossed with tears. Disappointment surfaced on her face and I held her hand. A tear flew down the hill of her cheek and she wiped it off with a tissue.

"I took one for the 'hood. I guess that makes me gangsta, huh?" She tried smiling, and seconds later closed her eyes to rest.

The doctor nursing Felicia stopped by to check on her. Noticing the snoring from Felicia, the doctor smiled at me and slipped her business card in my hand. I strolled out the room, and something told me to glance over my shoulder. I did, and the doctor stood there cheesing.

"Call me so we can have lunch or something," she whispered.

I was flattered by the gesture and slid the card in my back pocket. The African woman was attractive, but I didn't plan on dialing her number. If all else failed, I knew where to go if I needed a late night creep for a quick booty call.

I left the joint and swooped back to Fort Greene to check up on Caprice. She was staying with Felicia until her parents came back from their vacation in Aruba. I walked back with my head down facing the concrete, thinking about my old earth, as well as passing the LSAT to enter law school.

Chapter 25: Retired Jersey

I busted my tail in the Brooklyn library from noon until the joint closed at 9:00pm. Reading until my eyes swelled was a ticket out of heading nowhere. Mastering the art of strengthening and weakening cases were my strong points when studying Law, but I hated multiple choice when every answer looked correct. I would've breezed on to law school if the tests were based on mock trials. I could only fantasize.

Hitting the library everyday and attending a preparation course for the LSAT was like sparring for a heavyweight fight. I was like a man locked in solitary confinement until I was ready to leave the house. The only time I left the room was when I showered, ate, and relieved myself in the bathroom. Phone calls were brief, and I studied with nothing to lose. Zoning out by listening to smooth jazz on the iPod soothed me while I worked like a manic on a mission.

I also called the guy Wakeetah had insisted I should contact about scholarships and grants. He hooked me up with a few people, and I wrote several essays to prove myself (again) as a worthy student. Just like the justice system, earning grants and scholarship money for college is about whom you know; *what* you know kept you out of trouble.

After one night of studying, a tear raced down my cheek as my old earth's face dusted before my eyes.

***

I knelt down to the concrete and dropped a purple rose over the murder scene. No tears poured when I looked over the exact spot where she was iced. I spilled cries the first few times I visited the spot, but chilled out once I got older. A decade of purple roses on the pavement flushed away tears and turned my heart from slush to ice, realizing the only guarantees in life were death and Uncle Sam knocking on my door.

Twice I skipped school and called in sick for work to hike a cab to the Bronx on the anniversary of my old earth's passing. I was never in the mood to take public transportation when I needed time alone. Spending a few more dollars was nothing to me, as tolerating beggars in subways would've worsened my already somber mood.

The rose rested on the concrete that was once covered with Mama's blood. I stood upright and faced the sky. A cardinal swooped from the horizons and flapped around me. The red bird tapped lightly on my shoulders and rested there. Its feet playfully poked me, and I cracked a smile. Gazing over at the red bird, I saw the reflection of Mama through its eyes that were like the windows of heaven. Etched with three 7's on its forehead, the red bird squawked cries of truth, compassion, and nurturing; the trinity of what I'd missed in over a decade.

A storm brewed when thunder smacked the sky across the face. Lightning cracked between the light blue clouds with not a drop of rain falling on me. Shades of orange raked through the row of blue dimness with the flow of clouds clearing above me. The cardinal floated down beside the purple rose and took flight when the heavens bled sunlight. The sky looked like swizz cheese as the cardinal flew in one of the openings that reminded me of bullet holes. I walked away from the joint with my head high and chest poking out; ready to grab the world by its horns.

Riding the cab back to Brooklyn was like taking a shower after a mud fight. I detoured to Queens to stop by Wakeetah's grandma's house in Ravenswood to build with him. I had big plans, and I needed him on it.

I knocked on the door and a voice answered, "Who is it?"

"Deeeez Nuuuuuuts," I fired back, and the person opened the door. The door opened and I almost fell to the floor. I didn't know whether to hug him or stay silent.

Casper leaned forward and gave me a brotherly hug. "What's good, sun?"

Frozen by the element of surprise, I hesitated to hug him.

"I just came back from Pelan to pay homage to my old earth." I looked at him skeptically. "Did you bust outta Rikers or somethin'?"

"Nah, kid, they let me out early. For what? I don't know. I guess from overcrowdin'."

"It's good to see you home, man. A brotha is starvin'. What's good with grub?" I asked with my stomach fighting off hunger.

"Everything. You know grams always keep the grub on point. I know you don't eat the pig, so I got turkey sausages, pancakes, and scrambled eggs."

Casper fixed his meal and stacked eight pancakes on his plate with an egg and cheese omelet. A tall glass of orange juice rounded out the meal. The boy ate like a horse, but couldn't gain weight to save his life.

"Damn, sun. They didn't feed you in the joint?" I was wide-eyed at how high his plate was stacked.

"You know how it is. I wasn't countin' sheep. Ya' boy was countin' cheeseburgers, cheesesteaks, and omelets, sun. Oh yeah, thanks for the money you sent me."

"No doubt, man, I had to hold you down some way. So how was it in there?" Curiosity leaked through the tone of my voice.

"Nothin' major. Scar-lo's crew held me down. I didn't have to worry about gettin' robbed, stabbed, cut, or any other madness." Casper chomped on his breakfast that was fit for a giant. "What's good with you and the dark skinned honey you was messin' with?"

"She's pregnant," I said, *this* time knowing the woman he was speaking of.

"Word?"

"Real talk. She told me awhile ago when you was in the box."

"Get the fuck outta here! Join the club, sun." Casper gleefully pumped his fist in the air as if *he* was expecting a child. He stuffed his mouth with pancakes and swallowed like a vacuum. No wonder he liked eating swine because he was a pig himself.

While Casper ate, I couldn't break off not knowing why he'd taken the fall. Most so-called "gangsters" today would've ratted on everyone taking part in a crime by signing confession statements for a lesser charge. But Casper wasn't a gangster; just a stand-up dude looking out for his ace when he didn't have to. Our friendship was death before dishonor.

"Why did you take the rap for the thefts?" I asked, and Casper thought while chewing on pancakes. He paused and exhaled. His jaws slowly circled with food caked inside his mouth as swallowing was a chore.

"You got the world in your hands, Justice. I don't see myself doin' shit but hustlin'. I'd rather see one of us make it instead of us both livin' assed out." He gulped down half the glass of orange juice and sighed. "If I didn't take the rap, it would've been over for all of us. The cee-ciphers put the full court press on Fast Teddy to snitch on everybody. Money gave himself up, and I told them I was behind everything. *Everything*, sun. They never caught up with the rest of the crew because of me."

"Thanks, fam. I really appreciate that." I reached over and gave Casper a pound.

"It's all 'hood, baby paw. It just means I gotta go hard body hustlin' clothes. It's nothin'. I know those Euros ain't gonna hire a felon…a *Black* felon at that."

"I feel you, man. So how many years they were gonna give you?"

"Four years, sun. But they reduced my time from that to a few months. I'll have to serve the rest on probation."

"Wow. That's crazy."

"Like a donkey."

Even with Casper released from jail, I still felt bad. I dragged him in my own shit and *he* paid for it. Revenge was the gas that drove fools to their demise while the wise pumped the breaks and mapped out every move. The goodwill of working at Shoe Fetish ran out of gas when I got the brass to rob the store out of thousands. Ripping the store off with Casper making dough on the side was supposed to have killed two birds with one stone. The stone turned out to be a boomerang of bad luck that curved back and struck me in the ass.

Casper finished his plate and placed a hill of turkey sausages and scrambled eggs in a pot.

"Help yourself," he said. "I'm about to go and take a nap. I haven't had a good rest in months. I'll holla at you later." We hugged each other, and Casper went off to the guest room.

Our lives were heading up the fork in the road with Casper turning left while I broke right. Despite his criminal record and the plight of him finding a decent job, knowing how he worked erased worries of him shuffling through the revolving door of the beast. He had a knack for the legal hustle, all the while feeding his brain by reading books for spiritual healing. We vowed not to bubble crack for stacks of money as we loved to live a life without unnecessary setbacks. I strived for a greater ambition to leave the hellish conditions that left others in peril. Some brothers around my way lost their religion when hell was in their faces with a step from prison. The test of faith only made them more cynical, as ghetto scholars only biblical quote was "In God We Trust" on dollars.

The retrospect blurred away when my eyes scanned the living room. I saw Wakeetah playing with his daughter; laughing at Jerry making a mockery out of Tom by causing him to slip on bananas peels with mouse traps slamming his fingers. I sat on the sofa and nudged Wakeetah.

"'Keetah, I need a big favor. You still teach kindergarteners in the after school program at the school?"

"Yeah, what's up?" he squinted his eyes, and looked mad suspicious of my question.

"I have plans and I need your help," I said, and he still looked doubtful. "It has nothing to do with anything illegal. I just need you to do this solid for me. That's all."

"All right, put it on me." Wakeetah stopped watching television with his daughter and faced me with the "this better be good" look.

I laid down my plans with Wakeetah, and he was for the idea. All I needed was a third party. Luckily, I kept in touch with Shan, the brother working for the MTA, and asked him for a big favor. All was going as I'd planned.

***

Rehtaf tossed a football in the air and threw the pig skin when he saw me. I caught the football and raised my hands in the air like I scored a touchdown. I threw back the football, and we silently played a game of catch for a few minutes.

He'd called me to meet with him at a park next to the Brooklyn Bridge and I halfheartedly agreed. Dust of anger still lingered, but he tried sweeping away any ill feelings I harbored toward him. Calling me everyday just to see how I was doing was cool; we'd talked for a few minutes. He was late on the effort, but I still wanted to see what was on his mind. I also asked him the question I knew he could answer.

"Why'd you give Casper an early release?" I broke the million dollar question. He paused before tossing me the football.

"I did it because I owe you."

I laughed angrily. "Because you owe me?"

"Yeah, I do. I wasn't there to see you grow and mature into a man. I had to *at least* do something to bring back the times I missed."

"So why'd you leave me and Mama?"

He caught a pass and looked down at the grass. The winds blew strong gusts of air, but I didn't feel the chills. The wind breaker jacket I wore was too light for the hawk, but the coldness flew past me. Each question I threw at Rehtaf drew heat as my flesh cried wetness like morning dew.

"I wasn't ready for the responsibilities."

"But you were ready to open Mama's legs, right?"

"Yeah, you right, and I'm sorry, Justice. I was scared. I didn't know what to do and how to handle the birth of my first and only child. The best thing I thought about doing was running away." He tossed me a pass, and I held on to the ball, waiting for a better explanation. "I can't change the past. I can only better the present and move forward. Do you forgive me…son?"

He asked, and I tossed back the football. My mind said "no" when my heart pulled him closer for me to hug him. Maybe *I* was the reflection of him refusing to live with responsibilities: Staying with Felicia rent free, dating countless women, and not furthering my life by working retail with a college degree. Stabs of doubt had left deep wounds by carving out my drive to do better. I healed once I turned a blind eye to self-pity. As I looked at him disgustedly, I wondered if he was deepening the permanent scars he'd helped create.

I spiked the football to the ground and walked away without answering his question. His confession didn't move me enough to accept his apology. I left him with the blaze of wind slapping my back. His whole existence to me was dirt. I wanted to see him fall in a bottomless pit for neglecting me for all those years. Dreams of his demise overwhelmed my subconscious; visions of cutting his eyelids and forcing him to face the sun, driving back and forth over his body, choking him 'til his eyes popped out, cutting his body and pouring gasoline over the wounds, etc. Anything worst that was done to him would've gave me a good night's rest. He didn't want me as his child. I didn't want him breathe.

Splitting between cars in traffic, I fended off remorse. I grew up a blind boy walking on the edge of a mountain with the Sheppard on the other side of town with his pants down. The brute force of pain sowed the root of me pushing him away. I vowed to stay with Nandi and the baby, and not run off like a coward. I called Nandi and asked her to meet me at Penn Station so I could see her. Not allowing Rehtaf to steal my joy, I took the train and met my babygirl for the long awaited surprise I had for her.

***

"Why are we meeting here?" Nandi looked around the dilapidated City Hall train stop in downtown Manhattan that had been closed for years.

"What? This is heaven, baby. I could've sworn I saw Jesus down here." I kissed Nandi and caressed her stomach. Her breasts perked out the wool sweater she wore and her smile was syrup on pancakes. Covered up in a long, blue jean dress, her sexiness was still magnified, from the coils of her hair to the grain of her shoes.

"Nandi." I subconsciously tapped my beige pants pocket and deeply exhaled. "We've been together for awhile now, and I'm diggin' you. I'm diggin' you a lot."

I mustered the courage to spill my feelings. Letting a woman know how much I cared for her was a stranger to my tongue. She wasn't sure where the conversation was going, but I led the way.

"I don't think I can do this anymore." I forced out, and her forehead creased with confusion.

"You can't do what?" she asked.

"This…this life…I can't do this while…"

"While what?"

"While…you know. I really like you, and I don't wanna hurt you. So…"

"Hold up…are you breaking up with me?" She stepped back, and held her hips in a combative stance.

"Baby…no…what I mean is…I'm hangin' it up. I wanna settle down. I'm tired of runnin' around skirt chasin' and not gettin' anything but sex that doesn't even matter to me. I want something stable. And I'm feelin' *us*."

I felt Nandi's words slip off her mouth, unable to flow off her tongue. "Oh…Justice," She whispered, still scrabbling for the right words to say with her hand twitching inside mine. Her watery eyes hit me harder than a quart of hennessy and emptied me of all my thoughts by knowing she was meant for me.

"Yeah, I'm serious. I'm for real. A king needs a queen by his side on the throne. And I see you as the one walking beside me."

She stood speechless. I blew a whistle and turned to face the train that screamed through the tunnel like a hundred hawks. Specks of light beamed from the darkness, and the train screeched on the rail. I held Nandi's hand as the iron horse rolled by with giant painted letters covering the windows. Each train window had a letter that spelled out the words I'd thought would never leave my mouth; Wakeetah's students hooked me up and I was thankful for the favor. Nandi read the letters and covered her mouth as her eyes widened. Her voice muffled through her palms and she burst out in tears.

The three-car train wailed for a full stop, and she read…

WILL YOU MARRY ME?

Shan poked his head out the conductor's car and nodded. Standing with the ring case cuffed in my hand, words were stuck, but I managed to propose to Nandi. Tears crept down her cheeks and her hands were fidgeting.

"Nandi…will you marry me?" I proposed, still standing, and she paused. Overwhelmed with excitement, she fought away tears to answer me. Everything around us fell silent.

"Yes, yes…oh, yes."

I opened the black ring case, and the four canary diamonds smiled its shine on the ring that left her in awe. I mentally patted myself on the back; the ring would've broken a brother's pockets if it wasn't for an acquaintance giving me a favor for a favor because I protected his briefcase.

My player days were officially over when I slipped the rock on her left ring finger. Stepping out the game of meeting nameless faces with different traces of lipstick painted over me, I turned a new leaf with each minute I stood next to her. Scapegoating my runaway lusts with aimless hormones, I ran through a cycle of women that circled me like the earth rotating around the sun; adding cell numbers as quickly as deleting them if they failed to call me for a week. A slew of creeps, bastards, dogs, assholes and jerks that broken hearts hurled at me, I let good moments slip away through selfishness, but held them closer when I looked at my queen's eyes in the dimly-lit subway. Our lips met, our tongues wrestled, and our bodies locked together, with us looking forward to a new life.

Chapter 26: Ghost of the Past

I thought I was going to die. My stomach dropped and I felt like shitting bricks. Fixing my collar before stepping inside the classroom was torture; the clock ticked ten minutes before I was to take the LSAT. My life depended on me passing. I blocked out everyone surrounding me and remained focused on passing the test.

Listening to smooth tunes of John Coltrane's *Love Supreme* on my iPod was relaxing. I closed my eyes and pictured me strutting inside a courtroom, briefcase, suit and all, and shutting down the joint. I was destined for greatness, but the LSAT was another obstacle standing in the way of my journey.

The instructor stepped inside the class and sat his briefcase on the table. The tall, pale complexioned man wearing black-framed glasses and a suit two sizes small waited for the clock to pass the start time.

"Hi…my name is Mister Abore…We will start the session at noon," he spoke dryly to the packed classroom, like the Economics teacher on *Ferris Bueller's Day Off*. We weren't paying the guy any attention; we either stared off into space or meddled with our cell phones.

Both hands on the clock stopped at 12 and the test proceeded. He passed out the key to my future, and I threw down once he gave us the word to begin. The hard questions kept a brother on his toes. I pretty much knew almost every question the state flung at me as I bust my ass studying. Mentally chiseled from bench pressing knowledge on the brain, the test was a piece of cake to me.

Some had argued that the LSAT was culturally biased against inner city students. I got past that issue by studying the "King's English" as a shorty. Through tutoring and checking out books from the library about the English language and other subjects, I didn't want any excuses for why I failed the tests. I can come off as street, but I knew how to go into a job interview and get down with the suits when needed to.

During intermission I bounced to a Jamaican food joint across the street and ordered me a few beef paddies. The 15-minute break between sections gave me enough time to grub and sit down to briefly go over my notes. While I waited for my food, my past strolled through the entrance. The sun was beaming on the frame of cocoa blessed by God; her long, jet black hair danced on her shoulders. Her round, dark brown eyes drew over me, and she shot a smile while rushing over for a hug.

"Long time, no see, stranger." Nadeejah kissed me on the cheek and sized me up. "Damn, man. You've been hitting the gym or somethin'?"

"Well, you know, a brotha gotta stay in shape," I responded, and caught her looking at the engagement ring on my left hand.

"Is that what I think it is?" She shrieked, and I nodded while smiling.

Nadeejah was an ex-fling I had to leave alone because she was a crazy chick. I'd come to the conclusion that pretty girls were more insecure with their looks than average looking chicks because of constant competition with their own shadow. A woman glancing at her mini-mirror every five minutes was half crazy to me. Nadeejah's possessiveness also got on a brother's nerves. I caught her raiding my celly looking for girls' numbers. Needless to say, I deaded her afterwards.

"When did this happen?" she asked me about the engagement, still shocked from the news.

"A few months ago. We haven't set a date yet. I got a son on the way, too."

"Wow, congrats. It's about time you retired your player's jersey and traded in your mack card."

"Yeah, well...the *right* one will do it." I emphasized "right," and got Nadeejah back for her smart remark. Her smile bent to a frown. "But don't worry. I'm sure one of those swole strippin' dudes you like will sweep you off your feet."

My sarcasm punched a hole in her ego. I didn't care. Hey, she asked for it.

A man behind the counter with a heavy Jamaican accent called Nadeejah for the food she'd ordered for delivery. She clutched her designer purse to grab the grub and walked back to my seat. She fumbled inside her purse and handed me her business card. As a semi-famous plus-sized model touring in fashion shows overseas, she was doing well for herself. Gracing the pages of major magazines and appearing on talk shows brought more notoriety to her name.

"Keep in touch, babe." She kissed me on the forehead before walking out.

Nadeejah waltzed out the store, and I stared at her modeling card. She would've got the serious gas face if she was any other shorty. I was surprisingly cordial with her when she handed me her business card. Taking a final glance at her card, I tossed it in the trash without regrets of doing so. I maxed the beef patty and was ready to knock out another section of the LSAT.

I stepped out the joint refreshed about going on with my life. As I walked back to the school, a homeless man stepped to me with his eyes begging of a favor.

"Hey, brotha. Can I get some change so I can buy me a sandwich?" he asked, and shivered from the light breeze. He tried holding his brown leather jacket together that was riddled with dust and holes.

I reached in my pocket and gave the man a ten dollar bill without thinking of it.

"May God bless you, brotha," he said, and limped off around the corner.

Usually I would've ignored the bum types and kept it moving. For some strange reason I didn't.

A flock of cardinals circled the block and formed a heart, similar to what I'd seen on top of Casper's grandma's building in Ravenswood. A red bird broke away from the formation and swooshed down to my shoulder. The bird danced a short jig with crescents in its eyes before rejoining her crew in the sky. Strips of gray smeared from the sunshine and faded to blue, erasing touches of a rainy day. The sun shone on me, as if its proverbial shine was anointing me to succeed. As the cardinal flew away from my shoulder, greatness was passed on when the bird soared high above the clouds before disappearing in the pit of the sun.

I Hate My Job

Epilogue – Karma is a Bitch

Coldness inside the jail chilled my bones, and I wobbled my legs to keep warm. Wintry air swarmed near the holding cell and seeped through my long johns. I clenched my fists and winced angrily while digging my clipped nails into my palms. Harboring exhilarated thoughts of running away, I sat calm with my patience riding on fumes. My mind drifted to ignore the cold, shielding myself from freezing.

I turned, and my eyes lit with relief. Rehtaf walked out the men's bathroom and strolled my way.

"You ready to roll?" he asked.

"Yeah, it's cold in here. Y'all don't have heat in this joint or somethin'?" I sat perturbed while sitting across from a holding cell.

Rehtaf laughed at my question and shrugged. "We're working on it, son. We're working on it."

Rehtaf was escorting Attorney James Porter and me to the courtroom in downtown Brooklyn. Since Nandi had given birth to our son, I patched things up with him. I cracked the hate that cemented my heart and accepted the events that shaped me as a person. Robbing my son of not knowing his grandfather was putting a band-aid over a gun shot wound, but I still refused to call Rehtaf "Pops." I wasn't letting him off the hook that easily.

Job shadowing Attorney Porter for a case meant more experience for me. The case was an R&B singer suing his record company for failing to pay royalties from publishing and album sales. Working as an aspiring entertainment lawyer was cool, but it wasn't all lights, glitz, and glamour.

Besides meeting celebrities and building a star studded clientele, researching every contract and statement to find cracks in a case was hard work. Prior knowledge about the music industry over the years had helped me dearly. I dropped my passion as a rapper even though I knew how to rhyme better than my potential clients. I'd rather make money staying in the background instead of living famously broke. A lot of artists in the music industry weren't as rich as they said they were. No big deal. I guess everyone has to fake it before they make it.

Passing the LSAT was a sigh of relief. I'm in my final year at a prestigious law school on the East Coast and doing quiet well for myself. Keeping close with family in New York was a must, especially since Nandi and I had bought a brownstone in the Stuyvesant Heights section of Brooklyn. Some say it's *still* Bed-Stuy, but I guess that depended on who you asked. We planned on buying land in other parts of the country for an extra source of income once we saved more money. There was no way I was leaving Brooklyn like a lot of New Yorkers was and is doing. My heart was a big apple that bled the grind of the five boroughs, and I wasn't jetting anywhere.

Rehtaf and I drove through Brooklyn one gloomy morning and spotted a crowd of folks lining outside a white stoned building. Besides the clothing they wore, they had nothing but sleeping bags and frowns. The line snaked around the corner, and cee-ciphers patrolled the sidewalk, directing traffic. Dark clouds blackened the sunlight as drops of rain sprinkled on the colorless scene. We drove past the joint, and I turned to Rehtaf to find out what was going on.

"What's good with the line?" I asked.

Rehtaf rolled down the windows to smear the rain for a clearer view. "Oh, those are families who lost their brownstones. It's a shame, but hey, what can you do?" Rehtaf answered carelessly. He refocused his eyes back on the road. "Gentrification has been going on for years. It's nothing new. Black folk came to New York from the south by settling in Greenwich Village before moving to Harlem and Brooklyn. It ain't nothing that we can do about it."

Astounded about the brief history lesson, I murmured, "We *can* do a lot."

I glared away from the sea of sad faces that reminded me how economically powerless we were as a people. Slipping on concreted soap with question marks above their heads, lost souls scrambled to pick up the pieces of scattered possessions left tattered by pine boards and bulldozers. While some sulked in misery, others recessed their focus on hope; a change for the better. The sun arose and casted a dawning of a new life after the storm weathered their faith; roaming their eyes with fog lights through the haze of doubt. But *I* saw something. I saw strength in a time where handshakes and contracts wrenched away their shelter; a girl patty-caking with her younger sister, and a boy tossing a football to his father. With bitterness frying inside their veins, a part of them died, only to resurrect by them having each other.

I told Rehtaf to stop at Felicia's old brownstone for a minute on the way downtown. The "For Sale" sign hanging on the front window had stood there for a few years. The joint was a shell of its former shelf; the ivy on the bricks had dried out and looked like a road map of sticks; waves of dirt haired over the stoop with cracks lining each step. No one bought the brownstone since the country was suffering from a deep recession. Felicia had foreclosed the joint and moved down to Florida for a new marketing gig. The rest of her family lived in Florida, so she chose to stay closer to relatives. I guess all that marching did nothing after all.

I was told awhile back that many people in New York City were suffering from Predatory Lending, the practice of a money lender tricking home owners to agree to unfair and abusive loan terms, or systematically violating those terms in ways that make it difficult for home owners to defend against. The failing economy had forced people to lose homes and brownstones they had owned for years. The practice had caused many foreclosures in NYC, and the majority of people foreclosing their homes were Black American seniors.

I poured out some water on Felicia's old stoop in memory, and carried on to the courthouse. Police cars packed the front of the courthouse, and we wormed through the news media circus. Scar-lo stepped outside a police van with four federal agents. Donning an orange suit with chains locked around his wrists and ankles, he arrogantly sliced through the sea of reporters with a grin before entering the court building.

The security guards frisked him as he took baby steps through metal detectors. He turned and his eyes spotted me. He smirked as more federal agents lurked behind and hauled him into a courtroom. I returned the nod, and he looked away before entering inside the court next to where I was headed.

A herd of news cameras flashed at Scar-lo for the last time and trailed him like a bunch of groupies. I didn't feel sorry for Scar-lo even when it saddened me to see another brother fall in the system. He had enough brains to run a fortune 500 company, but decided to run the streets instead. I never got down with his crew because I could've been locked up along with him. I caught wind that he was facing a LIFE sentence with no parole for running an ecstasy ring along the east coast, as well as countless murder charges. Wiretaps along with members of his crew snitching did him in. Another one had bit the dust, and I asked myself, "was it really worth it?"

After Scar-lo disappeared inside the courtroom, I followed Attorney Porter inside the next room and shook hands with the client. The judge gave us fifteen minutes to go over the case. I was giddy about my first real life experience as a lawyer, or at least an assistant. The empty courtroom was a far cry from the circus next door, but I didn't care. For once in my life the attention was irrelevant to me.

I looked forward to a new career and way of living. After struggling with finding my way in the world, I finally found the missing pages and wrote new chapters in my book of life. Waking up every Monday was like my Fridays, and I didn't have to push myself out of bed…I no longer hated my job.

I Hate My Job

Closing: Dreams Are Visions

If you see it, reach it,
And hold on so forever you keep it,
When you think of it, go after it,
And don't let anyone shatter it
Because dreams are nothing but visions,
And visions are nothing but potential,
But what's good is that potential, if not sought for?
As talent without drive is like birds without wings,
Or a song that never sings, or a bell that never rings,
Don't let anyone hold you back,
Or talk you down and hold you off track,
Strength comes from within, so forever hold your head up when down,
Get back up, brush it off, and work even harder,
Through earthquakes, hurricanes, snow storms, and heavy rain,
Always stay focused and keep your eyes on the prize,
Because inner-visions live forever, like a spirit that never dies.

Friday, October 31st, 2008 12:53pm

Glossary

"40 Going North" - phrase for speeding; going too fast
Abuelos - Spanish for "grandparents"
"Beast, the" - prison
"Beastin'"/"Beasting"; "beast, to" - overly anxious
"Blunt, a" - marijuana rolled in a cigar wrapper
Bodega *(boe-day-gah)* – Convenience store
"Box, the" - jail or prison
"Cee-cipher" - police officer; cop
"Cee-rule" – crack
Chuck Brown - known as the "Godfather" of Go Go, a sub-genre of funk music that originated in DC in the 70's.
"Columbos" - detectives
"Cream" - money
"Deaded" - to dump, or no more
"Dee-bo, to" – to strong arm, take over.
"Dragon, the" - bad breath
"Duff, to" - to punch
Earth – a woman; female
Emmett Till - a Black American boy from Chicago who was beaten and shot in the head in Mississippi for allegedly flirting to a white woman
"Food" - a mark; victim
Football Numbers - phrase for a long prison sentence
"Frontin'"/"Fronting"; "front, to" - faking; lying; or to show out
"Ghost, to" - to lose someone or thing; to leave
Haile Selassie - born Tafari Makonnen, Emperor of Ethiopia from 1930 to 1974; a make-believe housing project in Harlem used in the book (Haile Selassie Housing Projects)
Hard Body - hardcore; to go at something, or someone all the way; strong
Hermano - Spanish for "brother"
Hija de Puta - Spanish for "daughter of a whore"

Huey P. Newton - co-founder and leader of the Black Panther Party for Self Defense, a Black American organization established to promote civil rights and self-defense

"Joanin'"; "to joan" – a roast of jokes

"Jumpoff, a" - a promiscuous female; place or thing

Kemet - original name for Egypt

Kente Cloth - a royal and sacred cloth of the Ashanti worn only in times of extreme importance.

"Knocked" - arrested

Kunta Kinté - one of the main characters from the movie "Roots"

Kwanzaa - a week-long holiday celebrated throughout the world, honoring African heritage; observed from December 26 to January 1 each year

"Lampin'"/"Lamping"; "lamp, to" - to relax

LSAT – Law School Admission Test

Luego - Spanish for "later"

Marcus Garvey - Jamaican-born; founder of the Universal Negro Improvement Association and African Communities League (UNIA-ACL)

Mecca - nickname for Harlem, NY; and/or Manhattan

Medina - nickname for Brooklyn, NY

Migenté - Spanish for "my people"

"Mo' better" - sex; intercourse

"Motivate, to" - to leave

Nat Turner - an American slave who started the largest slave rebellion in the antebellum southern United States, in Southampton County, Virginia in 1831

New Jerusalem - nickname for New Jersey

Now Cee - nickname for North Carolina

Old Earth - mother

"Oo-wop" - gun

"Package, the" – AIDS/HIV

"Peckerwood" - unfavorable name for whites; Caucasians

’elan ***(pee-lawn)*** **-** nickname for Bronx, NY
‘Pigeon, a” - a loose female; promiscuous
“Poli-talkin'”/”Poli-talking”; “poli-talk, to” - lying or deceiving
“Politickin'”/”Politicking”; “politic, to” - conversing; talking
“Power-U” - vagina
“Pum Pum” ***(poom poom)*** - vagina
R.B.G. - Red, Black and Green; colors of the Pan-African flag
“Rest, a” - home
Sak Pase - Kreyol for "what's up?"
Son - a male; the common, commercialized version of "sun"
“Stack, a” - a thousand dollars
“Sun” - a male; term of endearment for a male who has the shine of knowledge
Swahili - a language of East Africa
The Oasis - nickname for Queens, NY
Tommie Smith and John Carlos - famously known for the "Black Power Salute" while receiving their medals during the 1968 Olympics awards ceremony
“What's the Science?” - phrase for "what's up?"
“Whip, a” - vehicle
Zulu – the largest South African ethnic group